JAMES ARNESS

JAMES ARNESS

An Autobiography

by James Arness

with James E. Wise, Jr.

Foreword by Burt Reynolds

To Ruth Hay,

Regards,

James Arness

McFarland & Company, Inc., Publishers

Jefferson, North Carolina, and London

Frontispiece: John Howard Sanden, *James Arness—Matt Dillon.* **Oil on canvas, 46" × 44",
1981, 1982.05, National Cowboy & Western Heritage Museum, Oklahoma City OK.**

Library of Congress Cataloguing-in-Publication Data

Arness, James, 1923–
James Arness : an autobiography / by James Arness
with James E. Wise, Jr. ; foreword by Burt Reynolds.
p.   cm.
Includes index.
ISBN 0-7864-1221-6 (library binding : 55# alkaline paper) ∞
1. Arness, James, 1923–   . 2. Actors—United States—Biography.
I. Wise, James E., 1930–   . II. Title.

PN2287.A695 A3   2001   791.45'028'092—dc21 [B]   2001045222

British Library cataloguing data are available

Manufactured in the United States of America

*McFarland & Company, Inc., Publishers
Box 611, Jefferson, North Carolina 28640
www.mcfarlandpub.com*

For Janet, the heart and soul of my life.
Without her love and support,
this book would not have been possible.

Contents

Foreword
by Burt Reynolds

For many years (45 to be exact) I have been asked, "What were the best times for you growing up as an actor?" Without hesitation, I have always said, "The 2½ years I was on *Gunsmoke*." They were for me "the best of times." There were many reasons, but the main reason was that it was then I learned how actors on a film set should behave. What it meant to say someone is "really a pro."

I learned that acting isn't an easy career—long, tough hours sometimes—but it can be a wonderful time. That the working environment really can produce a "family" with real warmth among the cast and an honesty that you may or may not share again, but you will always be striving for from that time on.

It's no secret that such an environment starts at the top. If the "star" or top-billed actor displays no fits of temperament or unprofessionalism and makes no ridiculous demands, then it becomes almost impossible to act like a total ass if you're billed below that actor. It doesn't stop people from trying, but in those days a professional environment was very effective in stunting the growth of temperamental types. Young actors who are totally unprofessional today couldn't have lasted back then. They just wouldn't have been around very long.

The biggest surprise for everyone who had the good fortune to work on a few episodes of *Gunsmoke* in those days was Jim Arness. He was funny. I mean get-the-giggles, wrap-up-for-the-cast-and-crew, "time-out"-and-get-it-together funny. I've known professional funnymen. It's no surprise to people that Dom

DeLuise could (as I have done in return to him) practically put me in a coma laughing. Yes, David Niven was the best storyteller (raconteur if you will) I ever worked with. Jonathan Winters and Richard Pryor could always put me away. But for sheer surprise ("Where did that come from?") no one could top Matt Dillon. First of all, he was a very large, imposing, strong man. Your first thought always was, damn, he's bigger than I thought he would be. He had that wonderful ability to surprise you, make you laugh at yourself or the situation that actors often find themselves in.

Just as surprising, he was *totally* without ego. He never imposed his position on anyone. Not once did I or anyone else ever see Jim being rude, overbearing, self-righteous or selfish to anyone, whether crew member, extras, day players or co-stars. I've done over 200 TV shows (the only actor canceled by all three networks ... twice) and over 75 features and I can't think of any actor whose behavior on the set and off was more unpretentious than Jim's. He just didn't or wouldn't play the "star." I think the mere thought of it would have made him laugh.

Yes, of course, my time spent with Milburn Stone, Ken Curtis and Amanda Blake was priceless. I have hours of stories about the wonderful quality time spent with each and every one of them. But in the end we all followed our tall, self-effacing leader. We all hated "acting" that looked pretentious. If you could catch us "working," it wasn't good. We worked hard to make it look effortless. That's why those shows, although now thought of as part of the "Golden Years of TV," were not as honored by our industry as they should have been. Who knew when we watched Gleason, Lucy and Andy that we were watching irreplaceable performances? Only now when every episode is being collected and sold over and over again do we finally get it.

I left *Gunsmoke* only because it was time for me to move on, but I left with everyone's blessing and best wishes. I've had a hell of a ride since. A movie career that I never could have dreamed of. But when I think of those episodes of *Gunsmoke* on that wonderful old stage—sitting and telling stories in front of the Long Branch Saloon with Matt, Kitty, Doc and Festus—well, it just never gets any better than that.

This will embarrass Jim, to hear me say that he was and is so loved and revered by all of us. But you have to face it, old friend. Like it or not, you and that show are what the word icon really represents.

—Burt Reynolds

Introduction
by James E. Wise, Jr.

When I arrived on a lovely, bright morning, Jim Arness swept me into his home like a long-lost friend. I was doing research for a Naval Institute Press book, *Stars in Khaki*, about actors who'd served in the U.S. Army and the air services. Knowing that Arness had been wounded at Anzio in 1944, and as a longtime fan of his Marshal Matt Dillon character on *Gunsmoke*, I'd hoped he would grant me an interview. He did much more than that: he and his wife, Janet, granted me their friendship.

Because of my Navy background, Jim wore a USS *Enterprise* ballcap, received years earlier when he'd visited the aircraft carrier. He'd laid out all kinds of World War II mementos from his days in the Army. Quietly he told me about his experience. Before being shipped "over there," like many other young American men during World War II, he'd thought of combat as a new, exciting adventure. He couldn't wait to get overseas and fight for his country.

James Aurness (he would later change his last name to Arness when he began his acting career) was assigned as a buck private to the 2nd Platoon, E Company (rifle), 2nd Battalion in the 7th Regiment ("Cotton Balers") of the famed 3rd Infantry Division. (Audie Murphy, the United States' most decorated soldier during World War II, also served in the 3rd.) As a replacement soldier at Monte Cassino, Italy, he witnessed brutal fighting and killing. He and his comrades remained anxious to join in, but their zeal took on a more sober tone.

1

They saw that their chances of survival were diminishing, especially after they landed at Anzio. There, they faced an overwhelming enemy force. The 3rd Division suffered some 3,000 casualties during its first ten days of combat.

Jim's leg was shattered during a night patrol on 1 February 1944. He was transported by ship to a hospital in Tunisia, then Stateside to an Army hospital in the midwest where he spent one year recovering. When he left the war behind him, he wore a Combat Infantry Badge, a Purple Heart, his campaign medals, and, eventually, a Bronze Star.

When Jim and Janet asked if I would help write Jim's autobiography, saying yes was easy. I'd gotten to know him as an unassuming, charming man full of enthusiasm and wit. We were both from the midwest, and we'd both spent happy, carefree childhood summers in upper Minnesota and Wisconsin. Our recollections meshed so often that it seemed as if we'd hung around the same country stores.

As we wrote this book, I couldn't help but feel that I was also in the company of Matt Dillon. The actor and the character he portrayed on TV for twenty years are one and the same. Both are honest and strong, born leaders. Few actors are cast in a role that so deeply fits their true selves. Fortunately for all of us who spent a good part of our lives watching *Gunsmoke,* Jim Arness is one of them.

—James E. Wise, Jr.

Prologue

When troops prepare for war there is not much time for quiet reflection, but on a January day in 1944 I made what time I could. With bagpipes playing as we marched down the streets of Naples to our landing craft, I tried to keep my mind apart to think about my life so far.

Many hours later we were lying off the port city of Anzio, ready to storm the beaches of Italy. We heard our craft's engines revving up; then we moved out toward our assigned beaches. As we waited for incoming fire, I tried to concentrate on images of home. So much that was unknown and frightening lay ahead, while behind me lay everything I knew and everyone I loved.

I kept the pictures in my mind for as long as I could.

Part I

The Early Years

When my grandfather landed at Ellis Island in 1887, his name was Peter Aursnes, but "I had to throw away the s in the middle of my name," he reminded his father and brother in a letter dated 4 September 1893. Because the Americans could not pronounce the Norwegian, his family should spell the name "Aurness" when they wrote to him.

Thirty years old at the time of his arrival, Peter "Aurness" had studied medicine in Oslo (which at the time was called Kristiania). In America he made straight for Minneapolis and the Norwegian community that lived there—we assumed he must have known others from his homeland who had settled in the farmland community. He enrolled at the University of Minnesota to complete his training, and eventually he graduated from their School of Medicine.

Peter also experimented with medical equipment that he designed himself, running a mail-order business out of his home. He sold his own patented stethoscope; we still have among our family mementos the patent documents and a few of the instruments. His medical practice was quite successful, and by the time he met my grandmother, Ida Cirkler, he was a prominent physician and surgeon.

Ida was the child of German immigrants in New Ulm, Minnesota, about 75 miles southwest of Minneapolis. It was mostly farm country. When she was a baby, in the summer of 1862, the Minnesota Sioux and four Dakota subtribes known as the Santee attacked the town. The natives had signed a treaty in 1851 but had been cheated in their reservation rights, and after a clash on 17 August 1862, warriors asked fifty-year-old Little Crow to lead them in an uprising.

According to my mother, the family historian, they set out to kill all whites in New Ulm.

It became known as the 1862 Massacre. As the whites drove the natives out of Minnesota to join the other Dakotas on the plains, 700 settlers and 100 soldiers were lost, with 100 Santee killed on the other side. Three hundred and three Santee were captured, 38 of whom were hanged. President Lincoln pardoned the others. A number of New Ulm residents escaped the massacre, among them the Cirklers. My mother said the family had been forewarned by Indians with whom they were on friendly terms.

Little Crow retreated to the plains, from where he led a small band into Canada. But they found few friends there, and eventually Little Crow and his son returned to Minnesota. On 3 July 1863, a farmer saw them picking berries and shot at them, killing Little Crow. After covering his father with a blanket, the son withdrew.

Little Ida survived and eventually met her future husband, my grandfather. They were married in Minneapolis and had one son, Rolf Cirkler Aurness, in 1895.

During his early years, my father lived the formal lifestyle of his parents. Peter wanted him to study medicine, and Rolf enrolled at the University of Minnesota. But he was not overly studious, and when World War I broke out he joined the Army. During his two-year tour he contracted the Spanish Flu, a mysterious disease that killed some 70 million worldwide. Surfacing in 1918 in the Middle Eastern battle lines, it spread rapidly north and west and then to America, where it caused the death of 400,000 otherwise healthy people between the ages of 20 and 40. In mid–1919, the unexplained, untreatable epidemic came to a halt and disappeared.

Dad, who never left the States, was one of the lucky ones to survive. He returned to the

Mom and Dad pictured in 1918. Dad was an Army officer in the Cavalry during World War I. The picture was taken in Minneapolis while he was home on leave. My parents had the picture taken, standing on top of a railroad car, in a spirit of fun and joy in seeing each other. (Arness Collection.)

university after leaving the service, but he dropped out. He just wasn't interested in academics. But he was intrigued by a young lady, Ruth Duesler, and it wasn't long before they were going steady and talking about marriage.

Ruth was a highly intelligent young woman. While dating Rolf, she won a university contest that resulted in an all-expense paid trip to Europe. While they were apart, their romance blossomed by letter, and they decided to get married upon her return. When she disembarked from her ship in New York, Rolf was there to meet her. Everything was already arranged, and they were married in the Church of the Transfiguration, known as the "Little Church Around the Corner," in downtown Manhattan.

Mom and me, age 2. Mom was probably pregnant with Pete when this was taken. You can tell from the photo that she always liked me to be well dressed. (Arness Collection.)

They returned to Minneapolis, where they lived in a small apartment. At first Rolf managed a drug store owned by the Cirkler family, but then he got a job as a traveling salesman for Becton Dickinson & Company, a New Jersey medical supply firm. He worked for them from the time I was born right up until World War II.

I joined the Aurness family on 26 May 1923, and Pete followed in 1926. It was around that time that we moved to a house on Cromwell Drive, an idyllic setting for kids. We were outdoors most of the time building forts, fishing, playing in dense forests. During the winter months we went ice skating and sledding, and often just rolled joyously around in the snow. When I reached the age to go to John Burrows Grade School, I found that I had real difficulty sitting inside for eight hours a day. After all the freedom we had enjoyed during the previous years, it just was too confining. I looked out the window and just waited to be let out. Then I'd walk home on a path that wound alongside a running creek, with sunlight filtering through the oaks and other trees. It was nature at its most beautiful.

I played football as a youngster but was not interested in playing in high school or college. I belonged to a boy's athletic club where I also participated in basketball, baseball and hockey. (Arness Collection.)

Every Sunday we went to our grandparents' Victorian house for dinner. Mom spruced up Pete and me and reminded us of our manners, and we'd enjoy the warmth of their home. They had a big old touring car, in which we got to ride for picnic outings. They also had a barn in back of the house, where they kept several horses. Pete and I were allowed to ride them during our Sunday visits.

We were very close to my father's parents. They died within a few years of each other, in the late 1920s.

On Ruth's side of the family, her mother came from a little town in North Dakota where she had worked as the postmistress. At some point she relocated to Minneapolis, where she met and married Hess Graves Duesler. Her name was Mabel (Schroutenbach), but we knew her as Grandma Duesler. She could usually be found in her kitchen, cooking up the most scrumptious delicacies while a victrola played opera at full blast.

I used to sit there for hours, listening to Caruso and the other great singers of that time. Once in a while she'd play Al Jolson, singing "California Here I Come." I didn't realize then how prophetic that song would be for me in later years, as I headed west to seek my fame and fortune.

I never got to know Grandpa Duesler as well—he was more distant, and was usually at work. He was assistant treasurer at the Minneapolis Gas Light Company.

Dad worked a lot too, but I got to go with him sometimes. He'd take me on some of his trips, and I saw parts of Wisconsin and Michigan and the Sault Saint Marie Locks, all of which was a thrill for me. To watch the huge ore ships go through the locks was awesome. Dad loved the outdoors, and hunting and fishing. Along with the medical supplies he stored in the trunk of his car, he always carried fishing gear or hunting rifles, depending on the season.

When I was eleven years old, Dad began to teach me everything he knew about hunting. He bought me a .22 caliber rifle, a Browning semi-automatic, it was as good as any gun out there today; there haven't been many advances made in the .22 Browning. It was a beautiful gun but very tricky and could be fired accidentally if it wasn't handled carefully. My Dad was very safety conscious and taught me how to handle the gun and others we used later on. He took me hunting with him during my teens and we never hunted deer or larger animals; bird shooting was his passion, particularly pheasants. Minnesota was a pheasant hunter's paradise in the fall. Outside of the city was all farmland and that's where we'd find them. My Dad knew a number of farmers who would let us go on their farms when the corn had been stacked up and the pheasants would be feeding on corn shocks that were scattered around the fields. We'd usually hit a wooded area first and then walk onto a corn field and flush out the birds. We had a dog, a Springer Spaniel named "Lucky," who would flush the birds out for us and we'd shoot at 'em and always get a few. My Dad would frequently bring a few pals with him, who were good shooters and would take time to teach me how to hunt properly. Shooting birds in flight is not easy when you're first learning, but in time I got to be a pretty good shot.

I remember a time when my Dad and I and some friends, Lloyd Pattee and his wife, went up to Leach Lake, a great place to hunt ducks. We got in a boat and motored up into a bay on the east end of the lake which was a huge rice paddy that was owned, I believe, by an Indian tribe. We'd cruise among the four foot high paddies until we found a good hiding spot, then wait for flocks of ducks to fly over. Often hundreds of them would fill the sky and we'd shoot away dropping a number of them. One time when I was on the lake in November it was freezing cold and snow was in the air. As some ducks flew by I stood up to fire my 12 gauge shotgun, lost my balance and dropped the gun into the water. I knew the water was only a few feet deep and instinctively jumped overboard to retrieve the gun that was somewhere down among the rice shoots. My Dad and his friends were surprised at this and hollered for me to come back. Within minutes I had found the gun and climbed back into the boat. I was soaking wet and Dad immediately motored us ashore and built a big bonfire. I had to take off all my clothes and wear what clothing our friends could spare until my own dried out. Mr. Pattee got a big kick out of my effort to recover the gun in spite of the weather, and after that incident he treated me like a real hunter. He was very proud of me.

The Pattees ran a wholesale jewelry business in Minneapolis. He and his wife, DeeDee, came from Spokane, Washington, where she had gone to school with Bing Crosby at Gonzaga University. As a youngster, I was always looking

Family picture taken in 1936 when I was about 13. Left to right: Pete, Dad, Mom and a sprouting future U.S. Marshal. The photograph was taken in front of our home on Cromwell Drive in Minneapolis. We lived there from 1925 through World War II. My parents built the home, which was on the last street in town. A few blocks from our house was a dairy farm, and once in a while a cow would come wandering down our street. It was my job to return all such escapees to the farm. (Arness Collection.)

for ways to make money and Mr. Pattee offered me a job at his business; I ended up as a sort of courier. He would give me a package to take to some other jewelry store or up to Donaldson's department store and I would deliver the package that I assumed held jewelry of some sort. I appreciated his trust in me at an early age and I felt that he was teaching me to be responsible. I remember his office, which was on the second floor above a big hardware store in downtown Minneapolis. Their establishment consisted of one big room, and Mr. Pattee didn't have a private office. He sat down at the end of the room where he could observe his employees to make sure that everyone was working. I think he paid me $13 a week. I found a way to make the money look a little more valuable. There was a vat of cyanide in a back room that was used to clean jewelry and precious metals. When I got paid I'd go to the bank and get 13 silver dollars and take them back to the office where a guy in the back room would lower them into the cyanide vat. The result was 13 silver dollars that looked like they had just been minted. I would place the coins in a marble bag I carried and put them in my pocket. Man, I felt like I was really a wealthy person. It was great to walk around with that feeling! Whatever the money would buy, I bought it, though I did save a little of it.

While Dad was teaching me the ways of an outdoorsman, Mother was instilling another trait in Pete and me by encouraging us to read. She read to us every evening while we were young, from all kinds of children's books. She had quite a dramatic flair. She could read almost like an actor, and really got involved in her performances. Reading was a very big part of her life, and she wanted it to be equally important in ours. I still have some of the books she used to read to us. When I got old enough to read on my own, she would provide me with different ideas about what I should read. I always favored adventure books. One time I had this complete dream of going to sea in a small sailing boat. Maybe it was part of my "Norskie" heritage. Knowing how much I enjoyed these types of books, she would direct me to authors like Richard Halliburton, a prominent American travel and adventure writer, who spent most of his life exploring the world. His adventures included following Ulysses' route through the Mediterranean, emulating Lord Byron by swimming the Hellespont, swimming the Panama Canal and climbing the Matterhorn, Mt. Olympus and Mt. Fuji. In one of his

Me at 15, enjoying the wonders of nature on our island at Ox Lake just north of Brainerd, Minnesota. Pete and I slept in this tent at night, and the little cabin that was on the island was occupied by the women—Mom and her two sisters and my cousins. We did all our own cooking on a cast iron stove, and I was the official wood chopper. (Arness Collection.)

books he made the comment, "Well, I've grown up now. But as yet I haven't a son or any daughter to go traveling with me. And so, in their places, may I take you with me?" In his short life span of 39 years, he wrote numerous books which I practically devoured. They included, *The Glorious Adventure*, *New Worlds to Conquer*, *The Flying Carpet*, and *The Orient*. His ending came rather unexpectedly when he left Hong Kong in March of 1939 aboard a motor-powered Chinese junk, *Sea Dragon*, en route to San Francisco. He, his crew and boat disappeared after encountering a severe typhoon 1,200 miles west of Midway Island. The last radio message received from him read, "Southerly gales, squalls, lee rail under water, wet bunks, hard tack, bully beef, wish you were here—instead of me." I've been an avid reader my whole life, as a result of that early exposure to books.

Mother was also the disciplinarian in our family. She encouraged Pete and me to do something with our lives, and she was a major factor in teaching us courtesy and the social graces. Mother took us to symphonies and the opera, ensuring that we would grow up to be well-rounded young men. She was always cheering on her boys to excel in whatever we attempted; she was just a "you can do it!" type of person.

I only dreaded one thing upon which she insisted: dancing lessons. Each Saturday night we attended a session in which the girls were on one side of the room, while we boys nervously paced across from them on the other side. When directed, we had to walk up to one of them and ask them to dance. It was all very awkward for us.

My mother loved to walk. She'd take me with her and we'd hike out into the farmlands just beyond where we lived. We'd also hike several blocks from our house down to Lake Harriet and walk around the lake which was a pretty good hike. While we walked, she'd speak about her hopes for me, things that I could do. She would emphasize that I just had to form the right moral habits. She was a wonderful person, great at building a fire under you to get you doing things you never dreamed possible. My mother wanted Pete and me to be more involved in activities in school and at work and socialize, i.e., be a part of what was called in those days "the polite society." My preference was to escape "polite society" and stay out in the woods and fields.

During his travels, Dad learned about a cabin that was for rent on an island in the middle of Ox Lake, near Brainerd, Minnesota. It was about 90 miles north of Minneapolis. We went up and looked at the place and fell in love with it. The cabin rented for $300 for the entire summer. This island became our second home. I spent all my summers there, from about the age of 7 until I began to work at various summer jobs when I turned 16. Those times on the lake were filled with swimming, fishing, sailing, and just enjoying the serenity of the place. I had my first experience with sailing while summering on Ox Lake. We had a row boat that was designed and built by the "Scandahoovians" in Northern

Minnesota. The design actually came from Norway dating way back to Viking times. The boat was called a lap-strake, round bottomed boat. It was a common boat used on the lakes up there and I believe it was the best boat in the water compared to others there at the time. I got to thinking about converting the boat into a sailing ship and my Dad was all for it. He found a lateen sail which had a triangular sail affixed to a long yard or crossbar, mounted at the middle to the top of a mast and angled to extend aft far above the mast and forward down nearly to the deck. The sail, its free corner secured near the stern, was capable of taking the wind on either side and by enabling our boat to tack into the wind, the lateen greatly increased the potential of our "sailing ship." My Dad installed the lateen on the boat and using an oar for a rudder at the stern we went out on the water, caught some favorable winds and we were indeed sailing! It was a galvanizing experience for me and I knew that from then on I wanted sailing to be a part of my life. We also had an X-class boat, a 16 footer, that belonged to the owner of the island.

When summer ended we'd take our boat to Lake Calhoun near Minneapolis where we could use it right up until the local lakes began to freeze. Then we'd store it for the winter and in early spring we'd get it back out, put it on the lake and go sailing. I've traveled far and wide since then, but the memories of Ox Lake are among my happiest. It was there that I began to wonder about bigger waters—the ocean. What was it like not to be able to see the other side? How towering were the waves? The mere idea of an ocean fascinated me. Someday I hoped to see those waves for myself.

Often my summer days included bike hikes where I'd just roam around the countryside. One of my favorite stops during these ventures was the local airport. I was fascinated watching airplanes take off, fly around the field, then come in to land. One day a guy who worked there invited me into a hangar to see an old Waco biplane up close. He let me climb into the cockpit and sit in the pilot's seat! As I looked over the instruments, I imagined myself in the air. I didn't know it then, of course, but eventually flying would become an important part of my life.

Aside from discovering spots of secluded beauty, Dad also showed us more populated parts of the world, such as a fair in Minneapolis with rides and sideshows. One of them had a barker yelling, "Come in and meet Jack Johnson, World Heavyweight Champion!" Dad and I were into boxing at the time. Soon we found ourselves inside the tent facing Jack Johnson, who was sitting on a little raised platform. He was really a massive guy. He smiled at us, and Dad introduced me, and we shook hands.

Later, as I became more familiar with the sport, we'd sit by the radio and listen to Joe Louis fights. It was a popular neighborhood pastime. In fact, if you stuck your head outside your house during the fight, you'd hear radios blaring all up and down the block, all tuned to the same bout. After each round we'd run out into the street and talk excitedly, then dash back into our houses as the bell rang, signaling the start of the next round. In later years, I got to meet Joe Louis, Jack Dempsey, and Rocky Marciano in person.

Fighting was big in those days, and not only organized bouts in the ring. Back in the '30s, gangsters like Al Capone, John Dillinger, and "Baby Face" Nelson were in their heyday. Shoot-outs were commonplace in broad daylight, between police officers and criminals on the run.

One summer our family went for a picnic to the St. Croix River up near Stillwater, north of Minneapolis. We drove through one small town and saw cops all over the place, some carrying Tommy Guns. We stopped, and Dad asked someone what was going on. Dillinger might be in the neighborhood, he was told. There was a prison in Stillwater, and Dillinger might be planning to break someone out of the place. Mother got worried, so we turned around and found another picnic area some distance away.

I read later that Dillinger was not in the Minneapolis area at the time. But the infamous gangster "Baby Face" Nelson was holed up in our sister city, St. Paul, which had a hideout arrangement for criminals. It was called the St. Paul Layover. From the beginning of the century to the late '30s, St. Paul was regarded as the safest place for gangsters to hide from federal and local law-enforcement officers. Around 1910, Police Chief John J. O'Connor put out the word that out-of-town criminals could "lay over" in St. Paul and enjoy the offerings of the city, as long as they broke no laws. As a result, crime statistics were practically nil, and gangsters from all over the country could be seen eating in St. Paul's best restaurants and spending their money freely. When a criminal arrived in town, he was required to report to Paddy Griffin's lodging house on Wabash Street, where he was assigned a room and charged an exorbitant fee.

O'Connor's operation was the result of the political clout of his younger brother, Richard, recognized as the boss of the city and state Democratic party. He was well known for his dedication to protecting the poor, and the layover system seemed to complement his philosophy. The people of St. Paul didn't seem to mind the arrangement, since they enjoyed a crime-free environment where a woman could walk down the street at night alone. But the system started to unravel when Chief O'Connor retired because of poor health, and his brother shifted his attention to national politics.

Paddy Griffin was replaced by Dapper Danny Hogan. He made incoming criminals report to him at the Green Lantern Saloon, within sight of the state capitol. The new chief of police opposed the operation but could do little, since the system was so deeply ingrained in the city. Then Hogan was killed by a car bomb, on 5 December 1928.

His partner, Harry Sawyer, took over. Local politicians and city officials saw no reason to continue St. Paul's special status, and crime soon returned to the once-peaceful city. Sawyer joined an underworld gang and eventually went to prison on a life sentence for his part in the kidnapping of a banker.

It was in this world, in some places tranquil and in others fraught with brutality, that I finally graduated from John Burrows Grade School. I must admit that I had been a poor student, struggling all the way through and not getting good grades. I entered Ramsey Junior High at the 7th grade level not knowing what courses to take, since those offered seemed so difficult. While I was trying to decide, another student approached me and suggested glee club. This sounded pretty soft to me, so I signed up and wound up really enjoying the club. The other courses, I just sort of endured.

But there was another problem even further alienating me from school. I suddenly started growing like a weed. Up to that time I had been tall, but in the same realm as my peers. Then I began to shoot up, and in one year I was four inches taller than anyone else in my class. By the time I finished junior high, I was 6' 7". I took a lot of razzing from other students asking me how the weather was up there and other such remarks, poking fun at me. Kids are cruel, and I resented their teasing. Seeing how this bothered me, my mother wrote me a poem, "To a Young Giant," assuring me that one day my height would be a sign of distinction and that I would go on to great things. I treasure that poem still.

I'd had it with school anyway. I didn't want any part of it. My glee club director encouraged me to stick it out and even cast me in a school play, *The Emperor's Clothes*, which turned out to be a great personal success. I played the tailor. Another student had to be fitted for the big fancy dress ball, and I had to measure him. In our scene together, I held one end of a long tape measure on the floor, while I reached up with my other hand to his full height. We kept a humorous dialogue running for the whole scene, and everything came together. We had a great time doing the scene. The families in the audience loved this bit of comedic business, and I got the biggest hand of anyone in the play. It was the only time in school when I enjoyed being tall.

After barely getting through Ramsey, I went on to Washburn High School. The next thing I knew, the football coach had me in his clutches. Once he saw my size, he told me that I just had to try out for the freshman team. I did, but soon found that I didn't care for the discipline involved. Somebody always seemed to be hollering at me to do this or that; I just couldn't get into it. I talked with the coach and told him football wasn't for me. He let me go, and that was the extent of my high school football career.

I went through Washburn still feeling a sense of alienation because of my size, especially since girls had now become a factor, and I wanted to date. But again I felt awkward, and as a result wasn't very successful. I could only get dates with girls that I'd known before, and then we'd just go to movies. No dances or social gatherings. I felt like an outcast all the way through school.

When the lakes froze over around Minneapolis, ice boats began to appear and I mentioned to my Dad that it looked as if we might be missing a lot of fun. I asked him if we could build one of our own. He was all for it and we collected

TO A YOUNG GIANT
(Jim, age 14 years)

In sunlight you cast a shadow tall
Each ounce with the bounce of a ping-pong ball
I delight in your sapling strength
But you abhor your special length.

You'd shrink I think if you could be
Cut to your age-pattern, sparingly
Head and shoulders above the throng
Makes you feel you don't "belong."

But Oh my fine rebellious son
Your life-span has but begun
Tall distinction to you now, so poor
Will be envied by others when you're mature.

If I could only foretell to you
The limitless things you may live to do!
Stand tall son, clear-eyed, fearless
Be a giant-hearted giant … peerless!

Mother
1937

My mother and the poem she wrote for me in 1937.

all the necessary materials and built ourselves a boat which was first class. He loved that kind of work and particularly liked carpentry. Once the boat was completed he got some wooden runners made and had some angled iron bent to fit on the runners. We put it on Lake Harriet and man I was in hog heaven. That boat got me through the winters because I couldn't take it in school and every time I got the chance I'd be on Lake Harriet racing with some of my Washburn school buddies. It wasn't unusual to reach speeds of 40 miles an hour when strong winds swept over the lake. Later I bought a larger boat with some help from my Dad. I worked on the side through all these times, delivering papers, selling magazines door-to-door, always looking for a way to make a few bucks. My Dad always operated on the premise that when I'd earn a certain amount of money he'd kick in some matching dollars (often exceeding my share) and we'd buy more new sporting equipment, a longed for shotgun, things that we could enjoy outdoors. However, we almost had one mishap which could have cost me and my Dad's boss our lives and of course Dad's job. Dad's boss came out for a visit from the Becton Dickinson factory in New Jersey. He was a very nice guy and my folks took him around to meet our friends and enjoy several parties. He knew that I had an ice boat and I asked him if he'd like a ride. He said sure and since this was late in the spring, the ice had melted along the shore so you had to walk on a wooden 2 × 12 plank from the shore to the ice a little further out to man your boat. The best sailing was in late spring. All the snow had melted into the ice but it left a great crust on top which the runners could really bite into. In the fall right after the lake froze it was great if you could get it before a snowfall, because it was like a sheet of glass. But at the same time you could slide easily. If you broke the louvered runner loose, the thing would just go into a big 360 degree spin which happened plenty of times. We tipped over quite often. When I took my Dad's boss out to the lake and he looked over the situation, he said, "Are you sure it's safe to walk over these planks to get to the boat?" I answered that it was and we both made it out to the boat and there was a heck of a nice wind blowing. We ripped across the lake at about 40 miles an hour, sailed to the other end and started back. I was facing forward, holding onto the tiller and laying forward in the netting. He sat in front of me and kept looking behind us. Finally, he said

My Dad and I built an ice boat which gave us many hours of enjoyment skimming across Lake Harriet in Minneapolis during the frozen winter months of 1938. The ice boat would go up to about 40 miles an hour with the right wind and ice conditions. If I was in school and saw the wind pick up, I'd duck out of class with two or three of my pals to get the perfect ride. On ideal days the lake was teeming with ice boats crisscrossing each other. We had many a close call. (Arness Collection.)

"Look behind us!" I looked back and saw that the ice was sort of gently rolling behind us. I realized that we could have broken through at any time. I hadn't experienced this before and kept on going because there had been a number of occasions when people broke through the ice on the lake and drowned. That happened fairly often during the winter months, and the spring and fall. I ended up sailing the boat full blast right up onto the shore. I heard from him years later when I was on *Gunsmoke* and sure enough he'd always mention that frightful experience in his letters. By the way, Dad continued to work for the company for many more years, so no harm was done by our little adventure.

We loved to skate, and especially to ski. There was a ski jump near Bush Lake, and we used to go there and watch guys go off it. It all looked pretty dangerous to us, but they were good and very few suffered any serious falls.

We skied all the time in the winter. There was a hillside behind our house, sloping down into a little valley. We'd jump off frozen turf and go a few feet in the air, hoping someday to become good enough to join the jumpers at Bush Lake. I always aspired to be a part of that group, but I never made it because it took so much practice. I did improve my skiing skills, though, when the Norwegian brothers Anders and Lars Hougan came to America and settled in Minneapolis. They were marvelous skiers, and when they started giving lessons, it seemed like everyone wanted them, including me and my folks. They taught us not only downhill but cross-country skiing out in the farmlands. The Hougan brothers stayed in the city for years.

While I was still at Washburn I got into trouble skipping classes, running around and being a little wild and crazy. The school officials finally caught up with me and decided to take some action. The principal called me into his office and said, "Look, you know things aren't too good for you. You're getting bad grades and you're in trouble with your skipping classes and rousting about with other classmates. In summary, you're setting a bad example for the other students." He further stated that West High was just as close to my home as Washburn, in fact I lived in the West High school district. He suggested that I transfer to West High which I did, not knowing what to expect.

I found a completely different atmosphere at my new school. Washburn was in a sedate neighborhood, while West High was a much older high school, farther west in town. The students were far more friendly, and I made some new friends there who were sort of rebel types. Like Oswald Wyatt and my other pals, they didn't care much for school. We'd take off from our classes and just sort of bum around together.

My mother had graduated from West High (one of her teachers was still there), and she was delighted with my new life, as was I. I joined a choral group and, as before, excelled in this class, encouraged by my music teacher. Of course I still had to struggle with the other subjects.

As I sat in class, I listened for the whistling of the freight trains coming down the track near school. They began to fascinate me. At night a bunch of us would go down to the yards and climb into the boxcars. Often we'd run alongside a moving car and practice jumping into it. Two or three trains would go by every day, and it was as if they were calling me to leave with them.

Finally I just had to do it: a few of us ducked out of school and jumped a freight headed for Lake Minnetonka, 30 miles west of Minneapolis. We started going often. Sometimes we'd hop a freight train that took us a bit farther down the line, and when it slowed we'd jump off and hike around the countryside, then hitchhike home. Our train excursions began to cover longer distances, and sometimes we'd stay overnight at a rail yard and return the next day.

On one occasion we decided to hop a freight and go to Wilmer, Minnesota, 'cause the parents of one of our buddies had a cabin just outside of the town. Wilmer wasn't too far, maybe 70 or 80 miles, and though it was freezing cold we went down to the yards and caught a train rolling through the yards headed towards Wilmer. We managed to get on but got onto an open "gondola-like" car; we couldn't find a box car that was open. We sat in the car as we went alongside the highway. We noticed a lot of loose wood in the bottom of the car and we were so cold that we built a huge fire to keep warm. Of course this caught the attention of those driving by and it was a wonder that we didn't burn up the whole car. Luckily no one reported us to the railroad security guards. During the spring when we would be riding the rails several of us used to get together and read poetry to each other. We read Robert W. Service, a popular verse writer who was often called the Canadian Kipling. His best known work in those days was "The Shooting of Dan McGrew." I can remember many of the lines of Service and other poets to this day. We dreamed up a fantasy where we were going to go up to the Great Slave Lake in northern Canada and escape from school and home and live in a cabin. Robert Service's poetry described some of that country, wild and free, a place you could be a million miles away from anywhere.

One of my friends, Bill O'Brien, moved to Fargo, North Dakota, with his family and a couple of us decided to go visit him. We located a freight train that was going to Fargo and hopped on board. When we were about halfway there the train stopped at a little town to take on water. We were sitting in a box car with the door open and right across the tracks I saw a little grocery store on the edge of town. I told the others that I was going to run over to the store and get some candy bars and potato chips and jumped out of the car. When I was in the store, I heard the whistle of a train coming fast down the track and I had no idea what was going on. I ran out of the store and saw our train slowly pulling out, headed west and coming toward me was this fast moving train heading east for Minneapolis. I knew that I had to catch our train or be left stranded far from home. I ran for our train with the eastbound train fast approaching and got between the trains running alongside ours hoping to reach my buddies and be pulled in or grab something that I could use to pull myself up onto the train.

There was little room between the cars of the opposite going trains and I was right in the midst of the screeching sounds of rolling cars and rumbling wheels. It was a deafening noise and as I looked ahead I saw that I was headed for a signal light embedded in my pathway. I decided to run as fast as I could and hope to get aboard the train before I got to the signal light. If I didn't get aboard before the signal light became a serious problem, I planned to drop to the ground and let everything pass by. At the last minute my buddies hauled me in as the light signal flashed by the open door. I was lucky not to have been killed. The whole thing was completely crazy.

On another occasion while I was riding the rails, two of my buddies and I decided to meet on a street corner on a Saturday morning sometime between Christmas and New Year's and hike out to the Minnesota River. We had some hot dogs and snacks with us and were going to build a fire and just kind of do a winter camp outing. When we met on the street corner it was absolutely frigid and we weakened in our resolve to hike to the river. Instead we decided to thumb a ride. A guy finally stopped and we jumped in. He asked where we were going and we told him the Minnesota River. He answered that he was going all the way to Marshalltown, Iowa. Since one of our gang had just moved to Des Moines, Iowa, we decided to take the ride to Marshalltown and then catch a freight train to Des Moines via Ames, Iowa, which was a short distance away from our destination. We arrived in Marshalltown at dark and we hung around waiting for a train going west. Within an hour or so the Corn King Limited of the Illinois Central line out of Chicago arrived and took on water and passengers. It was not a passenger train so we waited until it started to pull out then leaped aboard the coal tender. We hopped off when it reached Ames, Iowa, and calmly walked into the station house. I thought the local station keeper was going to faint. It was about 3:00 in the morning and we couldn't understand his reaction until we looked at each other and saw that we were filthy with coal dust. The steam from the engine had combined with the coal dust to cover us with wet, black grime. We told the man that we were just some high school guys trying to get to Des Moines. He became quite friendly and said he'd get us in the baggage car of the next train going there. We arrived in Des Moines and our buddy picked us up and took us to his home. His mother washed our clothes and we were treated like celebrities since we had ridden freight trains some 400 miles to come visit a friend. We spent a very delightful New Year's Eve in Des Moines. We called our parents at the insistence of the lady whose home we were in and although our mothers all wanted to send us bus tickets to return home, the fathers insisted that since we found our way to Des Moines on our own we could use the same ingenuity to come home. The next morning we caught a passenger train to Minneapolis and once again found ourselves riding in a coal tender. We finally pulled into the South St. Paul freight yards in the middle of the night and I caught a streetcar back home. My father was waiting up for me and took me down to the basement into the laundry room where I cleaned up, washed my clothes and went to bed. In the morning when my mother woke up I looked halfway decent. I've often thought back on those days when I was riding the rails and since it was in the '30s and the Depression was on, we'd ride with men who were down on their luck and hoping to find work in towns along the rail line. They were all nice guys, friendly and willing to share what food they could spare. Even though they probably knew that we might have had a little money on us, there was never a hassle with any of them. Trying to travel the same way today I imagine would be quite risky since many petty criminals ride freight trains these days.

Across the tracks from where we used to hop on the freight trains there was a block of apartment buildings. The bottom story was half underground, it was almost like a basement but was half way up. We used to go down some steps to a little corner grocery store in the building and the grocer had a back room where he used to store his goods. He liked us 'cause we used to visit his store and spend money buying snacks almost daily. He'd let us go into his back room and we'd spend our time playing penny ante poker. We'd use an old carton for a table and sit around it playing by the hour. Guys would come and go, most of the time skipping classes. I have to admit that this was the fun part of going to West High. Attending classes and getting serious about school work was still a problem for me. What I really enjoyed was singing with choral groups, glee clubs and an "a cappella" choir. I continued to improve and my teacher told me that I might have a career as a singer. He suggested that I consider trying out for the Hennepin Avenue Methodist Church Choir since it was the top choir in Minneapolis. My mother further encouraged me to join, so I went to see the conductor of the choir, Turi Fredrickson, to get an audition scheduled. Fredrickson was either a Swede or a Norwegian and was considered to be one of the finest church organists in the country. When we met it was obvious that my teacher had told him about me and after a pleasant conversation he said, "Well, why don't you sit in tonight for choir rehearsal and just listen and see what you think?" I listened to the group and knew immediately that I wanted to be a part of it. Within a week he gave me a tryout and eventually had enough confidence in me to put me in the choir. I was about 16 or 17 at the time and very proud to be a member of the prestigious Hennepin Avenue choir. Following a rehearsal on Thursday we'd go to the church on Sunday morning, put on our robes and file down into the choir loft which was behind the pulpit in front of the organ. The pipe organ was huge and from the loft we looked down on the entire congregation. The church was a beautiful Gothic cathedral and for two years I became totally engaged in the spiritual atmosphere of the church, the sermons and the wonderful old Protestant hymns we sang. It was so uplifting that even though I was still riding the rails, I was diligent about being back in town to sing with the choir for two services every Sunday. I loved being a part of that experience back then. I think in a way it balanced the scales for me.

By the time I was 18, I was looking for farther-flung adventures than train hopping. Ships intrigued me, and in the summer of 1941, I read that people could book passage on freighters. I talked it over with my folks; Dad said that if I worked for half the summer, he'd match whatever money I made. Then we'd check it out to see if it was doable. Ironically, I found a job in the Minneapolis freight yards loading and unloading boxcars.

At first my mom made lunch for me, but before long the other guys asked me to join them for lunch at a local restaurant. A whole plate of chicken, beef, or meatloaf with mashed potatoes and a vegetable and bread cost twenty cents. I often ordered two plates—chicken and meatloaf—and downed the food with coffee at five cents a cup. Lunch became a great treat for me. I worked in the yards for several weeks, then Dad matched what I made and we lined up a trip.

I took a train from Minneapolis to Houston, Texas, then a bus to Galveston. When I got to Galveston, I immediately went down to the dock where my ship was tied up. I remember looking at the ship and thinking, *man*, this is a life's dream come true, to get on a ship and head out onto the ocean. The freighter, operated by the Lykes Shipping Company, was small, maybe 2,000 tons. That's tiny by today's standards. I went aboard and met the crew and other passengers and was just thrilled about my new surroundings and the forthcoming voyage to the Caribbean. I always had a fantasy about going to sea, however, living in land-locked Minnesota was as far away from salt water as one could get. We left the dock and made our first stop at Beaumont, Texas. There was a young man aboard who acted as the ship's purser. He was a student at Texas A&M and a little older than I was but we easily developed a friendship and were pals during the course of the trip. We next headed for Cuba and docked at a little town, Cienfuegos, on the southern coast of the island. It was a fairly good sized town and it was well known as the home of Bacardi rum. Since we were scheduled to spend a few days there, someone suggested that we take a tour of the area and visit the Bacardi factory. About ten of us got on a bus and toured the city and ended up at the factory. Most of the passengers were school teachers and later during the trip we exchanged information about ourselves, where we came from, what schools we attended and so on. I told them that I was a poor student and I remember sitting on the deck with several of them around me encouraging me to go back, study hard and continue with my education. They were all very nice people but we didn't have much in common when it came to academics. When we arrived at the Bacardi factory we were greeted by the manager of the facility and he personally took us on a tour, proudly showing us the workings of the plant and stopping now and then to introduce us to some of his employees. Everyone seemed to be delighted to see us and it was obvious that they took pride in their work. After we completed the tour they took us to a patio where we sat and were served drinks. In fact, we could have as many drinks as we wished and as usual when people are on vacation and in a festive mood, the rum kept flowing. We all got so completely plastered that we barely could find our tour bus! When we arrived back at the ship the crew was taking aboard cattle and putting them in pens which had been built on the deck of the ship while it was in Galveston. Believe it or not they had a real cowboy on board (probably the first real one I had ever seen) who was in charge of handling the deck load of cattle. The ship's next port of call was Colon, Panama, where the cattle would be offloaded.

We left Cuba and headed for Colon. I found it fascinating to be on a freighter in the open seas with a deck loaded with cattle. I used to visit the young purser who had a small office aft of the bridge. He introduced me to the captain, "Wee Willy" Henderson, a Scotsman who spoke with a brogue. Years later when I was doing *Gunsmoke*, I mentioned that Caribbean experience during an interview and a few weeks later the studio got a call from Henderson's granddaughter who lived in Texas. She and her family came to California and visited us on the set. We had a wonderful chat about her granddad and his ship.

There was a small dining room where the passengers ate their meals. Captain Henderson would sometimes come by and chat with us. I think he took a liking to me because he could see how totally stoked up I was by being at sea on his ship. As a result he often invited me to visit him on the bridge. About the second day out we ran into a major tropical storm, huge waves were washing over the deck and the bow was plunging in and out of the sea. I was standing up on the bridge, getting soaking wet from heavy rains and loving every minute of it, although I don't know why. The worst part of the storm lasted about a day, then the wind let up and the sea became calm. Unfortunately, about half of the cattle drowned and the cowboy had to dispose of them over the side. When we got to Colon I helped unload the remaining cattle. Across the pier where we were tied up was a freighter with a Nazi flag waving from its fantail. It was the summer of '41 and I had heard about the war in Europe but knew few details about it.

Colon was a busy port servicing ships from all over the world, including those that passed through the Panama Canal. One can only imagine the intrigue in the city, with spies from various countries packing the bars collecting intelligence information.

We spent a few days in Colon and one evening several of us decided to go into the city and just cruise around. At the time the city was a duty free port. In other words you could buy anything in the shops and not have to pay taxes. I bought a few Panama hats that were rolled up in a tube, some ivory figurines and a Japanese-made fan for my mother. The cowboy and the purser were with us and early in the evening we all decided to go into a bar in the middle of town. It was a wild kind of saloon, packed with people standing and sitting almost on top of each other. Luckily we found a table, sat down and ordered a few drinks. Our festive mood changed somewhat when we found German sailors sitting all

High school graduation picture, age 18. (Arness Collection.)

around us. There was kind of "Casablanca" air about the place. We soon returned to the ship. We departed the next morning for Colombia and visited two ports, Cartagena and Barranquilla where we unloaded and loaded various types of cargo. We finally headed for New Orleans and home. I arrived back in Minneapolis by train, just in time to start my final year at West High.

It was quite a change, but once back in school I got into the old routine. I sang with the Methodist choir and struggled through my regular courses, attempting to get passing grades to graduate. One Sunday morning in December 1941, we were all home kicking back when the whole neighborhood erupted with the news of the Pearl Harbor attack by the Japanese.

My folks were pretty upset about the war, but I, a high school kid, was still more focused on escaping from West High with a diploma. Then, a week or two before graduation, the principal called me to her office and proceeded to lecture me. She said something to the effect that she was going to allow me to graduate even though I had been a poor student and had skipped many classes. She said that if it hadn't been for the memory of my Dad's dad, she wouldn't even consider it. Her decision, she said, was based solely on the fact that my grandfather had medically treated her family during the Depression and never asked for remuneration. She told me to get my act together and do something that would make him proud of me. With these words ringing in my ears, I received my high school diploma in June 1942.

That summer, a bunch of us went to Idaho to work in a logging camp. I think the reason they put out a call for younger people was that they were losing their regular workers to the service. We took a train out to Lewiston, Idaho, which was the center of the state's logging industry then. From there we were bused to a small town called Pierce.

That town was close to what Dodge City must have looked like, back in the frontier days. There were no guns or gun play, but plenty of brawls and fist fights. While we were up in the mountains cutting timber, we stayed in bunkhouses that were adjacent to a cook house with a dining room. And, of course, there were outhouses. One night I was sitting in one of them when I heard a banging on the door. Thinking maybe it was some impatient joker, I opened the door to tell him to kindly wait his turn. My heckler, however, was a big black bear that took no notice of me as I went streaking for the bunkhouse!

We worked in forests of old-growth timber. When we first got there, they put us to work piling brush, i.e., gathering all the brush and limbs that had been cut from the timber and stacking them into large piles to be burned. Then I became a bumper (cutting the limbs off logs with an axe) and stamper, which meant hitting the log in several places with a chopping maul whose metal stamp marked the wood as belonging to our camp. During my last days there I became a choker setter, meaning I'd wrap steel cable around one end of a log; the log was then attached to a caterpillar tractor, which towed the timber down to a truck.

The truck took the logs down to a man-made lake and dumped them in the water. They floated out through a wooden trench called a flume, constructed to use lake water for moving timber into the Clearwater River. From there, the logs floated down to Lewiston.

Our pay was $90 a week, which seemed like a lot of money for the work we were doing. We occasionally got letters from home, and we all had to read our letters aloud, so the others could hear news that made them feel closer to their own kin. There was a radio in the dining room, and we frequently listened to Gene Autry singing "There's a Star-Spangled Banner Waving Somewhere." With the war on and Americans going off to fight for our country, the patriotic song inspired everyone.

I enjoyed the whole experience. Years later, when reading about the Lewis and Clark expedition, I learned that they had journeyed just a few miles south of our camp at Pierce.

My mother wanted me to go on to college, and her letters pleaded with me to return home by September 5th, in time for university enrollment. I made it home, but destiny soon took me to Anzio.

Part II

Anzio, 1944

Mother was quite concerned about my lack of interest in higher education. Even though I barely made it out of high school, she was dead set on college. I had a good pal, Oswald Wyatt, who was also a free spirit—we'd often hit the road together just to see what was over the next hill. Finally, our two mothers got together and decided to send us to a small college in Wisconsin—Beloit. A small campus of 500 students, they hoped, would be an ideal place for us to settle down and study.

So we went. But we got somewhat distracted, since we immediately pledged a fraternity, Beta Theta Pi. Studies kind of went out the window—in fact, we never did study. Every night the frat members had a sending-off party for brothers going into the service. Some were drafted and others volunteered, hoping to get into the service of their choice; for most, this was the Army Air Forces.

As for me, I wanted to join the Naval Air Force and become a fighter pilot. As a kid, near our home I'd watched Navy planes taking off and landing at the Wold Chamberlin field (Naval Air Station, Minneapolis, by 1942; George H.W. Bush took his primary flight training there in 1943). There'd been one hangar dedicated to Naval reserve training, and fleet planes were biplanes in those days. They were hot—really hot! My God, I thought, if I could fly one of those fighters, I'd be in hog heaven!

Now, with the war on, it was time to seriously consider a military service rather than waiting to be drafted, which usually meant a quick track into the

27

Army. My father knew how much I wanted to fly and arranged for a naval aviator friend on the base to interview me, to see if I was Navy flight cadet material.

I knew I had little chance of being accepted, because of their stringent requirements. I didn't have 20/20 vision; I had something like 20/40 or 20/80. There were reports out in those days that carrot juice improved eyesight, and I must have downed four quarts of that terrible stuff before my appointment.

Upon my arrival, I was given a cursory physical and eye exam, then ushered into a room where the naval officer awaited me. His expression was not very encouraging. Then he initiated the interview with, "Well, Jim, we're stuck." In the Naval Flight Program, a candidate had to have at least two years of college, with a high grade level.

At that point, I knew I was sunk. He went on to say that I was too tall: the height limit for aviation candidates was 6' 2". At 6' 7", I would be disqualified automatically. So my dreams of wearing Navy wings quickly vanished as I departed the base.

Some of my friends were talking up the Merchant Marines. Though manning Liberty ships that brought supplies to our troops overseas was important to the war effort and sounded adventuresome to me, I didn't seriously consider this option: my mother was still pressing me to stay in school until I got my draft notice. Nevertheless, like many other American boys at the time, I was at the point where I was tempted to volunteer for any military service, just to join my friends who were fast leaving our circle. One of these was Dick Bremicker, who joined the Navy and became a pilot. We'd bummed around throughout our childhood, and later we would strike out for California together.

After the disastrous naval aviator interview, I was so impatient with my situation that I actually wrote my draft board in Minneapolis, asking that they call my number as soon as possible. Evidently my initiative did the trick, for within a few weeks I received my notice. I believe it came in February 1943.

It was a blessing for me, since I wasn't doing well academically and couldn't wait to leave college. But I was in good company when it came to academics: the famous pilot Charles "Lucky Lindy" Lindbergh lived in Little Falls, Minnesota, close to Brainerd, where we spent every summer. He had flunked out of the University of Wisconsin!

I was ordered to report to Fort Snelling on 20 March 1943, for induction into the Army. I'd heard that a special group of soldiers was being training at Aspen, Colorado, to be mountain ski troops. Since I'd been born and raised on skis, this sounded like my kind of action. So during the induction process at Snelling, when asked what my preference was in the Army, I wrote down "Ski Troops."

The officials seemed to approve my choice and wrote "Ski Troops" on my official induction papers. I was really excited about the whole idea, and I passed through the rest of the process with flying colors.

Next we were all loaded onto trucks and taken to a train station, where we were jammed into railroad cars packed with recruits. As we headed south, I was still thinking I was en route to a ski trooper training camp. When I noticed that we were going south along the Mississippi River, I asked a nearby sergeant if we would stop soon so those of us slated for ski troop training could head to our camp out west. He looked rather perplexed. "Ski Troops!" he said, "Boy! You're headed for Camp Wheeler, Georgia, for infantry basic training!"

I thought to myself, my God, there goes the ski troops. But I adjusted to this unexpected turn of events. I decided to give my all to whatever lay ahead. If I was to be an infantryman, I would be the best!

At Macon, Georgia, trucks transported us to the gigantic Wheeler training camp. It was set up in battalion-size groups, each with its own quadrangle where we worked out and did our calisthenics and close-order drill with rifles. We had coal miners from Pennsylvania, mountain men from the Appalachians, laborers and accountants from big cities, and college guys like myself who'd left school to find adventure in serving their country. I watched newsreels with these new buddies, and we talked about what was happening "over there" and how much we wanted to get into the fighting.

Many in our training group were born hunters. We had one recruit who was a real sharpshooter. We were on the rifle range much of the time, and this guy was phenomenal. He'd fire off 20 rounds with his M-1 Garand rifle, and his accuracy was incredible.

I enjoyed our 13 weeks of basic training: it was a great time for me. It was like an adventure. Our days were 12 to 14 hours long, starting with the sound of reveille. We'd be up at the crack of dawn, make our beds to perfection, shower and dress, eat chow, and start the day's training. Twenty-mile marches were common. At 6' 7" and 190 pounds, I was lean and mean, nothing but bone, muscle and sinew. Not an ounce of fat on me, and I could walk. I could knock off one of those 20-mile hikes like it was nothing. I hardly broke a sweat, and this was in Georgia—south Georgia, in the summer, when the temperature was about 100 degrees and the humidity 99 percent.

As we set out on one of these marches, I was given the job of guidon for our company. What that meant was you carried the guidon, a high pole with a flag atop it, and led the marchers. This kept the group marching as one and in a straight line. Of course, platoon sergeants alongside us barked orders to keep in step. My God, it was marvelous. I had more doggone fun doing that. I seemed never to tire.

I got through everything like gangbusters. I was stoked by our routine and had a blast. The regimentation and discipline demanded by the instructors was fun. And being a part of a whole group of guys gave me a great feeling, something I hadn't experienced much before. During my childhood I'd only had a few friends at a time, but now I was part of a group. It gave me a new sense of worth and belonging; those were happy days for me.

Private James K. Arness, U.S. Army, 1945. This picture was taken after I came home from overseas. (Arness Collection.)

After we graduated from Basic, I was called in to see the training sergeant, Bunch. I'll never forget him. Sergeant Bunch was a tough southerner, a straight-talking son of a gun. He kind of liked me, I guess, because of my attitude. I was always gung-ho to do stuff. So when it came time for me to leave, he said, "Look, I'd like to keep you on here. I'll promote you to corporal and make you part of our training staff."

Trying not to upset him, I told him I had different plans, that I really wanted to move on. He looked at me like I was some kind of nut. I'm sure he was thinking this kid didn't know what was ahead of him. He finally nodded his approval, still wearing a perplexed expression. I went home on a five-day pass and cruised around the city, enjoying myself.

My mom was very anxious during my short stay at home. She had enough sense to know where I was probably going, since I'd had basic infantry training. She knew I wasn't going to wind up being a rear-echelon chef or supply soldier. But she was also very encouraging. I would do just fine, she said; I was to do my duty and be a good soldier.

When we said good-bye, her eyes mirrored her fear that she would never see me again, a feeling shared by thousands of mothers as they watched their sons go off. When someone in a family was away in the war, a blue-star pennant was hung in the window. If a gold star replaced it, a son or a father had been lost. Our neighborhoods in Minneapolis had more than their share of gold stars.

My leaving was tough for my mother, but not so much for me. I was ready to get rolling on the ultimate adventure in my young life. I traveled by train to Fort Meade, Maryland, the collecting point for guys from all over the country who'd finished training and were headed overseas. During our week's stay at Meade, we trained some more. Wherever we moved and had time on our hands, we went into immediate training. I guess they didn't want us to lose our edge.

Next stop was Newport News, Virginia. We were marched to this huge camp, back in a forested area just outside of town. The thick undergrowth had all been cut down, and there were squad tents as far as the eye could see. Camp-fires burned at night, and the whole scene reminded me of a Civil War camp. I don't know how many men were there, but there must have been thousands.

We all knew that within a few short days, we would be on our way across the Atlantic. We imagined they would land us somewhere in Northern Africa, where our troops had landed in late 1942 and were presently converging on Tunisia. For a change, we didn't do any training at this new camp. We just rested, ate, and slept, waiting for something to happen. Many of the men shot craps and wrote letters home to while away the hours.

Finally a large convoy of trucks drove into the camp, loaded us aboard, and headed for the docks. As we stood there in groups after offloading, a number of soldiers were coming off a ship that had just tied up. They were a raggedy-looking bunch, and as they marched down the dock toward us, we realized they were German and Italian prisoners of war (POWs). I would think about this moment later, when I was in combat and all hell was breaking loose.

I wondered whether the enemy soldiers I was facing would be sent to America, if they surrendered. Not a bad deal, I thought, going from fierce combat to hog heaven back in America. I eventually learned that they were dispersed all over our country, to work at various military installations. Some even worked at Schick Hospital in Iowa, where I later spent time recovering from my wounds. By the end of the war, we held over half a million German and Italian POWs in 511 camps, converted Civilian Conservation Corps (CCC) camps, high school gyms, and local fairgrounds. Santa Anita race track, in California, was a holding area for thousands of incoming German Afrika Korps captives.

They loaded us right onto the ship, with duffel bags slung over our shoulders. We were directed to the hold, just forward of the bridge, then down two stairways to the bottom of the hold, which had been converted for transporting troops. There were vertical rows of bunk-like hammocks, consisting of two poles with a piece of canvas stretched between them. They were about two feet apart, and 500 men were jammed into this space. Because of my size I couldn't get comfortable, so I spent most of my time on deck.

As we left the dock and moved up the channel, other ships joined us. When we were out at sea and darkness fell, I went below and ate chow, listening to others talk about where we were going and when we would see combat. Soon we bunked out for the night, though unfamiliar ship noises and the sway of the sea interrupted our slumber.

Next morning, we found ourselves in the middle of a huge convoy steaming along at about 10 knots. That was the top speed designated for the convoy, but destroyers ripped up and down its edges at about 30 knots, searching for German U-boats.

They told us that morning we'd have to go on limited rations, because our stores had been inadvertently left on the dock! We grumbled over this news, of course, but it wasn't long before food was the least of our concerns. Far out to sea, the ship ran into a violent storm. Practically everyone became seasick, and within a day or so, the hold was a stinking mess. Everything was plugged up, and the deck below was covered with the retching of hundreds of men. I went back down, gathered my gear and a couple of blankets, and found a gun turret on the forward deck. I think there was a 4-inch gun mounted in it, and a metal shield around it was about three feet high. I'd found a home for the trip. I had protection from the wind and October chill, and, above all, the air was fresh and invigorating.

About the third or fourth day out, the commanding officer of our group approached me and said he was going to put me in charge.

"You're about the only one not seasick and still on your feet," he said. "I want you to communicate any needs the men might have." He himself was too sick to carry out his duties. He made me a temporary master sergeant and pinned new stripes on my uniform. I was somewhat surprised at my change in status, but I carried out his orders for the remainder of the voyage. As soon as we reached North Africa the stripes were to come off, making me a buck private again.

As the men became more accustomed to sea travel and began to feel better, it was clear our limited food rations weren't going to satisfy their hunger. Guys began scrounging around the ship. During the middle of the voyage, some of them broke into one of the holds and found all kinds of stuff, gasoline, ammunition, bombs, and so on. They also found some food—candy bars, cookies, crackers, all kinds of snacks. The men just broke open those crates and took everything.

Our commanding officer, a really nice guy, got us out on deck and pleaded with us to maintain order. "Look," he said, "this is a violation of everything and I need to know who did it!" No one ever came forward individually. But you couldn't argue with what had taken place. Good God, the fools had left our food on the dock! The troops had to eat something. Because I was on deck so much of the time, periodically I'd go back to the merchant marine quarters. They had their own galley, and they took pity on me and shared their food.

Then, early one bright morning amid calm seas, we sighted land. The troops were elated as we entered the port of Casablanca, French Morocco. Back at Camp Wheeler I'd seen the movie *Casablanca* and envisioned a rather exotic city, complete with smoke-filled cafés and French police officers roaming the streets. I thought maybe I'd even bump into a few Humphrey Bogart–like characters, so I was really stoked up about being there. We had to wait a long time outside the harbor because it was cluttered with ships, but finally we entered and tied up to a large wharf.

Everyone was on deck with their duffel bags, ready to depart the ship. Under the wharf was a huge pile of coal, maybe 20 feet high, and on top of it a bunch of Arab women in long dresses waving and yelling at us. They spoke in broken English, taunting us in a very seductive way. This certainly got a rise out of the troops. It was a welcoming committee, but not the usual type: our greeters to Africa were "ladies of the night."

On shore, we piled into trucks and were driven through the city, down narrow streets crowded with Arabs going about their business. Finally, just outside of town, we arrived at a huge tent city. Thousands of soldiers bivouacked there, waiting to be moved closer to combat areas. We were briefed on the local situation—unfriendly at best—and warned not to leave the compound at night.

We were strictly forbidden to fraternize with Arab women. At night, we heard female voices calling to us to leave camp and come to them. Like the ladies on the wharf, they described the services they would offer to "Yankee" soldiers. They waited on a nearby hillside that was covered with shrubs and low grass. A few soldiers disregarded orders and ventured out into the darkness, seeking their enticing callers. Next morning, guards patrolling the camp boundaries found their bodies, with throats cut. In one way, they saw us as an invading force and resented our presence. However, they also knew we had not only money but also personal possessions that were of great value in their markets.

We did get passes to tour Casablanca and bargain for trinkets and souvenirs, but before leaving camp, we were again warned to stay away from the women. We were also lectured on how to behave in an Arab city: always bargain before purchasing souvenirs, watches, gold chains, and trinkets of any kind. Negotiating was part of doing business in the country, we were told. There was a French government office in the city, with French police on patrol.

We made our way to Casablanca's center, where French restaurants and outside cafés surrounded a park. Most of us just basked in the sunlight at those cafés, watching the scenery go by. Unfortunately, some of the guys we sat with still didn't get the message that not all Arabs were our friends, and succumbed to the nods or gestures of passing females. After following them through narrow streets to exotic-looking destinations, they were beaten, stabbed, sometimes killed.

Arab men usually controlled the activities of these women, profiting from the oldest of professions. However, there was also an underlying hatred of foreign soldiers coming on to their women. Most of the time, though, it was only robbery that was the motivating factor.

Within a week we were on the move again, this time loaded aboard what were called "40 or 8" French railroad cars from World War I, designed to hold 40 men or 8 horses. We traveled to Oran, Algeria, passing through the snow-covered Atlas mountains, which reminded me of the Rockies.

Tragically, we lost several more men on the journey. The train stopped periodically during the night for us to relieve ourselves, and a couple of guys never came back. We never learned why, but we assumed they'd been robbed and killed.

Oran was warm and sunny, and we enjoyed the weather and pleasant countryside. Later, in Southern California, I would note the similarities.

Two days after arriving, we were loaded aboard what appeared to be a passenger liner and shipped across the Mediterranean to Naples, Italy. Luckily our crossing was uneventful, because the calm, deep blue sea was a haven for German U-boats.

Naples had fallen in October 1943. It lay in ruins due to German demolition and Allied bombing, but within a week the wreckage was cleared and Allied soldiers and supplies were moving through the city. When I arrived a few months later, buildings still showed the effects of the fierce bombardments.

We hiked through the streets amid waving crowds, though I did note that many of the men who watched us showed no enthusiasm. At the time there were still people sympathetic to the Fascist cause, and we remained the enemy in their eyes.

We ended up at what appeared to be a large fairground, with an auditorium-type building. We learned later that it was called a "Repple Depple," or Replacement Depot. Here recruits were assigned to battle-front units that had lost men in combat. There were tents scattered everywhere, and for the next few days we just lolled around.

Then we were loaded aboard a convoy of trucks and were taken northward, out of Naples. It was December 1943. Our convoy stopped around noon for chow, and a bunch of us got to gabbing with soldiers who'd been at the front and were going back after having wounds treated. Their stories were sobering, but I was still feeling adventurous.

Nevertheless, the reality of what we were about to get into started to sink in, at this point. These guys told us about combat, what to do and what not to. The first thing an infantryman learns when bullets start flying, they said, is to hit the dirt and find some cover, a shallow ditch, anything. After that, as a buck private, you don't do anything until someone tells you what to do. The vets were helpful in their advice, but I could see the mood of the replacement troops changing after our talks with them. Before, there'd been no fear of death. Now there was uncertainty.

As darkness fell and we started to move forward again, we heard the thunder of artillery up ahead. It had been raining most of the day, and when we arrived at our destination it was mired in mud. We were immediately assigned to squad tents and just crashed for the night. Next morning we were told that we were situated on a hillside above the town of San Pietro, about twenty miles north of Naples in the Volturno Valley.

I also learned that I'd been assigned to the 2nd Platoon, E Company (a rifle company), 2nd Battalion, 7th Regiment ("Cotton Balers"), of the 3rd Infantry Division.

About the same time we arrived in camp, the 3rd Division got there too. They'd been withdrawn for rest and receipt of new replacements, and the vets told us of the fighting they'd gone through. Of course they were happy to see replacements like ourselves, ready to fill their depleted ranks. In battle, a unit can lose over half its soldiers within a few weeks.

We began each day with breakfast, powdered eggs that tasted god-awful, rubbery bacon, and the soldiers' favorite fare: Spam. We ate that canned meat at all meals, so much so that even today, almost sixty years later, I've only eaten it once or twice, and even then, purely for old time's sake.

After chow, we marched and marched. We hiked through hills outside of San Pietro. Our clip was a bit faster than we were used to back at training camp. We soon learned that we were marching the "Truscott Trot," an accelerated pace named after and ordered by our division commander, General Lucian K. Truscott, Jr., who demanded that his troops always be in top shape. Before long we were knocking off 15 miles a day with ease.

Meanwhile, just north of us a major battle was about to begin. It took four such efforts to dislodge German forces from their entrenched positions on Monte Cassino, a towering (1,693-foot) rock with an ancient monastery on top. This mountain was a formidable obstacle to Allied forces who were fighting their way toward Rome, about 75 miles north of Cassino.

We were told that we would be joining the front-line troops. First, though, we needed amphibious training: to get to the action, we would have to ford the Volturno River. Practicing out of harm's way, we used rafts to cross and recross the river near San Pietro. We also learned how to leave the river and carry our rafts along hillside footpaths, which were narrow and often hazardous.

One day as we made our way along a path, we came upon a German soldier's body. His remains were in an advanced state of decay, so it was obvious he'd been dead for days. This was our first experience of this kind, and it made a deep impression on all of us. It certainly brought home what lay ahead.

A few days later, some American bodies strapped to mules were brought down from the mountain into our camp. We quietly stood aside to let the entourage pass through our ranks. They were from a different division but wore the same combat clothing we did, and for the first time we were seeing guys like ourselves who had been killed. The war instantly moved much closer to us. The images of these dead men lingered with me for some time. My enthusiasm for adventure was waning rapidly.

We spent Christmas 1943 waiting to go into battle. On Christmas Eve we were called out of our tents, after a particularly hard day of training. Outside of our platoon area, the noncoms had set up a Lister bag, normally used to fill canteens. It was made of canvas with a waterproof lining, maybe four feet high, and it hung from a tripod. A bag held about 50 gallons of drinking water, but that night it was wine. We heard that every company in the area was getting a Lister bag of wine to celebrate Christmas. Our platoon lined up, and everyone got a canteen cup of wine.

After slugging it down, the guys loosened up and started talking about home. We didn't talk about what carnage lay ahead, but reminisced about families, girlfriends, where we were from, home life, and above all food. That subject always seemed to be on everyone's mind. We went into great detail, describing menus of steaks, real eggs, homemade bread, fried chicken, the works. In reality we knew it would be canned Spam, as usual. But it was fun just thinking about the past, and the wonderful lives we had led.

We talked like this a lot, during breaks from training and in the evenings, when we sat around and didn't have anything to do. As I look back on those times and the friends I made during the war, I can still see their faces. I can't remember their names, but their faces are clear.

Several days after Christmas, we were ordered to quickly pack our gear and be ready to move, not toward the battle line but away from it. This came as a surprise, but we packed our duffel bags and were loaded onto trucks headed for Naples. After bouncing along dirt roads for an hour or so, we offloaded onto large open fields just north of the city.

We camped there and kept on training, until we were taken down to Naples harbor and loaded onto landing craft. For several days we practiced beach assaults on various stretches of land, on the island of Capri, and at Salerno.

A few days before the action, our platoon leaders warned us that it was likely to be horrendous. We were told that when we landed, we could be met by a determined veteran enemy force right there on the beach. They were trying to prepare us for the worst. They said, "You've got to do it. Your mothers can't do it, or your brothers, your father, your sisters … you've got to do it!"

Of course we were all in the dark regarding where we were going, except we now knew we weren't going to be part of the ongoing Cassino assault.

One morning as we traveled through the streets of Naples on our way to another day of amphibious-landing training, we were overwhelmed by what we saw ahead of us in the harbor. A massive number of American and British combatant and support ships were all jammed in, and we knew the real thing was about to happen. There were thousands of new troops, on top of the 15,000 soldiers of the 3rd Infantry Division.

After the day's training was over, we were sent back to camp to prepare for a voyage and destination unknown to any of us. We were to leave Naples in about three days, time we spent training. One day we were on a ten-minute break, and everybody was sitting around on the ground lighting up cigarettes. A jeep pulled up to us—it had a .50-caliber machine gun mounted on it—and a one-star general jumped out. It was General John O'Daniel, second in command of the 3rd

Division. We'd all heard of "Jack Daniels" but had never seen him before. He was a rough and ready guy, and he gave a marvelous pep talk about the assault and what it was going to mean. We had to do this, he said, and it might be very tough fighting, and some of us wouldn't make it. Jack Daniels wasn't a large man, but despite his small stature he exuded a powerful presence.

While he was speaking, we heard an aircraft engine sputter and then rev up into a screaming pitch. We all looked up. Several thousand feet above us, a P-51 fighter was going into a spiral dive straight for the ground. All eyes were riveted on the aircraft, and all of a sudden a parachute popped out of the plane. The P-51 hit the ground no more than a quarter-mile away from us. Everyone, including the general, rushed to the crash site and watched as the pilot drifted to earth almost in the middle of the 3rd Division.

I didn't get that close to him, but many shook his hand and asked if he was okay. Word got around that he was from a P-51 squadron flying out of Foggia, a large airfield outside of Naples, and that he'd been on a reconnaissance flight over Anzio and taken flak damage to one of his wings. None of us made the Anzio connection, and after the incident we went back to our training.

Other than that crash, the few days we spent training were a peaceful time of preparation. We weren't near enemy troops, and we heard no shooting or artillery fire. A day or so before we departed Naples, squads were brought individually into a standard-size Army tent and briefed on what our responsibilities would be once we hit the beach. A three-dimensional map was laid out, with markings on it that showed landing areas, mine-swept channels for landing craft, and fire-support sectors. The 3rd Infantry Division was to land on X-Ray beach, which was divided into two quadrants: Red and Green.

Our platoon was assigned to Red beach, which was marked "Nettuno" on the map. We were to fight our way inland until we reached our objective, five or six miles inland. Every detail was covered—except where along the Italian coast the landing would take place.

We all felt it had to be either north or south of Rome. We were certain the invasion was to be a flanking movement to pull German forces from the Cassino area, hopefully breaking the stalemate. I wouldn't learn until much later that Field Marshal Albert Kesselring, commander of all Axis forces in Italy, and his staff correctly surmised that such an assault was coming. However, they assumed it was going to be north of Rome, so they held a number of divisions in reserve in that area.

The briefings took most of the day, and as we were waiting in line for chow, someone came by and said there was going to be a chaplain in camp in about twenty minutes. Without a word being spoken, we kind of drifted out of line one at a time, and found our way to where he would speak. I don't know whether he was Catholic, Protestant, or Jewish—it didn't matter.

The chaplain read from the Bible, and then he just talked to us as men who were about to face combat and perhaps death. Everyone listened to him quietly. It was very spiritual and beautiful. Throughout the fighting that followed, the hymn "Holy, Holy Holy" kept running through my mind.

The next day we marched down into Naples in full battle dress to embark in our landing craft. British troops went with us, their bagpipers leading us through the city. They were part of the invasion force.

We left Naples during the early hours of 21 January 1944 and headed north. In our convoy, which stretched as far as the eye could see, there were more than 200 landing craft with about 40,000 men loaded into them. Aside from these, there were cruisers, destroyers, and support ships. It was a sunshiny day, and as the ships took their positions and moved as one, it was a breathtaking sight. I felt a great sense of pride as our convoy made its way north. The men seemed ready for what lay ahead.

As we sat on the deck of our LCI (landing craft, infantry), a British destroyer cruised slowly up beside us. Suddenly a voice boomed from a megaphone: "Men of the 3rd Infantry Division: we want you to know that we are embarked on a magnificent maneuver today." As the gung-ho speech continued, we learned it was coming from a British admiral unknown to any of us. But his words inspired us: we Americans and British soldiers and our feats, he said, were going to go down in history.

Ammunition for our weapons was distributed. Our M-1 rifle bullets were carried in clips that held eight rounds each. We were given bandoliers that accommodated about six clips, and we strung three or four of these bandoliers over our shoulders. We filled our jacket pockets with hand grenades. We were so busy getting prepared for what was to come that we didn't stop to think that we were about to land on enemy-held territory to kill or be killed. It all still seemed remote to us, yet we were filled with anxiety.

We arrived off Anzio during the night, and we could hear all the engines shut back to idle. At the time we still didn't know where we were, but it didn't make any difference. We were just anxious to land and get on with our mission. We were all belowdecks, packed like sardines and waiting for the order to go up the companionway and down off the ship. All was quiet as we waited.

Suddenly we heard our combat ships, which were a few miles farther out to sea, open fire. The barrage thundered overhead and lasted for about half an hour. The men were mostly subdued. All eyes were riveted on the forward end of the landing craft, where we would be jumping off once we hit the beach. Word began to spread that we were laying off the port city of Anzio.

Then, just as quickly as the firing had started, it stopped. At that moment our engines revved up, and we moved out toward our assigned beaches. As soon as we touched bottom, the men would move quickly to the offloading ramps and scurry onto the beach.

We anticipated stiff resistance and expected to hear incoming fire at any

U.S. troops landing at Anzio, 1944. The landing itself was almost bloodless, but within 24 hours the Germans had begun to ring the beachhead with eight divisions to our two. (National Archives, Rockville, Maryland.)

minute. It was the supreme moment: we were filled with thoughts of the fighting ahead—and with fears that death lurked just a short distance away.

My reflections were interrupted when I was told to come up on deck and report to our squad sergeant. He handed me two fairly good-size packages, wrapped in burlap and connected with a strap. My instructions were to carry them ashore. He slung the strap around my neck, so that I had a package on each side of me.

"Someone will get these from you when you hit the beach," the sergeant said.

"What's in them?" I asked.

"Oh, just some TNT charges for blowing bridges," he said nonchalantly. "You'll go first down the ramp on the beach. That way we can check water depth. If you go under, we know we have to move closer to shore. Good luck!"

So here I was with dynamite under each arm, acting as a depth finder because of my 6' 7" height. I went down that ramp like a shot, and the water was waist high. Any second I expected to hear heavy gunfire open up on us. The troops from the other landing craft were scrambling ashore, and soon there were 15,000 of us stretched out on the beach for maybe a mile.

Within seconds after getting ashore, we realized that we weren't going to die. Not a shot was fired. It was an incredible moment. I've never forgotten it—first a feeling of sheer terror, fearing you were going to die as you stepped off the boat. Then there were 15,000 soldiers standing on the beach, all with the same sense of relief. The landing had been completely unopposed.

There was kind of a noise, a roar, something indescribable, as 15,000 men realized they were still alive. Then we silently moved inland toward our objectives without meeting enemy opposition.

Three U.S. Ranger battalions quickly captured the port city of Anzio, and the 509th Parachute Infantry Battalion encountered no resistance in occupying the adjacent town of Nettuno. The British troops landed north of Anzio and began a 20-mile march farther north, to the Alban Hills just south of Rome.

While that was going on, we were ordered to start moving inland immediately. Just before leaving the beach, two guys, part of a demolition team, relieved me of the TNT I was carrying.

We cleared a small patch of trees and found ourselves moving across open farm land, with little stone and stucco houses scattered around us. After walking about five miles or so inland, we came to a rise that gave a good view of the distant lowlands. We could clearly see a road with trucks and vehicles moving south toward Cassino. It was one of the supply routes—highway 7, the Appian Way. Our mission was to sever it, cutting off this supply line to Cassino.

The Germans had no idea that they were being observed by our invasion force. We were ordered to remain in our positions, so we rested, lit up cigarettes, had a bite of D-bar (chocolate), and watched the scene below.

About an hour later we were ordered to do an about-face and pull back, toward the beach. We walked about 3 or 4 miles and then made camp in the woods and stayed there for the night. Still no shots were fired. As far as we knew, the enemy did not know of our presence.

The pullback had been ordered by the commander of the Anzio invasion force, U.S. Army Major General John P. Lucas. General Lucas didn't want to overextend his troops, since he felt his initial invasion force could not withstand a serious German counterattack. Thus he hesitated, awaiting reinforcements before attempting to cut the supply routes to Cassino.

We found out later just how wide open the area was for an advance by our forces. Two American soldiers took off in a jeep down a road leading northward, and since they weren't challenged, kept going until they came over the crest of a hill and looked down at Rome. They kept driving, right up to the outskirts of the city, and then they parked for a while. They lit up cigarettes and sat there like part of the scenery. Nobody detected them. After a while they thought they'd better get back to their unit, before something happened.

When they approached our lines, they were challenged. Asked where they were coming from, they simply said Rome! Their commanding officer heard of this, of course, and there was hell to pay.

With only two divisions ashore, we probably would have run into real trouble had we continued our advance and attempted to take highway 7. Unbeknownst to us, the Germans were rushing massive reinforcements toward Anzio. Had we gone on, we might have ended up as prisoners of war in short order.

Our commanders got word about German troop movements, so scouting parties were ordered to find out just where their lines were starting to form. About the third night, we were out on patrol walking across the countryside in a spread-out formation. All of a sudden something shot up and burst high in the sky. A flare floated down in a parachute and lit up the whole area. "Freeze!" hollered our squad leader. We stood there not moving a muscle as the flare descended: objects are much harder to detect at night when there's no movement.

Just as the flare burned out, the Germans opened up from several positions across a small hill. I stood frozen, almost in a trance, watching tracers kind of float toward me. Between each of these rounds were several dark rounds—from 20mm guns, I was told later. Then a tracer brushed by my face, and I just panicked. I started to run, but two guys grabbed me and held me to the ground. They were both vets and knew what to do.

We returned fire and scrambled away from the shooting. Then we reported back to our officer-in-charge, who marked the incident on a map. He was noting where our troops encountered the enemy, so he could plot out their positions. That was my baptism of fire: facing a 20mm automatic weapon. If you get hit dead-on, you just explode.

More firefights followed during the next few days. On one reconnaissance patrol, we came upon a farmhouse the Germans were occupying. They were positioned behind a low stone wall surrounding the house, and bullets flew all around us as they opened fire. We threw ourselves into a ditch, but it was shallow and we were just barely able to keep below the German line of fire. A couple of our guys got hit during the first volley.

"Three guys in the haystack!" yelled our sergeant, and we all fired in that direction. Within minutes, three Germans fell from the haystack.

They were rushing periodically between the stone wall and the farmhouse, probably supplying fresh ammo to the soldiers at the wall. We took machine and rifle fire with no letup. Finally we were able to bring up a light machine gun, but we were still outgunned. Then we heard an explosive round behind us, and we realized we were now facing mortar fire. When the next shell hit in front of us, we knew a spotter was bracketing our position. One of the next few shells would definitely reach us.

Looking around, we saw that about 100 yards downhill from our shallow ditch, it joined a great big one. Just as we were about to take off for it, the guy next to me popped up and took another shot. At that moment a mortar shell exploded in front of him, and he rolled back into the ditch. His face was gone. Pieces of his flesh splattered on me, and I was just paralyzed. I couldn't move.

The guys in front of me ran toward the big ditch, but I blocked those behind me. The sergeant, seeing what was happening, yelled, "Aurness, you son-of-a-bitch, get down that ditch or I'm gonna kill you!" Man, did I move fast then. First I had to crawl over the guy who got hit, and he was still moving, kind of twitching. It was horrible. To this day I don't know why I didn't take some shrapnel from the explosion, since I was right next to him.

We all made it, crawling on our bellies. It was a drainage ditch, about eight feet deep, crisscrossing the beachhead. As we piled in, we saw that another American soldier was already in there with us. He'd been spotting German positions, and for the rest of that day, a major artillery engagement raged on. The Germans had strengthened their lines with tanks and artillery, while we fired back with 105mm howitzers and support from heavier naval guns behind us.

The firing only stopped when darkness fell, and we were able to work our way back to our lines that night. We'd lost several guys from our platoon during the battle. From that day on, we knew we were up against a formidable enemy. Until we could get more reinforcements ashore, they were going to outman and outgun us. But the beach was soaked with rain, and the weather wasn't getting any better. It was slow going, and our trucks and tanks got mired in a sea of mud.

Within hours after our landing, Kesselring started moving the Fourteenth Army from Northern Italy down to Anzio. Elements of eight divisions quickly headed south, commanded by General Eberhard von Mackensen. The Fourteenth Army was to drive our forces into the sea, while at the same time protecting the rear of their Tenth Army fighting at Cassino.

On our side, after a few days on the front lines we were ordered back from the shooting, to rest and be held in reserve. We were bivouacked on a hill just a few miles behind Anzio, and we had a clear view of the harbor and all the activity down there. We had ringside seats to the continuous unloading of our ships, as well as to all the action in the air.

The German Luftwaffe was making daily raids on our ships and our shore depots. Focke Wulf 190s and Messerschmitts dived down or made low-level runs over the water. They dropped their bombs and raked machine-gun fire over our ships and support troops onshore. The ships were so tightly packed in the harbor that their bombs and fire could hardly miss. The Luftwaffe also used glider bombs, carried under the wings of attacking aircraft, and guided them to their targets by radio control.

Our fighters were in the air continuously, and dogfights were a daily occurrence. The air was full of all kinds of debris, and as the ships were hit and our ammo dumps ashore exploded, fireballs blew skyward. Our antiaircraft guns filled the sky with flak. Periodically one of the attackers exploded and fell into the harbor.

Offshore, our Navy guys had to fight off German E-boats. Similar to our PT boats, these high-speed craft made their runs after dark. They launched torpedoes and then disappeared back into the night. The Germans were relentless in their attacks on our ships. One-man human torpedoes called Marders were also used, without much success. Those who manned them rarely survived.

We watched all this daily, as we cooked our rations, wrote letters, cleaned weapons, and tried to enjoy our rest period. Soon we were sent back to the front lines. By now the 3rd Division had been assigned to fight its way up the Nettuno-Cisterna road to the town of Cisterna, which had been one of our main objectives from the time we landed. It sat on a hillside in front of mountainous terrain, and highway 7 ran right through it.

Farther to the northwest, the British were in furious combat with German troops and artillery along the road that went from Anzio to the Alban Hills, about ten miles south of Rome. Their primary objective had been the Alban Hills when they'd landed.

But our forces reached neither Cisterna nor the hills during the early fighting, due to General Lucas' hesitation and the quick response of the Germans to our invasion. Now it would take months before the U.S. 5th and British 8th armies could break the Cassino stalemate and relieve the German entrapment at Anzio.

Upon rejoining our troops, we resumed our daily reconnaissance patrols. One morning we were walking across farmland, when I found three bodies laying out in the field. They were Americans, and one of them was still alive. He was terribly wounded by shrapnel, and just lay there moaning. I yelled for a medic, and he raced over and tended to the guy. As we moved on, we found more bodies and assumed they'd been killed during the night.

Then we sighted some of our Sherman tanks up ahead, arranged in a skirmish line. We were ordered to stay behind them: troops usually followed tanks into a skirmish. For the next hour or so nothing moved, until we heard a creaking noise a short distance ahead. Over a hill toward us lumbered several "Tigers," German tanks armed with cannons that fired 88mm shells, deadly when they struck their target.

The Shermans and Tigers started firing at each other. We stayed behind our tanks, ready to fight any German infantry that might appear. A couple of ours were hit and caught fire; luckily, the crews were able to escape before being trapped. The tanks exploded into fireballs as the Germans continued to target them. The battle went on for an hour or so before both sides disengaged.

No enemy infantry were sighted, so we continued our patrol up the Nettuno-Cisterna road. It was frustrating, because when we made these patrols we could see Cisterna in the distance. But German fire always stopped us from advancing too far, and it seemed to increase by the day. The morning after the "Tiger" battle we were at it again, only this time the enemy was in a farmhouse.

After coming under machine-gun fire from a second-floor window, we fired back. Two of us were ordered to crawl up an embankment and get behind the house, to determine if we could take out the machine-gun nest from there. As we got close to the rear of the building, we saw an outside stairway that went up to the second floor, and at the top, the door was open.

We crept up the stairs, threw in a couple of hand grenades, and ducked. The second they exploded, we rushed through the door and sprayed the room with gunfire. The German machine gun was now a piece of twisted metal, and three gunners lay sprawled around the small room.

Satisfied they were dead, we started back down the stairs. We were startled by—and almost shot at—several Italians who jumped up from a ditch and ran toward us, waving and shouting. This was their house, they made us understand, and they could never thank us enough for rescuing it. Of course, we had no time to do anything but accept their thanks and move on.

When we caught up with our platoon, we learned they'd taken out another machine-gun nest farther down the line. Firing in the area ceased, for now, and I had a moment to look around. For the first time I noticed that a major battle had taken place just a short distance away from us. We'd been so intent on taking out the Germans along our line that we hadn't seen a German tank burning only a hundred yards or so ahead of us. A cloud of black smoke fumed from it, and two dead Germans hung out of the top of the turret, both burning.

During the early weeks of the fighting, each side was sending patrols to make contact with the other. At the same time as our platoon would be engaging the enemy, there were often several other skirmishes close by. We never knew what was happening to our other units; it was just continuous fighting throughout the rolling fields, farmhouses, ditches, and tree lines as we tried to reach Cisterna.

On 30 January, Lucas ordered a daring attack on Cisterna using three Ranger battalions. We watched silently as hundreds of these elite soldiers filtered through our lines toward the embattled town. Before they could reach their objective, they were ambushed by German troops, tanks, and heavy artillery. More than 700 Rangers were pinned down, subjected to withering crossfire, and only six men made it back to the beach. The others were either killed or captured. I heard later that some of the latter escaped while being transported to Rome.

On the night of 1 February 1944, we were on the front lines and assigned to reconnoiter a certain sector there. With no moon, it was a pitch-black night.

There were three squads in our platoon, and each had a point man leading the way. I was it for our squad. Our troops were spread out to lessen casualties, should we come under fire.

Having been on these dark patrols before, I knew that we developed a sixth sense about where our buddies were as we moved together. As point man that night, I was probably 40 to 50 feet ahead of my squad. I picked my way over the terrain—since I couldn't see ahead of me, I never knew whether I'd walk into a big rock or step off into a four-foot ditch. For the first twenty minutes I didn't hear or see anything. I remember looking down and not being able to see my feet step in front of me. Finally I would just set one foot down slowly, to see if the ground was solid. Then the other. I felt my way along. It was the same for the point men on either side of me, and for the troops following us.

We were under strict orders not to speak as we crept along. Except for the night sounds, the air was completely quiet. We were particularly careful not to break a twig, stumble on rocks, or make any noise at all as we stepped through brush-filled terrain. Most of the farms had small vineyards, maybe three rows of grapevines planted four feet apart. They'd been trimmed down to a height of about three feet for the winter.

I was walking through one of them when I heard voices 50 feet ahead of me. In what seemed like seconds later, a guttural voice yelled and enemy fire burst out in front of me. I'd walked right into a German machine-gun nest. I was hit in the right leg but was able to leap over a row of vines anyway, out of the line of fire.

Then I fell to the ground in excruciating pain. It felt like the bones in my lower right leg had been shot all to hell. Intense fire started coming at me from both sides. I was almost killed when a "potato masher," a German concussion grenade, went off near me. The explosion literally lifted me off the ground.

The Germans had two machine-gun nests, with infantrymen spread out on either side. The firing was low, about 18 inches off the ground, so I had to practically hug the earth not to get hit. There were about 15 Germans; we had 40 riflemen firing and throwing grenades, backed up by a light machine gun. The shooting was intense, but eventually our guys overran them and took them out.

I don't know how long I laid in the vineyard, but I remember feeling that I was going into shock. In my semi-conscious state, I heard guys coming through the vineyard, checking on our wounded and dead. The point man next to me, Jim Rosen, a soldier I had befriended at Anzio, had been killed, as well as several others. Finally my platoon reached me. "Where are you hit?" someone said.

"In the leg," I answered, but since I couldn't move, I wasn't too sure what other wounds I might have suffered. Soon a medic appeared, took a look at my leg, and cut the pants open. He inspected the wound and said my leg bones had been severely splintered. Penicillin wasn't used at this point, but sulfa powder did an adequate job of sterilizing wounds. He poured some on and gave me a shot of morphine, jamming the needle into my stomach since he didn't have time to turn me over and remove all my gear to shoot me in the rear. Then he wrapped the leg with gauze-like material. Before leaving, he said he thought I had a ZI wound (Zone of Interior). That meant an eventual ticket back to the States for treatment and rehabilitation.

Many others who got hit were in terrible condition, so I was lucky. My wound was not life-threatening, nor would it affect my future, though over the years it's been troublesome, requiring several surgeries.

The medic came back, briefly, to let me know a medical team would be coming through soon, with a doctor. While I lay there waiting, I could hear groaning from Germans who were still alive in the machine-gun nest. Our guys had driven through their position, assuming they'd all been killed. It was an eerie thing, lying there in the pitch black listening to one of them call out a name in German that I didn't understand—perhaps a loved one. I had no idea what was going to happen to these soldiers.

Finally I heard voices behind me and recognized them as Americans. I yelled for a medic, and within seconds one was at my side. He was an MD, assigned to go out with the medical teams and give emergency treatment to the wounded. Other medics joined him, and they put a splint on my leg and wrapped it tight. I was still in a lot of pain, but one more squirt bag of morphine took care of that problem. They left me to attend to other wounded men, and a little later a team of guys came along and put me on a litter. By then I wasn't feeling a thing.

It was still dark when they lifted me and started back to a collection area for the wounded. Evidently they were walking along a ridge line when one of them slipped, and I fell off the litter and rolled down an embankment. They came running down, concerned that I'd been additionally injured by the fall. I told them to forget it—I was of course in no pain.

The collection area, a way station before moving us to the evacuation hospitals on the beach, was at one of the old farms to the rear of our lines. I was offloaded into a barn, full of other wounded. They put me right next to a dead, bloated cow that must had been killed the night before. I hadn't thought about animals being killed before, but I guess during engagements, anything that moved was fired on by someone.

An ambulance arrived about dawn, and I was hauled down to the 95th Evacuation Hospital, on the beach in tents. I was lifted onto an operating table, and some medics examined me. I was pretty groggy, but still aware of all the activity around me. That's the last thing I remember before they put me out.

I came to lying in a narrow bunk in another tent, somewhere away from the operating room. My injured leg was wrapped in a heavy cast, which immobilized me. I learned later that they'd cleaned my wound and repaired the damage

95th Evacuation Hospital at Anzio, 1944. I was brought here after being wounded, and I was there about three days before being shipped back to Naples. (National Archives, Rockville, Maryland.)

to my shin bone the best they could, then covered it with sulfa powder and wrapped my leg with cotton bandages before putting the cast on.

The cotton bandages soaked up the blood that was still seeping from the wound, and it accumulated under the cast. By the time I got back to the States, some blood had soaked through the cast and I smelled terrible. Most orthopedic wards in those days smelled bad. But none of this bothered me, because I was going home!

The tent was packed with patients. Their wounds ranged from injuries like mine to some terrible ones. The guy next to me had been shot in the abdominal area and died that same night. The nurses there were truly angelic. They did a tremendous job with our troops, especially those in the evacuation hospitals. I don't know how they took it. It must have been a traumatic thing to live day after day caring for guys who were filthy, caked with mud and blood, and suffering from horrendous wounds.

I remember one in particular, from Minneapolis. She was the first American

Wounded Anzio soldiers awaiting evacuation by sea. I was in one of these groups. The harbor was often dive-bombed by the Germans while our wounded were waiting to be evacuated. (National Archives, Rockville, Maryland.)

woman I'd seen in months, and it was like talking to my mother. We talked a lot about home, and she was a great comfort to me.

Medical facilities were bombed and shelled frequently. After I left, I learned that a German fighter bomber dropped a load of antipersonnel bombs on the 95th Evacuation Hospital, killing 28 patients and hospital workers, including three nurses. Mine may have been among them.

I was at the 95th a very short time, perhaps 48 hours, after which an ambulance took me down to the harbor. I remember that day well because, for a change, it was sunny. They laid a number of us out on litters on the docks. We were strapped to the stretchers to ensure we wouldn't fall off as we were transferred to hospital ships. I had kind of mixed feelings as I lay there—on the one hand I was elated that I was leaving what had now become a hellacious struggle. At the same time, I feared that I would be killed while strapped onto a stretcher, should an air raid occur. While I was thinking about all this, in zoomed the Luftwaffe on one of their daily raids.

I knew the dive bombers were concentrated on harbor targets, but they appeared to be heading right for me.

After surviving that raid, we were loaded onto a British hospital ship that headed out to sea, then down the coast to Naples. A mine-cleared lane had been established for shipping back and forth between there and Anzio, but German U-boats still did their share of damage to transiting ships. Two weeks after our voyage, on 16 February, U230 would sink LST 418. Two days after that, U410 would send the British light cruiser *Penelope* to the bottom with three torpedoes, as well as sinking the American LST 348 on 20 February.

Luckily, we had an uneventful trip. We arrived at Naples and were taken to a large auditorium, the same building I'd been to when I'd first arrived in Italy last December, just two months ago. The entire floor was now covered with beds of wounded soldiers. I spent three days there, resting and listening to the comforting music of home—Fred Waring and his Pennsylvanians, Tommy Dorsey, and Benny Goodman. "Smoke Gets in Your Eyes" was one of my favorites.

Many of us were put in ambulances and driven to the airfield near Foggia, where they loaded us onto C-47s. We flew to Tunisia, North Africa, the first place the 3rd Infantry had engaged the Germans in 1942. Just outside Bizerte, a major coastal city, they settled us into a hospital that was another tent facility, with a little more room than we'd had at the 95th. We were placed in beds here, much more comfortable than the cots I was used to.

In the meantime, General Clark and General Sir Harold Alexander, Commander of Allied Armies (15th Army Group) in Italy, decided to let Lucas establish defensive positions until more reinforcements could be landed. On 2 February 1944, the 1st Special Service Force and British 56th Division joined the Anzio operation.

At Campoleone, German General Mackensen's 14th Army hit the Allied lines hard with infantry and armor, seeking a quick tactical advantage. The British, initially driven back, stiffened their lines and after fierce fighting regained their positions. Meanwhile, German forces won the battles at Aprilia and captured the town. At dawn on 16 February, Mackensen launched a massive assault that was to drive Allied forces into the sea.

The Berlin-Spandau Infantry Lehr Demonstration Regiment, ordered to lead the attack, moved down the Albano-Anzio road toward the American 45th Division. The 45th counterattacked, and the Germans, unable to stop them, swiftly retreated.

The Germans attacked the 45th through the night of 16 February, with continual aerial bombardment and strafing supported by two additional divisions, the 29th Panzer Grenadier and the 26th Panzer. The 45th fell back to the rearmost beachhead line. When the Germans succeeded in breaching the Allied lines, Lucas ordered more artillery and air support. He also asked for and got concentrated naval fire to stem the advance.

The next day, 17 February, wave after wave of Allied bombers and incessant fire from American cruisers hit the Germans hard. Mackensen threw more soldiers and tanks into the battle, but the Allied line held. By 19 February the Germans had had enough, and they began to retreat.

In spite of the successes Lucas had begun to realize, he was removed from command of the VI Corps and replaced by General Truscott. On 29 February, Allied armor and massive air strikes stopped a strong German assault near Cisterna. The 3rd's successful counterattack ended the Germans' last major offensive at Anzio.

Now there was a stalemate at Anzio and along the Gustav Line to the south, at Cassino. Both forces at Anzio seemed to have had enough of intense confrontation, and for the next two months there were only raids, skirmishes, and artillery and air attacks. At Cassino, the U.S. 5th and British 8th armies now comprised as many as twenty-eight divisions, with twenty-six nationalities serving in them, including Algerians, Basutos, Brazilians, Canadians, Greeks, Indians, some Italians, Moroccans, Nepalese, Poles, and Yugoslavs. The fiercest fighters, most feared by the Germans, were the Moroccan goumiers. Operating mostly at night, they thrived on mountain combat using long, razor sharp knives as their main weapons. Fifty thousand men of the II Polish Corps had also joined the fighting.

The Allied command decided that the only way to realize a breakthrough was to overpower the Gustav Line by massive force. The Germans were outnumbered three to one in artillery, armor, and aircraft.

On 11 May 1944, the entire Allied front opened fire. The Gustav Line became a hellish battleground. Fourteen fresh Allied divisions, previously scheduled for the invasion of Southern France, were moved into the sector. The Allied force attacked 14 badly depleted German divisions, and the Gustav Line was finally broken. Led by Lt. General Wladyslaw, Polish troops were the first to take Monte Cassino. Kesselring, facing setbacks along the entire front line, ordered a fighting retreat.

With the breakout in the south, Truscott's VI Corps began a major offensive on Cisterna, using massive artillery bombardment and hundreds of Allied aircraft that practically pulverized the town. With seven divisions now at his command, Truscott found enemy troops ready to fight to the bitter end. But they were no match for the 3rd Infantry, and four months after the landing at Anzio, Cisterna was in Allied hands.

On 25 May 1944, the VI Corps was finally able to join up with the U.S. II Corps that was moving up highway 7 from Cassino. During the evening of 4 June, General Clark and the U.S. 88th Division entered the Piazza Venezia, Rome.

Of course I missed all this, being on the mend in Tunisia and then the United States. One of the enjoyable features of our stay in Bizerte was when they rolled up the sides of the tent each dawn, so we could taste the cold morning air and watch the peaceful, flat meadows. Gradually the sun warmed the day into a Southern Californian balminess.

We stayed there for a couple of weeks, then were moved onto a train loaded with other wounded that took us to Algeria, where they carried us on board a hospital ship.

We docked in Charleston, South Carolina, on a sunny day. They took us off the ship on stretchers and laid us out on the dock. Soon we were surrounded by ladies who'd come to welcome us home. They brought encouragement, caring words—and ice cream, which really knocked us all out. We hadn't tasted this marvelous treat since we'd left. Those ladies were wonderful.

At a hospital in the city, we were told where we would be going for treatment and rehabilitation. The Army tried to place everyone as close to home as possible, to make it easy for relatives to visit their loved ones. In my case, I was destined for Schick General Hospital in Clinton, Iowa.

Then we were allowed to call home. What a joyous conversation I had with my mother! I spoke to my brother, Pete, later, since he was on duty in the Army Air Forces at the time.

Within a day or so we were loaded onto trains and on our way to our assigned destinations. During the trip, everyone went out of their way to ensure that we had the very best food and care. It was like a dream, since many of us had thought we'd never come home again, once we were in combat. It didn't really hit me that I was home until that train trip. We traveled through the heartland of America, the Southern states and the mountains of Appalachia, and beautiful countryside everywhere. I felt such joy—I just got this marvelous feeling, thinking about America and all it meant to me. I was proud to have fought in a war to save my country.

As soon as I got settled in Schick, I called my mother. She hurried down to see me, and I imagine seeing me safe from war's harm must have been like a miracle. For some reason, during my entire time overseas she'd never received any of my letters. She'd had no idea where I was or what was happening to me.

I'd thought she might have trouble seeing my blood-stained cast, which was elevated now as I lay in bed. Not only that, the condition of the other patients and the odor of the orthopedic ward were not easy to take. But she was so happy to see me that I could tell those things didn't matter at all. Her son was home. She talked to an Army doctor, and he assured her that with proper care and treatment, I would be fine.

But shortly after my arrival at Schick, they discovered that I had osteomyelitis in the bone, a serious infection suffered by many soldiers. Penicillin was just being introduced, but for many it was already too late. Thousands had lost limbs due to infection.

I was one of the lucky ones. My doctor said they were going to put me on this new drug—penicillin. I underwent intense treatment to save my leg. Every two or three hours, the nurse walked in with a humongous needle in a giant syringe, or at least so it appeared to me. I wondered whether horse veterinarians were lending the hospital these needles and syringes. Since the drug was new and thick, not watery liquid as we now know it, they kept the needle in me for several minutes every three hours to empty the syringe.

After a few days of being stuck, I was getting freaked out just seeing the nurse make her way toward me, but looking back over the years now, I thank God for penicillin. Eventually a doctor cut a hole in my cast, so he could gather tissue and analyze it to see how I was progressing. It took time, but the infection finally subsided.

When I was given my clean bill of health, the doctor said I'd come pretty close to losing the leg but was going to be okay. He said that after the wound was completely healed and I'd undergone some leg rehabilitation, I'd be good as new! I felt much better after that; I think the good news boosted my spirits to such an extent that it hastened my recovery. One of the medics suggested I get a lift for the right shoe, which I did. I have worn it ever since.

The doctor also cautioned me that as I got older, the leg might cause me other problems. He more or less forecast the future, because he was certainly right. Despite the lift, I walked with a bit of a limp for about the first two years. My right leg was now about 5/8 of an inch shorter, and over time, that throws the spine off center and starts a reverberating effect there.

By the time the doctors decided to take the cast off, it had been on since the 95th Evacuation Hospital had put it there, eight months earlier. My upper leg had shrunk to half the size of the other, and a regimen of massage treatments was begun immediately. I also began carefully exercising my knee and ankle.

Many other wounded were also in wheelchairs, and we'd race through the small building with a spacious connecting hallway. The staff didn't bother us—I think they felt these games meant we were ready for the next step in our recovery.

We ate wonderful food. Upon our arrival at Schick, the ladies of rural Clinton had come to the hospital and taken over the kitchen. You can't imagine the meals they made for us. They all had sons in the service, and they'd decided they were going to take care of us. We ate nothing but the best. Prime cuts of meat, mounds and mounds of creamy mashed potatoes, fresh vegetables, and delicious desserts of all kinds. All we had to do was suggest a particular food and it would be served at the next meal!

I'll never forget those wonderful, cheerful Iowa farm ladies who became the light of our lives at Schick. One condiment on our chow tables was olive oil. Many of us didn't even know what it was, had never tasted it before. Then we found out that a group of Italian POWs was working around the hospital, taking care of the yards and doing some gardening. They ate in the same chow hall we did, at a different time. They'd requested the olive oil, a staple for Italians. When we considered how brutally the German and Japanese military treated our POWs, this pampering seemed excessive to us.

My brother, Pete (also a future actor—Peter Graves), visited me too. He was in the Army Air Forces at that time, in training. I think he was a crew member of a B-25 medium bomber. Pete was three years younger than me, and he'd just gone into the Army Air Forces before I got to the hospital. He would serve for two more years before being discharged.

"Pete," I said during our conversation, "all this has made me realize how short life is. I really want to do something worthwhile, go back to school, find my way into a field where I can contribute, make a difference."

"Sure you do," said my brother, "you'll do all that, but first you just let these

Pete and I at home for some rest and recreation. Pete was going through training in the Army Air Forces. In the fall of 1944, I was still sporting a leg cast from my wounding at Anzio. (Arness Collection.)

people help you get strong again." Pete, like the rest of our family, was always sounding the positive note.

But I was apprehensive about returning to college, I told him, because of my past academic performance.

"You know Jim," said Pete, "at the University of Minnesota I took radio drama and announcing. It was great—I think you might really enjoy it too. If you don't take any more credits than you have to, you'll be able to fit it in."

Before entering the service, Pete had played in a well-known local band in elite resorts around Minneapolis. He knew what he was talking about when it came to performing, and his advice stuck with me after I was discharged. As a result, a whole new world opened up for me.

In early December 1944 I was shipped to Colorado. Camp Carson was being used as a center for servicemen with injuries requiring rehab. I stayed there until I got honorably discharged from the Army about six weeks later—29 January 1945.

I was eligible for a disability pension, about $56 a month, which kicked in when I left the service. It came in really handy when I later headed out to Los Angeles: I paid my rent with it. I still get that pension to this day. With cost-of-living increases, it's now up to about $500 a month.

Upon my arrival home, my mother packed away my uniforms and medals, and I forged ahead seeking a new life. But I've always cherished my Army time, and often I've thought about the war. Anzio was the most searing experience of my life.

My uniforms and medals had long since disappeared, but in 1999 I decided to find out if the Army would issue me a replacement set of medals. I wanted to leave them as a legacy for future Arness generations. After I'd completed the necessary forms, on 7 January 2000, Secretary of the Army Louis Caldera traveled to Los Angeles and presented me with these medals: a Bronze Star, Purple Heart, Good Conduct, American Campaign, European–African–Middle Eastern Campaign with three bronze star devices and an amphibious landing bronze arrowhead, and the World War II Victory Medal, along with the Combat Infantryman's Badge. All were encased in a handsome shadow box, complete with a folded 48-star flag. They are displayed proudly in my home today. I am at a loss for the appropriate words to express my appreciation and pride.

The following are remarks made by Secretary Caldera at the awards ceremony:

"It is my great pleasure to stand before you today, after almost fifty-five years, to award the Purple Heart, the Good Conduct Medal and Bronze Star to James Arness. For most of us James Arness is a childhood hero known as Marshal Dillon, one of the most popular and enduring television characters ever to appear on screen. Today, we recognize him for his service to our country in uniform, a role he played that is less well known, but equally deserving of recognition.

"Because prior to his storied acting career, James Arness was one of the Private Ryans, who selflessly answered our nation's call in World War II. In 1943, during his freshman year at Beloit College, Wisconsin, Mr. Arness was drafted into the Army, did his basic training at Camp Wheeler, Georgia, and soon found himself aboard ship steaming to the Africa Theater of Operations. For the next four months, as part of the 7th Infantry Regiment, 3rd Infantry Division, he would trek across Africa en route to the beaches of Anzio.

"The 'Rock of Marne's' famous march from Fedala, Morocco, to Munich had to first pass through seasoned German defenders in the mountains of Southern Italy. The Germans knew that an Allied foothold in Anzio would expose the heart of Germany to deep penetrating attacks. Their reaction was swift, and they raced fresh troops to stall the Allied advance.

"In the terrible fighting that ensued, over 6,000 soldiers would perish protecting the 100 square miles of the sandy Anzio beachhead. It was here that Private Arness would sustain devastating injuries while walking point for his platoon during a nighttime patrol. Walking point is one of the most dangerous roles for a soldier. It requires a soldier to travel ahead of his comrades in arms as a lookout to warn them of enemy danger. It was while walking point that Private James Arness was cut down when a bullet from withering German machine gun fire shattered his shin. The 'Cotton Balers' were in the path of a German counterattack. In the dark of the night an intense battle would run its grisly course. And though the German machine guns were eventually overtaken, the cost was high. Over the next four days, the 7th Infantry Regiment—the second oldest regiment in the Army—would lose 158 soldiers and suffer over 460 wounded.

"His fellow soldiers would move on, but Private Arness would be evacuated to receive treatment for his wounds—treatment and hospitalization that would last a year. From Schick General Hospital, in January of 1945, he was honorably discharged from military service with a Purple Heart, the Good Conduct Medal, and the European-African-Middle Eastern Campaign Medal. He should also have been awarded the Bronze Star. Today, we humbly correct his military records.

"Mr. Arness, from your service in uniform during our nation's time of need through your storied journey entertaining countless American families, you have stood as a proud representative of the Greatest Generation.

"At the beginning of the 21st Century, your service to our country is a proud example to a new generation of Americans that we must look to, to keep our nation strong. Thank you for allowing us to honor you today.

"It is my pleasure to present to you these awards for your distinguished military service to our nation."

Part III

Drifting into Show Business

Home is a magical word to those who have spent years away from their loved ones. Military men and women especially know the joy of returning to heartwarming surroundings where they knew love and support during their early years. I was gone just 22 months, and I think of the boys who spent years fighting a war in both Europe and the Pacific, then had to wait months before being brought home.

I had a joyous homecoming. Friends were loving, and my tearful mother had thought she'd never see me again. My dad, unfortunately, was not there: he and Mom had divorced while I was gone. Already off to the wilds of Alaska, he remained a big part of my life in the years to follow. He spent a few years working at Elmendorf Army Air Force Base, and he'd fly down to visit me after I moved to California. Eventually he relocated there too and spent a year in the Forest Service at Sequoia National Park, before managing my ranch at Simi Valley.

Mom was an aggressive woman, and very talented. She got a job with a Minneapolis newspaper, where she eventually wrote a daily column. As things settled down, we talked about my returning to school. She was thrilled with the idea, of course, and we went to the University of Minnesota to see what my status might be and what I would need to get started. The university had four- as well as two-year programs. My poor grades ruled out my getting into the four-year program, so my mom used all her powers of persuasion to get me into the shorter one. She even told the registrar that I'd been wounded in the war and deserved a chance. The poor man finally relented, despite his reservations concerning my prospects for success.

I signed up for the required courses, and also took the Radio and Announcing one that Pete had recommended. Luckily, I got the same professor he'd been so high on. Right from the start, I knew that this was for me. We were put behind microphones to read commercials, radio scripts from some old shows and newscasts. My other grades slipped, but I did well in this course.

I got to know the professor on a personal basis and learned that he was actually the radio-station manager for WCCO, a CBS outlet in Minneapolis. One day I stopped by his office and told him I didn't think I was going to make it in school, but I really enjoyed his class.

He was very encouraging and said I had a natural radio voice, and why didn't I consider attending a school in Minneapolis that specialized in training radio announcers?

I followed this advice and enrolled in the announcers' school. Of course I needed to make some money and started to look for work while going to school at night. I went to see our old neighbor, Lloyd Pattee, who had quit the jewelry business at the start of the war and joined a large company. Now he ran a big defense plant. He offered me a job at the plant and started me off at $90 a week, which at the time was good money. The job, however, turned out to be something not much to my liking. I sat on an assembly line for eight hours a day putting screws in a machine and testing them. I practically went nuts and knew I couldn't last long doing something so repetitive; I was just too restless. So I went up to Mr. Pattee one day and told him of my plight, and he said that he understood perfectly. He told me to go on out and do something else. He said, "You're gonna do all right and I'm proud of you." Many years later when I was on *Gunsmoke*, he and Deedee and my Dad came out to visit me. They had stayed in touch over the years and it was kind of funny to watch Lloyd and Dad. They were so darn proud of me playing Marshal Dillon, keeping law and order in Dodge. During one of our chats Lloyd mentioned Plummer's Lodge in northern Canada on Great Bear Lake. It was a retreat where big wheels went, like corporate heads and high ranking military officers. He had recently been to the Lodge and met Mark Clark, who had been the commander at Anzio. He told the General that I had been his neighbor and that I had been in the 3rd Infantry Division at Anzio. Clark had no idea who I was then, but by now I was sure that he was familiar with Matt Dillon.

I thoroughly enjoyed the radio announcer training, although working in the media served to remind me of a very sad event that occurred right after I returned home from the war. We first heard over our home radio that President Roosevelt had died. For our family he was a major inspiration and we felt that he was the right man in the right place to carry us through the war. We felt the same way about Winston Churchill in England. My mother had been a particular supporter of Roosevelt and his passing was very difficult for her. The whole nation mourned his loss. When Harry Truman took office we wondered what type of leadership he would provide. Was he up to the job? We were all kind of nervous about his running the country.

About that time the man who ran the school told me how pleased he was with my progress and said he was going to try and get me a job with a radio station located in our building. The regulars were going to start taking vacations, he said, and they needed someone to fill in. I jumped at the opportunity and spent the entire summer working at the station. By the end of the summer I was hired on as a regular working as a disc jockey. I had to spin records myself in a booth and learn how to move the needle to the correct spot when I announced the record so that there would be a smooth transition between announcer and the start of the record. In addition to doing the usual chores of a disc jockey, I had to do commercials. I remember one night while working the evening shift from 3:00 in the afternoon to midnight I was scheduled to interview a local politician, a man from the Fifth District. He arrived at the studio with a prepared script, including my questions. With his help, we got through the session with no hitches. He was a delightful gentleman by the name of Hubert Humphrey.

The station closed at 5:00 P.M. and only an engineer and I were left in the studio. He was in a booth right next to me so I could see him and he could see me, and we'd talk to each other over our mikes. I remember one night I was doing a commercial for Yellow Bowl Pipes. That was a pipe, well known at the time, which had a yellow bowl made out of a substance that supposedly took the bitterness out of tobacco. It was a commercial that I did every night and it was kind of a fast hustle plug. I'd say, "Folks, you men want a really good smoke, you pipe smokers try this Yellow Bowl Pipe," and so on. One night while I was doing the commercial and giving it a real push, I just happened to look up at the engineer who was in his booth and he had about six of these pipes in his mouth. They weren't lit up, but I cracked up and started laughing. Luckily I was able to put on a record which gave me time to control myself before I had to go on again. There would be many more times when I did radio shows, movies and television where funny things would set me off. This personal characteristic seemed to follow me throughout my show business career.

At the end of that summer of 1945, they hired me as a part of their staff. I also gave some thought to acting after seeing Tallulah Bankhead in a touring comedy called *Foolish Notions*. However, it was a fleeting thought on my part, since I felt at the time that radio announcing was my future.

Christmas rolled around, and my long-time friend Dick Bremicker, who'd been in the Naval Air Force, returned home. We met at the 620 Club, a bar and restaurant on Hennepin Avenue.

Dick was all fired up about going to California. A friend of his, another navy pilot who was from Santa Monica, had gotten him excited about moving to the coast, with its beautiful weather, women, scenery, and the enticing Pacific beaches. It didn't take long before that excitement touched the wanderlust in me, and I was ready to sign up. I figured I'd find a radio job out there.

Shortly after Christmas, I told Mom. "Just for a few weeks," I said. "I'd just like to go out there and have a look around, see if there are any good opportunities for me."

She just looked at me, sad. She gave me no argument, but I could see it was going to be difficult for her, losing me again.

"You'll never be back," she said.

Then I told my boss. He was dumbfounded. "You're making a big mistake," he said. "With your obvious talent for radio, you could have a very successful career in Minneapolis. Think about it. You're throwing away a good future."

But I was determined. I stood my ground, and thanked him for all he'd done for me.

Dick had heard that there was a housing shortage out there. So, through a newspaper ad, we found someone who needed help driving a trailer to California. We contacted the guy immediately, and he agreed to take us along. We thought this was a smart move, since we'd have a place to stay at night while en route. And perhaps we could talk him into letting us use the trailer in California.

Traveling across country with an aluminum trailer hooked onto our 1938 Plymouth was a great experience. We felt a total sense of freedom. Whenever we stopped to eat, the owner of the car, a young man like us, shuddered: he'd agreed to pay for our meals. I ate enough for three, and he was certain he'd be broke before we reached our destination. (To this day I have a tremendous appetite.) Dick and I talked a lot during the trip, wondering what lay ahead of us. We were two guys just back from the service, with no responsibilities. We were anxious to get out there, meet Dick's friend, who was an aspiring actor, and land jobs.

"Maybe we'll even find work as extras in movies!" I said.

"Sure," said my dark-haired friend, with a big California smile, "and we'll spend every evening at the ocean! We'll go swimming every day."

With our visions of paradise clear in our minds and our host no doubt rolling his eyes at our naïveté, we approached the Rockies. While climbing toward Flagstaff, Arizona, a large bank of dark clouds loomed up ahead of us. We cruised on into the mountains with snow beginning to fall, and soon we were in a full-blown blizzard. The heavy weather continued as we arrived in Flagstaff, so we just pulled off the road there to wait out the storm.

Somehow the rear end of the trailer slipped down an embankment, and when we tried to ease it back onto the road, the whole thing slipped down into a ditch. Finally we decided to leave it there and come back for it in the morning.

We registered in a hotel in Flagstaff, and the next morning it was still snowing. The trailer was buried in snow.

"Well, the heck with it," said the owner. "I've got business on the coast, and I can't waste time trying to save this trailer. C'mon, let's go."

So much for our first California home. We left it in the ditch and continued our trek westward. As we came down the mountains into the lower plains and desert country, we drove through Needles, California. Off to one side was Kingman Air Force Base, a wartime gunnery training facility.

This huge field was packed with every type of World War II aircraft. Awaiting salvage crews, the planes were parked wingtip to wingtip—B-17s, B-24s, B-25s, fighters, transports. There seemed to be miles of these old warriors, and all were nothing but scrap metal now. Eventually their disassembled remains would be used to build prefabricated housing. It was fascinating, and we stopped for a closer look. They let us wander around the field.

Many of the planes had insignia painted on their noses, and names given them by their crews. Images of voluptuous women adorned them, and many had row upon row of bombs painted on them, denoting the number of missions the aircraft had flown.

Around the country, there were other "bone yards" like this at the time. One was in Arkansas; another at Litchfield Park, a Naval Air Facility 18 miles southwest of Phoenix, Arizona. There was also one at Chino, California, that served as a setting in the 1946 Academy Award–winning movie *The Best Years of Our Lives*.

In one scene Dana Andrews, playing a recently discharged, troubled B-17 bombardier, visits the field and lifts himself into one of the battle-scarred bombers. He just sits in the bombardier's seat in the nose of the aircraft, reliving the war. He hears the plane's engines come to life, hears the roar of flight, and crewmen calling out positions of attacking enemy. He was bathed in sweat as those sounds faded away. That part of the film has always stayed with me. Perhaps, in a way, it reminded me of some of the emotion I felt in combat.

Within a few days after that, we were in Los Angeles. Everything was as I had imagined it. Palm trees lined the streets, the air was warm and sweet with the scent of flowers. Lawns were green, the streets clean and spacious. The people were friendly and relaxed. They were casual in their dress, and they seemed quite happy living in what looked to me like a paradise city.

Our driver left us at Pershing Square. So here I was, January 1946, in downtown LA. Dick phoned his Navy buddy, Ed Hampel, who said he couldn't meet us until the next morning. Between us, Dick and I had maybe a couple hundred bucks. We noticed a booth in a corner of the park, with a sign offering help to veterans. It was unmanned that evening, so we spent our first night in LA on

Pershing Park's benches. The next morning we were at the booth when a woman opened it, and she told us about a nearby YMCA that let veterans stay for five days. We checked in to our new temporary home, then went back to the park to meet Ed.

He was a real handsome guy, a total lady killer. Whenever we walked into a restaurant, all the women in the place looked at him, checked him out. They didn't even see Dick and me. Out there, we were a couple of hicks, at first.

Ed gave us a tour of the city. We started out on Sunset Boulevard and saw movie stars' luxurious homes and all the major radio and motion-picture studios. I, of course, was most interested in the radio studios. Radio was big, in those days before television. I had it in my mind that when we got settled, I'd visit one of these studios and tell them I was an announcer.

When I later did just that, a kind executive listened to me rattle off my experience; he even put me in a booth and let me read something. Then he said I needed experience, and that I should keep working to improve my skills. "Come back and see me in a few years," he added as I was leaving, "maybe we'll be able to work something out then."

After Sunset Boulevard, Ed drove us down San Vicente Boulevard to cliffs overlooking the Pacific Ocean. As I gazed out over the vast water, I remembered my Caribbean experience and my love for the sea. I knew immediately that I had found a new home in California. We looked down on the beach at people lounging around in bathing suits, soaking up the sun. The water was glass-like, with waves that broke out some distance from the shore, then dissipated as they reached the sandy beach. I noticed a couple of guys riding in with the waves.

"What are they doing?" I asked Ed.

"Body surfing," he said, not taking his eyes off them. It was a favorite sport in California, he explained. Ed, born and raised in Santa Monica, loved the water. He'd been a lifeguard before the war. A few days later he took us to the beach, so we could try what looked like a fun sport.

I'd spent many years swimming in Ox Lake back in Minneapolis, but I'd never experienced anything as thrilling as that first time I went body surfing using a pair of fins. I felt an almost spiritual connection with the water, and riding the waves seemed to capture my very being. I just couldn't get enough of surfing after that, and before long I was pretty fair at it.

Ed's main interest was in getting into acting, and he introduced us to a spot on the beach where actors hung out. Norma Shearer had a house there, with a big brick wall on its seaward side where the stars and their friends congregated and sunbathed. Ed, Dick, and I threw down our beach towels not far from the group and just sat and watched. We saw Peter Lawford, Van Johnson, and a few other familiar-looking faces. But our attention was drawn especially to one woman as she walked down the beach—we couldn't help but notice her, because of her incredible figure. It was Jane Russell, and soon she joined the other actors—she'd recently starred in Howard Hughes' film *The Outlaw.*

After our five nights at the YMCA, we found a room in a home on Olympic Boulevard. Now that we had a more or less permanent place to stay, Dick and I started thinking seriously about how to break into the movie business. One evening Ed had us over for dinner, and we met his parents, both of whom worked at movie studios. They were experienced professionals, she in wardrobe and he as a stagehand, or grip. When we told them what we had in mind, his mother suggested we enroll in an acting program to learn the basics of the trade and get some experience.

This seemed like sound advice, so we found a well-established little theater school in Beverly Hills, the Bliss-Hayden Theater. Harry Hayden and Lela Bliss were character actors, old-time pros in the business. We liked the couple, and they invited us to join their group. Our tuition was covered by our GI benefits.

Luck was with us, since at the time there was a shortage of men in the acting game—most servicemen hadn't yet arrived home from overseas. We started classes, which we really enjoyed, and spent our spare time at the beach body surfing.

Not only were we having fun learning the business at the theater, but we found ourselves surrounded by beautiful young women. Women from all parts of the country, who wanted to make it in the movies. They were all committed to some producer, agent, director, screenwriter, or someone in the industry, and a couple of dead-broke hicks like ourselves from Minnesota didn't stand a serious chance with them. But we all became pals anyway.

I noticed, while we were rehearsing scenes on the theater stage, that a guy would come in each morning and just sit in the back row. He sat there all day, never saying a word. Finally we introduced ourselves, and we went out for a hamburger together. His name was Bill Valkis. As we ate, we talked about our backgrounds and experiences, and I told him I'd been at Anzio. He'd been in the Army too, he said, stationed in the Philippines before the war. He'd been captured by the Japanese and survived the Bataan death march. Then he was taken to Japan, where he'd been held prisoner until V-J day, September 1945.

Once he knew we were combat veterans, Bill became very friendly and talkative. His sister, Joan Valerie, was a well-known movie actress in B movies. He drove us home in his Lincoln Continental convertible, and when he saw where we were living, he invited us to stay with him at his sister's house; she was out of town for a few weeks.

So for a short while, we lived in a gorgeous house. Harry Hayden knew Bill and his sister, and he told us that when he'd returned from his years in the prison camp, he wouldn't talk to anyone. Bill had been just a poor, lost soul. Joan asked if he could just come down to the theater each day and sit and watch the actors; she thought it would be good for him.

Well, it sure was good for him once we became pals. Each day we piled into his convertible, three guys and six gals from the theater group, and had lunch at the Farmer's Market. That led to parties at his sister's house, where we tried to empty her well-stocked wine cellar. Nothing happened with the girls, but something wonderful did happen to Bill. He came out of his shell and had a blast with his newfound friends.

This went on for several weeks, until his sister came home. And that was the end of it, but she wasn't angry. She was happy for Bill. Despite our having decimated her wine cellar and consumed all the booze in the house, she said we were okay guys. The improvement in her brother was obvious, but even so, the party was over. We returned to our rooming house and never did see Bill again.

A few days after the party ended at Joan's, Harry Hayden asked if I'd be interested in joining a group of actors who appeared in a play each evening at their theater. I was thrilled to accept, obviously.

The group was made up of students and professionals, who usually got the plum roles. The play that Harry wanted to put on had been a big hit on Broadway, and it was basically a two-man production. I was to play a detective who was taking a convicted mobster to prison. The setting was Grand Central Station—actually we were sitting on a bench onstage—with the two of us handcuffed to each other in the middle of the night.

With Harry directing, I really got into the part and became engrossed in the give-and-take between myself and the other actor. The play was called *Small Miracle on Broadway*, and it was later made into a movie titled *Four Hours to Kill*.

Years later, as a marshal in 20 years of *Gunsmoke* episodes, I probably took 500 guys off to jail. How ironic that my first play acting would be as a detective taking a guy to prison.

The play ran for two or three weeks, and I was unaware that there were people in the audience who worked for film studios. One night after a performance a lady, Ruth Burch, stopped backstage and complimented me on my acting. She asked if I could come out to her studio and meet her boss. I had no agent then, so I accepted enthusiastically. Next morning I hitchhiked out to Culver City and the old RKO lot. Miss Burch was there to greet me and took me into her boss's office, which was large but not too ostentatious. A gentleman sat behind a desk and she said to him, "Well, Mr. Selznick, this is the boy I was telling you about that I saw in the play."

David O. Selznick got up and came around the desk and shook hands with me. We sat and chatted for quite a while. He wanted to know all about me, my family, where I was from, the extent of my acting experience. He said he was thinking of producing a movie of Thomas Wolfe's first novel, *Look Homeward, Angel*. I'd read this classic years earlier, and it had been one of my favorites.

It's the coming-of-age story of a restless young man yearning to experience life to the fullest. The main character has three brothers, and during my conversation with Selznick it dawned on me that he might be thinking about my playing one of them. We chatted some more, and he said his office would stay in touch with me. Unfortunately I was never called, but it was exciting to meet such a Hollywood legend that early in my career.

Immediately after the show closed, people began wanting to talk to me—casting directors, talent scouts, and the like, who invited me out to their studios for interviews. I couldn't believe it was actually happening to me. I'd come to California basically hitchhiking, and here I was interviewing for parts at movie studios.

Another fallout from the play was a screen test at Warner Brothers. I wasn't offered a contract, but the studio executives said I had potential and should keep training. They said that with improved skills and more experience, someday I would make the grade. I found these words encouraging.

All this occurred within a few weeks of my meeting David Selznick, and I was kind of in a daze, wondering how it was all happening so quickly.

It was a different story for Ed and Dick, who weren't having this kind of luck. Ed stayed with it, even though he had trouble in front of a camera. His words didn't come out right, which happened to a lot of guys. Ed just would not give up on his acting obsession. He was extremely handsome and seemed always to be surrounded by beautiful women, but acting was not working for him.

Dick was still keeping after it too, but he was becoming discouraged. He had other options—his father owned a business back in Minneapolis. I tried to encourage him to stick with acting, but I could see it was wearing thin for him.

As for me, things just kept happening. It was almost weird. I met Leon Lance, an independent theatrical agent, when he walked backstage one evening and introduced himself. He was a gregarious little guy who seemed to know his way around the business, and everyone liked him. He asked if I could meet him the next day at his office.

I hadn't been there ten minutes when he said he wanted to take me to RKO. "I want you to meet some studio people," he said. We hopped into his '38 LaSalle Coupe, one of the prewar great old cars, and drove over to RKO, where we met a casting director and three other gentlemen. The one sitting behind a desk stood up to greet me and introduced himself as Dore Schary.

Later he would become one of the biggest movie executives in Hollywood and, eventually, the head of MGM studios. We would also become good personal friends, but at the time I really had no idea who these men were or what positions they held at the studio.

They were very cordial, and after we'd finished the meeting they asked me to take a screen test. This consisted of me talking on camera in a Scandinavian accent.

I passed the test. A few days later I had a contract for a part in a new movie,

The Farmer's Daughter, starring Loretta Young. They offered me $150 a week, which Leon managed to raise to $400.

The story concerns a clash between a Swedish maid (Loretta) and her employer (Joseph Cotten), the man she loves, over a congressional election. Loretta's character has three brothers, and I was to play one of these. I was a perfect fit, being from Minnesota and able to take on a Scandinavian accent almost at will, because of my upbringing.

I could hardly believe my good fortune. Here I was just out of the Army two years, and I was to be in a major motion picture with two of Hollywood's brightest stars. Loretta won the 1947 Best Actress Academy Award for that performance.

Shortly after signing on for the movie, I got a call from the studio informing me that I had to be at the Glendale Railroad Station within a day or so, a Sunday morning, as I recall it. The entire cast was going to San Francisco to shoot the first part of the film. I left the boarding house for a few hours to pick up some personal items for the trip, and when I came back, all my clothes were gone!

The lady who ran the place had overheard my telephone conversation, Dick explained, and while I was gone she'd come in and said that because we were behind in our rent, she was taking my clothes. I went right to her apartment (a small place over the garage) and found her, promising that she would get her money as soon as the studio began paying me. The landlady would not give back my clothing, and we both started yelling. Dick called the cops. When the officer arrived, I explained my situation, and he told the lady he thought it would be all right to give me back my clothes.

She finally relented, and I made it to the station in time. I was, of course, in a panic through this whole thing, imagining that I'd miss my first movie opportunity for want of some clothes. Dick had stood by me once again.

The whole movie entourage was on the train—producer, director, actors, actresses, and all the other people who make a movie happen. I met those who were to play my brothers: Keith Andes, who went on to sing in many stage and movie musicals; and Lex Barker, who later did a stint playing Tarzan. Lex and I would cross paths again in 1954, when I was working on *The Sea Chase* with John Wayne and Lana Turner. While we were shooting in Hawaii, Lex, married to Lana at the time, accompanied her. We had fun reminiscing about *The Farmer's Daughter*.

So, here I am among all these professionals—Loretta Young, Joseph Cotten, Ethel Barrymore, and Charles Bickford—never having been before a camera and about as green as they come. I was in awe. I could hardly believe I was part of this crew.

Dore Schary had come along too, and en route to San Francisco, he took Lex, Keith, and me to meet Loretta in one of the railroad cars that was packed

My first movie, *The Farmer's Daughter*, starring Loretta Young and Joseph Cotten. It was a wonderful experience. I played one of Loretta's brothers. The other two were played by Lex Barker and Keith Andes. Pictured left to right: Harry Shannon, me, Loretta Young, Lex Barker and Anna Q. Nilsson. Loretta won a Best Actress Academy Award for her performance in the movie. (Arness Collection.)

with people. As we were introduced, she said, "Ahh, my three brothers," and chatted with us in a Swedish accent. We, of course, responded using our accents, and we had a delightful time. She was beautiful and charming. When I think of movie crews that I worked with later and the problems that could arise after weeks of working together, this was by far the most congenial group of my film career.

In San Francisco we were met by limousines (my first ride in one) and taken to the Fairmont Hotel. We walked into a lobby with beautiful columns and a purple carpet. It was like paradise; I couldn't believe it. My room was the size of a tennis court, with a bathroom as big as a living room. I had the whole place to myself! This had to be one of the most beautiful hotels in the world.

The next morning we met in the lobby. The limos took us across the Golden Gate Bridge into Marin County, to a farm outside the town of Petaluma. We spent about three weeks out there. The director, H. C. Potter, wasn't too sure about me because of my lack of acting experience, but all went well. I wasn't much concerned about his opinion, because I knew he didn't have anything to say about my presence.

Each day we went back and forth between the farm and hotel. The studio representative in charge of expenses told us to charge our meals at the dining room, but of course he didn't know what a big eater I was. The first night, I downed three entrees. After a few days of this, he asked me what was going on in the dining room—I was charging a lot of money for food. Clearly he suspected I might have a kickback deal going with one of the waiters.

"Oh, don't worry," I told him, "everything's on the up-and-up. All those charges are valid. Would you like to join us for dinner tonight?"

Well, he did. And I thought, I'll do this guy in totally. I started with prime rib, then lobster, pheasant, and I didn't stop until he got up from the table and said, "Okay, okay." However, he did instruct Lex and Keith to inform him later whether I'd eaten everything I ordered. And that was the end of his interest in my food consumption.

After shooting in San Francisco, we returned to LA to complete the movie on studio sets. Dick and I settled up with the landlady, then moved to another rooming house in Beverly Hills. I wound up working five months on the film, while Dick kept going to auditions and trying to find himself a niche in the acting world.

One day I was walking up Beverly Hills Drive dressed for the beach, in an old, faded pair of pants and some kind of Hawaiian shirt. Just south of Wilshire Boulevard there was a theatrical agency—Berg Allenberg—housed in a beautiful, imposing building right on Beverly Boulevard. As I walked by, a man stepped out and stopped me, asking if I was an actor. I said yes, I was presently working in *The Farmer's Daughter*. He introduced himself as John Farrow and said he was directing a picture at Paramount and would like to talk to me. Could I contact him the next day for an appointment?

We met at the studio. His movie was about three brothers (again!) who'd been in the service, and how they fared during the postwar years. Farrow was thinking of me for one of the brothers—there must have been something about me that cried, "brother"! But I lost out to Sterling Hayden, Bill Holden, and Sonny Tufts. The movie, released in 1947, was *Blaze of Noon*. I later appeared in two John Farrow films: *Hondo* and *The Sea Chase*.

There were long periods when I wasn't included in scenes of *The Farmer's Daughter*, but even so I continued to draw my salary. I went down to the RKO paymaster's window every Thursday and asked for my check. The lady promptly handed me my money and I walked out. I was in hog heaven!

Dick still hadn't had much success in finding work in the studios, and finally he decided to return home and seek his fortune there. We didn't stay in touch regularly after that, but years later he visited me on the *Gunsmoke* set, and we had great fun chatting about those early, uncertain days in Hollywood. I've always felt indebted to Dick for encouraging me to go to California and try our luck in the business.

With my roommate gone, I rented a room in a Santa Monica private home. Later I moved to Newport, where I shared a room with another old friend from Minneapolis.

I spent all my free time down at the beach, surfing. At San Onofre, where the waves broke farther out from shore, I learned to use a surfboard. My first was made of redwood, twelve feet long and weighing 125 pounds.

For transportation, I'd bought a big old 1938 Buick convertible sedan, yellow with a black top. It had black leather seats, and big spare tires on the fenders. I think I paid two or three grand for it. I loved cruising around in that car, the California breezes tousling my sandy hair as I traveled from the movie studio to the ocean. Often I was the driver for groups of us, but sometimes I'd just get in the car and go for a ride by myself, to admire the beauty around me and think about my good fortune.

The Farmer's Daughter was finally completed in September 1946, and though I'd accumulated a lot of money, I was once again without a job. I contacted Leon Lance, who offered to help find me another part. He became my agent and went with me on all the interviews.

But by this time, many former actors were home from the war. They'd been promised that jobs would be waiting, and they were competing for roles. Earlier I'd been able to walk into a waiting room for an audition and find only a few competitors, but now I saw as many as twenty young, good-looking actors. I suddenly realized that this was going to be a whole different ballgame.

Not much was happening for me in show business, so I went home to Minneapolis for a visit with my overjoyed mother. She remarried, eventually, becoming Ruth Salisbury. She and John (of the Salisbury Mattress Company, Minneapolis) would come to visit quite often in California.

After relaxing for a while with Mom and old friends on familiar ground, I came back to California and practically lived at the beach. I actually gave some thought to the idea that maybe a career in this business wasn't going to happen after all. I stayed in touch with Leon anyway, just in case.

Eventually I got a job setting pins in a bowling alley on Balboa Island in the winter of '47, continuing to surf in my spare time. I surfed through the winter months, and at some point I totally lost touch with the acting business and Leon. Driving to San Onofre to surf and working odd jobs became a way of life for me, and often I even slept in my car or out on the beach. But such a leisurely life would not last long: soon I had another real job.

I was collecting unemployment insurance in Santa Monica for having worked on *The Farmer's Daughter,* and periodically the lady in the employment office would inform me of a job opening. Because of my radio experience she sent me to a local station, KOWL, which was located on the beach in the Ambassador West Hotel.

I got the job. Aside from doing regular broadcast work, I gave Santa Monica surfing reports, probably the first of their kind in California. Anyway, they brought in another announcer too, and we shared our patter over the airwaves. One day the radio manager got the idea of having me and the other announcer do rapid-fire commercials, which meant I'd fire off a line and he'd quickly follow with another, and we'd go on and on.

Finally one day while running these commercials, we both got into a fit of laughter and couldn't stop. Of course we both got fired, thankfully. My unemployment insurance had run out, and I had to find another job as soon as possible. I ended up working for a building contractor as a laborer and stayed with this until mid-'47. Then I kind of drifted into something else.

I surfed with a small group of guys, using the heavy surfing boards of those days. Our mecca was San Onofre, and we named our fast-growing crowd the San Onofre Surf Club. We often traveled to other beaches like La Jolla, and even spent some time in Tijuana, Mexico, below San Rosarito Beach. We just camped on the beach and spent a few days "catching the big ones."

Finally things got a little out of hand back at San Onofre, when we decided to take up residence in beach houses belonging to the U.S. Marine Corps: San Onofre was part of Camp Pendleton. One night a Marine officer showed up and told us to clear out the old furniture we'd brought in from a dump, and have our area cleaned up in two hours.

When he returned, everything was as we'd initially found it. We kept using the beach, but we were careful to keep our area pristine. We didn't mind indulging the Marines: just taking in the sun and surfboarding as we pleased was enough for us. It was beautiful there, an unforgettable experience.

One afternoon we were just kicking back, passing around a bottle of Muscatel while waiting for the evening tide glass-off, when a car careened down to the beach and pulled up in a cloud of dust. The driver jumped out and made straight for me—it was Ed Hampel, carrying a large cardboard box. He dumped a bunch of letters from it into my lap, accusing me of having received these fan letters from moviegoers who'd seen me in *The Farmer's Daughter*. Then he chewed me out for wasting my time lying on the beach when I could be having a career in movies. I just watched him, not knowing what to say. I liked Ed, and I felt badly for him because I knew how hard he'd been trying.

My beach bum friends had not known about my acting, and I was afraid that I'd be thrown out of the club if they did. But they seemed more amused than anything else. Ed was still running around Hollywood every day, going to interviews, trying to meet people, reading all the trades, and looking for that one lucky break. It must have been frustrating for him to see me lounging around

Party at San Onofre beach, summer of 1946, with my surfing buddies. I am sitting to the right of center, playing a ukulele, next to the gal in the striped shirt . Great parties, great friends and great surfing! During the 1940s surfing was a relatively unknown sport, but it was a big part of my life for many years. (Arness Collection.)

the beach, seemingly uninterested in the film business while having fallen into a feature my first time out.

As he stormed off, Ed asked for one favor: that I come with him to the Pasadena Playhouse that coming Sunday night. They had open readings for parts in plays being produced there, he said. Mainly to get him off my back, since he was embarrassing me in front of my buddies, I agreed.

The Playhouse had a big theater with a few smaller side ones upstairs, seating approximately 50 people. It seemed like all the theaters had productions underway continuously. The one Ed and I walked into was full of actors reading for parts in George Bernard Shaw's *Candida*. Of course I had absolutely no training or experience in anything British, and I was ready to leave when it came my turn to read. It was a three-character play, and as they whittled down the actors I found I was still in the running. In fact, they cast me in the role of a minister. Ed, unfortunately, was not given a part. But he was very pleased with himself for having dragged me along and gotten my career back on track!

Performing in the theater play *Candida* with my first wife, Virginia Chapman. (Arness Collection.)

The female director told me not to mind about my accent, that she would help me with it as we rehearsed. The other characters were the minister's wife, played by an excellent actress named Virginia Chapman who'd studied theater at UCLA, and an artist who'd fallen in love with her. Virginia was attractive and energetic, and she took her stage work quite seriously. We became very friendly, and soon I began to pick her up for rehearsals and take her home each evening after we'd finished at the playhouse.

Of course her parents were somewhat concerned, because I came by in my wreck of a car, not looking the part of a man who was serious about his work. They wondered what their daughter saw in me. Virginia had been married and divorced and had an 18-month-old child. We were getting serious about each other, and I could see that if I wished to hold on to her and gain the approval of her parents, I'd have to get off the beach and get a steady job, which is exactly what I did.

I applied for a job at the *Los Angeles Examiner,* a Hearst paper, and landed a position in the classified advertising department as a salesman. My client base was the real estate market. Using all the marketing techniques we were taught, plus a few of our own, I was supposed to hard-sell our clientele to take out larger display ads. I bought a modest-looking newer car and dressed up in a suit and tie and became respectable.

One day Virginia's folks, knowing how serious we were, suggested that after our marriage, we move into the house out of which they ran their wholesale china-ware business. They lived in Hancock Park but also had this old Victorian house on Beverly Boulevard, near Alvarado. Its first floor was filled with displays of china, and living quarters were on the second floor. Virginia and I were both enthusiastic about the offer; we moved in following our marriage in 1948.

Determined that I become an actor, my new wife had great faith in my ability and saw potential in me, something that I was blind to myself, at the time. I had just spent a number of months on the beach, and during that time I hadn't given any serious consideration to the profession. To me, it was still all a lark.

I continued at the *Examiner*, and life was beginning to take on some structure. I liked what was happening: I now had a woman whom I cared about deeply, her very kind family, a decent car, and a good salary. Life looked pretty good to me. The Chapmans offered to take me into their business and later retire themselves, leaving Virginia and me with a very prosperous livelihood.

Virginia would have no part of it. She was intent on us both becoming actors, and there would be little time for anything but study, auditions, and, hopefully, more work in the industry in the not-too-distant future. We would take anything at that time, cameos, small parts, even walk-ons, work that would give us the experience to make it someday. Virginia became my teacher, and gradually her acting career took a backseat to mine, common practice for women at the time.

We got back in touch with Leon and had dinner together. Virginia liked him right from the start, and the two of them practically made me sign a contract not to go to the beach anymore. I had to keep my nose to the grindstone and learn. Ed, of course, was delighted with these developments in my life. He considered himself responsible for getting my career going again—and, I had to admit, he'd indeed been a good influence on me.

While I was taking acting lessons, Leon and Virginia thought it might be wise for me to put on a few pounds, since I was pretty skinny for my height. So I joined the Bert Goodrich Gym and began to work out and lift iron. A lot of movie stars frequented the place, and one that I remember vividly was Mario Lanza. He tended to be heavy and had to drop pounds for his roles. One day after we worked out and were sitting in a sauna bath, Mario walked in and someone asked him to sing. Without hesitation he broke into a favorite of the time, "Because." What a treat to hear him sing that beautiful song with tenderness and great vocal power. For someone with limited formal training, he was awesome.

Steve Reeves was another regular, as were the famous golfer Frank Stanahan and "Mister World" George Eiferman. The workouts were paying off, and it wasn't long before I began to notice the addition of solid muscle and a weight gain.

Meanwhile, Virginia and Leon were setting up interviews for me, having put together a very professional resume package complete with handsome black-and-white still photographs. Everything was beginning to come together.

That's me sleeping on the floor (center) in *Battleground*. I worked with some fine actors like George Murphy, Van Johnson, Doug Fowley, and Jerome Courtland. This epic was directed by legendary "Wild Bill Wellman." Some of the actors later starred in *Gunsmoke*. (Arness Collection.)

Most of my early interviews were at Universal Studios, where I would eventually find a lot of work. In 1948, the same year of my marriage, I landed a part in a Warner Brothers western, *Whiplash,* starring Alexis Smith. It wasn't a major role, but I was pleased with it.

A year later I played in MGM's *Battleground,* the story of the Battle of the Bulge, which included a number of major stars—Van Johnson, John Hodiak, Denise Darcel, Ricardo Montalban, George Murphy, and Jimmy Whitmore. Leon thought that being a combat veteran, I would be well suited for this war movie. When we talked to the casting director, we were told that since it was a big-budget film, they were looking only for major stars. We were disappointed, and after huddling with Virginia, sent a rather tongue-in-cheek telegram to my old friend Dore Schary, who was producing *Battleground.* We mentioned my having worked for him in *The Farmer's Daughter* and wondered if there might be a place for another buck private in this movie.

A day later we got a cryptic call from the casting director, who said I was in the film and to report for work at the studio. The director was the infamous

William "Wild Bill" Wellman, a World War I veteran who'd flown fighter planes in the Lafayette Flying Corps in France. He was credited with a few aerial victories before being shot down himself. Bill often mused about the shootdown: he apparently felt he'd been the only Allied fighter pilot shot down by such lousy German machine-gunners!

Bill had directed the movie *Wings,* which had won the first Best Picture Academy Award in 1927. One never knew what he was up to when directing; he'd play tricks on cast and crew members, and "hotfoots"—a match stuck clandestinely into the sole seam of a shoe and lighted—were a favorite prank. His language was so salty that he always had a guy standing at the main door to the sound stage, so that if guests were about to visit the set, a whistle would warn Bill to tone down his language and tempera-

At Point Dume on the Malibu coast with my dog, Lady, 1948. She was a great beach dog who loved to chase butterflies. (Arness Collection.)

ment. He was a rough-hewn character and working with him was a colorful experience.

I had only a small part playing one of the many soldiers, but it was terrific watching Bill and the cast of stars work on that film. A few years later I would do another film with him, *Island in the Sky* (1953).

Fortunately, I spent several weeks working in the movie, and by that time Leon had my salary up to $700 a week, good money in those days. That same year I was cast in *Wagonmaster,* an RKO western, with Ben Johnson, Joanne Dru, Harry Carey, Jr., Ward Bond, and Jim Thorpe. Soon after that, Dore Schary got me a year's contract with MGM, which meant I'd be getting $750 a week for 40 weeks of work.

The early '50s were busy years for me. As a wrestler in Universal's *The Veils of Bagdad,* starring Victor Mature, I was among a group who were to put on a big show for a rajah. I remember one of the real wrestlers tossing me around as if I'd weighed ten pounds, and I was up to 230 at the time. He was a professional,

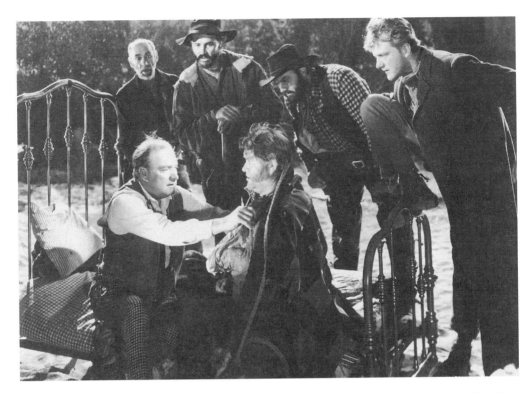

From the movie *Wagonmaster*. Famed actor Alan Mowbray is shown sitting on a bed tending to a wounded member of our gang (I am at the right). *Wagonmaster* was directed by the renowned filmmaker John Ford. It was a great experience for me as an actor learning from a man I highly respected and later befriended. The picture was filmed along the Colorado River in the wilds of North Utah. (Arness Collection.)

and though he promised he wouldn't hurt me as he spun me high over his head, I had my doubts during rehearsals and shooting of that scene.

Another of my early films was *Sierra* (also a Universal picture), which starred Audie Murphy, a former member of the 3rd Infantry Division and our nation's most highly decorated soldier during the war. We went up to Kanab, Utah, to shoot the film. While we were making it they'd pull him out to make personal appearances, be the Grand Marshal of a parade, make speeches about the war, you name it, they had him doing it. Of course the nation wanted to honor him in every way possible, but he wasn't into that sort of thing. He just wanted to be left alone and get on with his life.

He loved to shoot craps, and during every break, he and a bunch of the guys would be in a corner doing some serious crap shooting. He was a natural at the game and seemed to win everything. There was something unique about Murphy, a kind of mystique, which probably helped him through his harrowing war experiences. He was lucky, at that stage in his life; everything he touched turned to gold, and he was just on a roll. Sadly, in later years his luck ran out.

Universal's *Double Cross Bones* was kind of a spoof pirate film, a song-and-dance musical in which I played a member of the ship's crew. I performed the usual menial tasks portrayed in such period films. It wasn't much of a part, but I really enjoyed watching Donald O'Connor, who was—and continues to be—a great dancer and comic.

Jeff Chandler was a rising Universal star in those days. I worked with him in a prizefighting film, *The Iron Man*. We played brothers, born and raised in a Pennsylvania coalmining town. Every Saturday night, prize fights were held at a local saloon and Jeff won all his fights. His character was that of a natural-born fighter, and during the movie I had to take him on. Before shooting the scene I was sent over to the studio's gym to learn how to box. Since I had been working out and had put some weight on, I looked the part when I got into the ring with Jeff.

In all honesty, I

With Mari Blanchard in the movie *Veils of Bagdad*, in which I played a wrestler who was part of a band of men led by Victor Mature, trying to overthrow a despotic ruler of an Arab nation. Most of the band was made up of real professional wrestlers. In one scene one of the wrestlers actually picked me up and twirled me over his head. I was a little worried, but the guy was strong, I mean really strong. I think he was called "The Swedish Angel." (Arness Collection.)

I appeared (center rear) with several seasoned veterans and a few newcomers to the screen in the Universal movie *Double Cross Bones*. The cast included Donald O'Connor, Will Greer, Hope Emerson and a new guy on the block who was to become a huge star, Rock Hudson. Although the movie did not get very good reviews, watching multi-talented Donald O'Connor go through his paces was a delight. (Arness Collection.)

would have to say that my height and size contributed to the successes I've enjoyed throughout my movie and television career. They certainly were major factors when I was selected to play the alien monster in RKO's *The Thing*, produced by the famed Howard Hawks. It was a big-production science-fiction movie, about an alien from outer space who crashes in Alaska and is trapped there by a remote outpost of scientists and air force personnel. I was rather surprised by its initial popularity, and it seems to have evolved since then into a cult film. I still receive letters today from fans raving about that 50-year-old movie.

One of the tedious aspects of working on it was the many hours I had to spend with a makeup artist, one of the RKO-employed Westmore brothers. Several weeks before we started shooting, I had to go to the studio daily and sit while the artist tested makeup materials on my face and hands. On one occasion he covered my head with plaster of Paris to make a rubber and plastic mold, leaving only my nostrils open. Once he had finished, his arm accidentally brushed the mold and covered my only source of air. I made some frantic noises while motioning to my nose, and thankfully he discovered the problem. Quickly he cleared that area, and I breathed again. It sounds funny now, but at the time it was kind of scary, knowing how quickly plaster of Paris hardens!

After Westmore got the head piece finished, he worked on my hands. He built up their size using rubberized material, and attached big claw-like tentacles on every knuckle. I ended up with really gnarly looking hands.

Me as *The Thing*. Later, the picture became a sci-fi classic—who would have guessed it? I had great fun doing the picture even though each make-up session took 2½ hours. (Arness Collection.)

One day he suggested we go to a drive-in and have a bite of lunch, get a hamburger or something. It was in the middle of the day, and although I didn't have the head piece on I still had the makeup on my hands, and it looked very realistic. But Westmore had some more patch work to do, and he didn't want to undo his morning's work. We drove up to the drive-in, a few blocks away from the studio—in those days drive-ins were all the rage in California, the forerunners of today's fast-food outlets.

Before the waitress got to our car window, Westmore leaned over to me and suggested I take the menu from her with one of my made-up hands. This sounded like fun, so when the young lady arrived with a menu and a cheery "Hi boys, what'll you have?" I stuck out my claw. I just wish someone had had a camera. First her eyes widened, and I imagine she was thinking I was some sort of deformed person and she didn't want to say anything to offend me. She jumped away from the car and ran back to the counter. I yelled out that the hand was just makeup for a movie, and finally she came back then and took our order. But she remained wary of us until we drove away.

Part of the film was shot in the old LA ice house near the railroad tracks downtown. When we entered the large warehouse-looking building, the inside of which was freezing most of the time, we had to walk through slaughtered meat hanging from overhead hooks. I was glad when we finished those shots and moved on to Montana, where we finished the movie.

One day, we were done shooting at the ice house and riding back to the studio in our limo. I hadn't cleaned off my makeup, and we got stalled in downtown traffic. As we waited at a light, the guy I was with thought it would be funny if I jumped out and bought a paper at a nearby newsstand. So, in all my makeup, I went up to the stand and said something like "Hey, give me an L.A. *Times*, arg-gh-gh." I growled, thinking the joke would be obvious. But the frightened newsman abandoned his stand, and pedestrians stopped dead in their tracks. People just couldn't figure out if I was real or what. Finally they decided I was in costume, just another Hollywood screwball, and went about their business.

The picture did have some down sides, once it was released. I got a call one day from the studio, and it seemed a young boy had seen the movie in Georgia and gone catatonic. He was in a hospital and wouldn't talk to anyone. They asked me to go and see him, convince him the alien was not real and I was the actor. Of course I said yes, but before I could hop a plane, the boy recovered.

I think there was a lot of that sort of thing going on around the country, because the picture was so realistic and people were genuinely scared when they watched it. Perhaps memories of the 1938 Orson Welles radio show *The War of the Worlds* still lingered in their minds.

With money coming in and good prospects for more work, Virginia and I decided to look for a house of our own. I'd adopted Craig, her son from her first marriage, and within a few years we began to add to the family. In January 1950 she gave birth to our daughter Jenny at Good Samaritan Hospital. Shortly after that wonderful event, we moved to the Cape Cod cottage we built in the Pacific Palisades, on Benvenides Street. It was beautiful and brand new and all ours, complete with shingles.

Like me, my brother, Pete, had acting aspirations and moved to California after being discharged from the service. Using the name Peter Graves (a family name of our mother's father), he broke into films in 1950 with *Rogue River,* and fame followed with his superb performance in *Stalag 17* (1953). He starred for many years in the TV show *Mission Impossible,* and today he's a frequent host on *Biography.* Pete and his wife eventually bought a home near Virginia and me in the Palisades area.

Our second child, Rolf, was born in February 1952. With our growing family we went to the beach, enjoyed picnics, and just basked in our good fortune. Leon continued to get me work; by now I was making between 20 and 30 thousand a year. For the Arnesses, those were wonderful years. Our parents, of course, were thrilled with both their sons' success.

Later in 1952, I enjoyed working with Sterling Hayden in *Hellgate* even though he didn't care much about the business. It just didn't sit right with him. He felt as if he was pretending, instead of really living life. Hayden was born and raised in New England and was a master sailor. He was also a gifted writer. His two books, *Voyager* and *Wanderer*, were highly acclaimed when they were published in the 1970s.

In *Hellgate*, a Civil War epic, I was the heavy while he played the good guy. It was shot on a set that replicated a Yuma prison, and it was an intense experience. The producer, writer, and director was Charles Marcus Warren, who later became the first producer and director on *Gunsmoke*. For me, as I reflect back on all these early movie experiences, I can say that without exception, every set I worked on was fun. Nobody was uptight, everyone was very professional and friendly. I was relaxed, learning the trade and gaining experience. I always had a good part, a couple of pages here and a few scenes there. I didn't have to worry about demanding roles.

Sometimes I had a little too much fun on the set, and there were times when directors weren't too pleased with my shenanigans. I remember in *Horizons West* (Universal), which starred Robert Ryan and Julie Adams, we had some scenes at a Thanksgiving family gathering in a ranch house. Rock Hudson, who was just a kid at the time, and I started laughing about something and couldn't stop. The more we tried to get ourselves under control, the worse it got. They had to stop the filming several times, which interrupted the shooting schedule and cost money, and we rightfully got a thorough chewing out by the director. I guess in some ways I was still the mischievous boy back in Minnesota, staring out the classroom window waiting to hop a freight.

I had the unique experience of working with Spencer Tracy in MGM's *The People Against O'Hara*, a film in which I was cast for the first time in a major role. Tracy was a great actor, and it was fascinating working around him. He was very serious about his work, not a relaxed or easy-going guy on the set. In fact, when he came on the set, a buzzer went off and everyone had to quit smoking. He would come in and we would all sit down to rehearse a scene, sitting in a semicircle in canvas chairs with Tracy in the middle. The director sat facing the semicircle, and everything was directed at Mr. Tracy. We filled in various lines as we went through the dialogue. Tracy usually offered suggestions about what he thought would work, and then he went over to the director and they laid out the scene themselves and called us in later.

Pat O'Brien, an old pro, was also in that movie. He was probably one of the nicest persons ever to hit this town. We became good friends, and he was

People Against O'Hara starring Spencer Tracy. Shown here are Pat O'Brien at the left, me, and John Hodiak leaning across the desk. In this film I played a young fisherman who was falsely accused of murder and was defended by lawyer Spencer Tracy. We shot most of the scenes at the Fulton Street Fish Market on the East River in New York City. (Arness Collection.)

an enormous help in advising me on how to work with Tracy when I did a scene with him. As you can imagine, I was kind of overawed by this legendary star. O'Brien had played opposite Tracy many times, and he told me not to worry. "He's not going to bite you," O'Brien reassured me, "he just acts that way." But you could have fooled me. He was a real no nonsense guy on the set. I heard of an incident that happened during the production of the 1955 movie *Bad Day at Black Rock* in which he starred with Robert Ryan, Anne Francis, Ernest Borgnine, Lee Marvin, Walter Brennan and Dean Jagger. Tracy played the role of a returning World War II one-armed veteran who traveled to a remote western town to deliver a war decoration to the father of one of his buddies, an infantryman of native American descent, who had been killed in Italy. Tracy entered a run down saloon and was confronted by a host of "bad men" who were menacing in their attitude toward the stranger. When Tracy began his dialogue, Lee Marvin began drumming his fingers on a table he was sitting behind. After a few minutes Tracy stopped the shooting and walked over to Marvin. He glared at the young actor and said words to the effect that if he (Marvin) was going to steal a scene, he'd best not try it with him (Tracy). The shooting resumed as a chastened Marvin sat quietly in his place.

MGM cast me in the western *Many Rivers to Cross,* starring Robert Taylor and Eleanor Parker. The two of them couldn't have been nicer. I had a good part, so Taylor and I worked together a lot. He was the opposite of Tracy—easy going, friendly. Usually he just kicked back when we weren't doing a scene.

Greer Garson was a charming and gracious lady when we worked together in MGM's *Her Twelve Men,* released in 1953. Her English accent knocked me out! I had a small part as a gym teacher. Leon kept me busy landing other small but enjoyable roles, such as in *The Girl in White* (MGM), starring June Allyson. That movie was about the first lady doctor to work in a public hospital. Allyson's costar was Arthur Kennedy, a down-to-earth guy whom everyone liked.

Although MGM didn't pick me up again for a second year, I continued to get parts in a number of films, including *Stars in My Crown* (MGM) starring Joel McCrea, Ellen Drew, and Amanda Blake, who later played Kitty in *Gunsmoke.* I worked with McCrea in two other films as well, *Wyoming Mail* in 1951 and *Lone Hand* in 1953. In all, I appeared in nineteen movies during the 1950s, including *Carbine Williams,* with Jimmy Stewart and Jean Hagen; *Flame of the Islands,* starring Howard Duff and Yvonne de Carlo; *Ride the Man Down,* with Brian Donlevy and Ella Raines; and *The First Traveling Saleslady,* featuring Ginger Rogers, Barry Nelson, and Carol Channing.

In 1955, when I signed on to play Marshal Matt Dillon in the television series *Gunsmoke,* my movie acting became almost non-existent. Doing the weekly TV show became full-time work, and how could any of us know that the series would last twenty years?

Meanwhile, Virginia encouraged me to attend another acting group that she'd known at UCLA and the Circle Theater. It was called the Players Ring, and they had a little theater down in Hollywood—the New Hampshire Theater. I had to audition as an apprentice, since there were a number of major movie stars involved, like Akim Tamiroff, Anthony Quinn, Arthur Kennedy, and Richard Nash. In addition to practicing scenes from various plays, we frequently had guest lecturers who were renowned in the business. Michael Checkov was one of them, as I remember. Gary Cooper was a regular visitor who sat out front watching us go through our paces. I got to know him quite well as we drank coffee together during our breaks. He used to call me Slim. I've often thought about this chance meeting with him and our parallel fame in westerns, his already achieved at that time in *High Noon* and mine to come in *Gunsmoke.*

One evening a dance teacher was brought in to expose the group to what was called "pre-bodily freedom," just my thing! Each one of us had to get up on the stage and take turns letting ourselves go. I'd begun to question my presence

The First Traveling Saleslady, in which I co-starred with Ginger Rogers (left) and Carol Channing (right), along with Barry Nelson and Clint Eastwood. This film was made after our second season of *Gunsmoke*, when our ratings ranked us as the top television show in the country. *Traveling Saleslady* was a comedy and received favorable reviews. It was one of the first acting roles for Clint Eastwood. Shortly after this he starred in the TV series *Rawhide* and a legend was born. (Arness Collection.)

at the theater, what with the numerous movies I was involved in at the time. Still, I thought I needed all the experience I could get, and even working as an apprentice seemed worthwhile. But this night as we lined up in the wings getting ready to take the stage individually to go into our "bodily freedom" routines, I finally thought I'd had enough. I was next up, and I turned around to look for some way out the back door or something, and who should be behind me but Patricia Neal. She turned me around and said, "No, no, you can do this. Just go on!" Pat was a regular person, just offering encouragement.

The next thing I knew, I was out on the stage doing some really weird jumping around, all arms and legs. It must have been a howl, watching a guy of my size doing these bizarre contortions. I finally finished amidst muffled laughter from a small audience out front.

Later, another student said he definitely wasn't going to do it, and the teacher warned him that if he didn't participate, he would be expelled. Steaming mad over her prodding, he finally just lost it. He ran around the stage grabbing curtains, and he not only ripped them down, but tore them apart. We had to go out and subdue him, because he was intent on wrecking the place.

I also auditioned at the Players Ring Theater, at Virginia's urging, and was cast in several plays. One night after I'd appeared in a Greek drama, a man approached me and asked that I meet him the next day at the Charles Feldman Agency. This was a very big, important agency in town at the time, with major stars

Working in small theater productions proved to be an invaluable learning experience for me. Here I am appearing in the Greek comedy *Penelope* at the Players Ring Theater located on Santa Monica Boulevard in West Hollywood around 1951. (Arness Collection.)

under contract. I went, of course, and was told they might have a part for me. They wanted me to meet with some studio execs who were getting ready to make a movie. The day after that meeting, they called me and told me that I had an appointment with John Wayne.

Part IV

John Wayne

A few days later I met with Duke Wayne at Republic Studios. We sat down and had a friendly chat. He wanted to know where I was from, what I'd done, where I'd been to school, and had I been in the service. I answered his questions straight on, and after we finished, he said, "Well now, let's get down to the important part. Do you drink?"

I thought well, this is my kind of guy, a totally relaxed, real person. I told him I'd been known to take one or two here and there. He went on to describe the movie he was going to make. It was to take place during the House Un-American Activities Committee attempt to identify card-carrying communists in this country following World War II. There was a great deal of fear, at the time, that communism would envelop the world, including the United States. Subsequent wars fought by our soldiers and U.N. troops were directed at stopping such advances.

Hollywood figures and other high-visibility people from private companies were brought before the HUAA Committee. Many pleaded the 5th Amendment.

Wayne's picture, *Big Jim McLain* (1952), dealt with a communist cell in Hawaii. Duke and I played investigators for the HUAA Committee, sent to Hawaii to break up a conspiracy developing in the islands. It was a great part for me, playing opposite Duke. We had a lot of dialogue, and I was on camera a good part of the film. Unfortunately, I was done away with by the bad guys three-quarters of the way through the movie.

One of the real pleasures of filming in the islands was that I finally was able to realize a long-held dream of surfing in Hawaii. The crew was flown over in a Boeing Model 377 transport monoplane; there were no jets in those days. It was a big two-decker plane, with a bar on the lower level. Since it was a twelve-hour flight to Honolulu, we all managed to get drunk, sober up, and then get drunk again before landing at 9 or 10 in the evening.

Duke had flown over earlier and was settled in at our hotel, the Edgewater. It was a relatively small place, five or six stories high, and it had its own little restaurant, patio bar, and pool. I was ready to hit the sack right away, after the long flight and the free-flowing booze. However, we were informed that Duke was in the bar and wanted us to join him there.

I went down, and a bunch of the guys were having a great time. After a few more drinks, I felt right at home and didn't get to bed until about 1:00 A.M. It was still dark when I woke up the next morning—I hadn't yet adjusted to the time change. I stood peering into the darkness from my balcony, and I could just make out the ocean. The surf broke like thunder on the sand, and when it got light, there was Waikiki Beach stretched out right before me, with six- to eight-feet waves breaking.

I asked our assistant director, Andy McLaglen, who later directed 100 episodes of *Gunsmoke* and was the son of legendary actor Victor McLaglen, if my schedule would allow for some surfing. He said I was off that day, and after hearing how excited I was about board surfing, he called the Outrigger Canoe Club and arranged a temporary membership for me. I was in heaven. I was in Hawaii, cast in a role opposite John Wayne, and about to have the time of my life surfing in the beautiful island waters.

I quickly found a surfing partner, Duke's brother Bob Morrison, the second assistant director and an avid surfer. (John Wayne's original name was Marion Michael Morrison.) It took a number of weeks to shoot the picture, and every time Bob and I were free, we were on the water.

John Wayne was a special guy. I doubt if we'll see anyone like him again. He was one of a kind. He had a magnetic personality that immediately appealed to people, and there wasn't anything he couldn't get or make happen. Both the Navy and the Honolulu Police Department gave him unlimited support, and he gave the chief of police, Dan Liu, a pretty good part in the film. We were invited to a number of island social gatherings, and by the time we left, we'd become part of the Navy family out there.

In one scene, Duke and I went out to the sunken battleship *Arizona* to pay our respects, since in the script I'd lost my brother in the destruction of that battlewagon during the Japanese attack on Pearl Harbor. The beautiful memorial as we know it today had not yet been built; there was just a crude quarterdeck and a flagpole. Standing on the platform, we looked down right beneath our feet and saw the buckled hull. There was a big plaque mounted on the

With John Wayne at the Arizona Memorial in the movie *Big Jim McLain* (I'm at left). This was taken before the present-day memorial was constructed. *Big Jim McLain* was my first picture with Duke. Wayne was a great patriot and the Navy went all out to accommodate us. (Arness Collection.)

quarterdeck, describing what had happened to the ship and the 1,500 men entombed in it.

The whole crew was out there for the shoot, and when people read the plaque and looked at the wreckage, emotions were stirred. But Duke's business-as-usual attitude got us back to the matters at hand. He felt as deeply as did the rest of us, but there was a picture to be made. We shot the scene and left Pearl Harbor. Since then, I've returned to the memorial many times.

As it happened, Duke and I shared the same birthday: 26 May. Virginia had come for a visit, and we were invited to share in Duke's festivity at the Willows, a famous restaurant in Waikiki. Here I was an unknown actor, a brand new guy in the group, yet they treated me as one of their own. They were just a great, great bunch of people.

After completing the picture and before leaving Hawaii, I drove out to Makaha, at the west end of the island. Being at Makaha in the winter was the dream of all who loved surfing.

Back on the mainland, Duke offered me a contract. With Leon's approval, I signed on with his outfit, the Wayne-Fellows Company. His partner was Bob Fellows. I was paid $1,000 a week, with 40 weeks of work guaranteed. That was big money then, and I was overwhelmed by my good fortune. To be working with America's most popular star and making that kind of money was unbelievable.

There was a cloud on the horizon, though: once I became a member of Wayne's ensemble, my situation with Virginia began to change. She had more or less overseen my career up to that point, continually encouraging me to seek more substantive movie roles. She considered herself in part responsible for my success to date, and she wanted to keep playing a part in matters concerning my career. However, things changed when I signed with Duke.

The Wayne-Fellows group of actors consisted of all men. Women, especially wives, were not allowed to participate in film planning, script rehearsals, or any of the process. In other words, it was an operation strictly run by men, and all of them were loyal to Duke.

This greatly upset Virginia. One time she even got into an altercation with Duke, and he put her in her place. Things at home got a little testy after that. There were days when Virginia was unapproachable, and the situation didn't improve as time went on.

Shortly after I signed, Bob Fellows asked if I would go to Mexico and play a part in *Hondo* (1953), a western that was already in production. The movie needed a heavy, it seemed, and they wrote a part for me. Since I was under contract, Fellows could easily have said, "Get your ass down to Camargo and do this and do that," but the Wayne-Fellows folks always treated their guys with respect. As a result, they were a tightly knit group that worked in harmony. Their productions had a distinct quality to them that movie-goers recognized and appreciated—a reflection of Duke's style and personality.

The company had selected stage actress Geraldine Page to make her screen debut in *Hondo*, playing opposite Duke. Bob Fellows asked me to make a test with her, to get a feel for how she would look on camera. They set it up so I would read my lines offstage, and she would be the sole subject on camera. But Miss Page was uncomfortable with that arrangement, so I came onstage with her and we did a brief scene together.

In the movie, she not only held her own with Duke, she won her first Academy Award nomination. During her career, she was honored with eight Academy Award nominations and two Emmys. In her last screen appearance, *The Trip to Bountiful,* she finally won a Best Actress Oscar.

I went down to Camargo, Mexico, which is north of Durango. It was midsummer, and blazing hot down there. We worked 14 hours a day in the sun, under the direction of John Farrow. After each day's shooting, we'd all race back to our run-down Mexican motel and hit the bar to quench our thirst. We ordered

With the Duke and Ward Bond in *Hondo*. **I'm at right. I think they released this picture on TV in 3-D color for some charity. I have not seen it since. (Arness Collection.)**

anything, just so the glass was full of ice. After a few days, everyone came down with Montezuma's revenge.

I vividly remember being ill, but we had to keep working anyway. We'd be out in the blazing desert during a take on horseback, and the minute they'd say "cut!" we'd all jump off our horses, drop our pants, and hit it! It became a daily ritual. The problem was solved when we realized the water for the ice in our drinks was coming from a polluted river near the hotel. Another source for ice was quickly found.

Acting with Geraldine Page was difficult for Duke, since their styles were completely different. Here was dynamic Wayne, who wanted to move things right along regardless of meaningless details, and a very intense costar who wanted to know the meaning of every scene she was in. Duke was careful not to get her uptight, and in the end, as they got used to each other, things worked out fine.

In the middle of shooting, John Ford suddenly showed up. Since he'd directed a lot of Wayne's westerns, he'd taken it upon himself to see how this production was faring. Ford convinced Farrow that a second filming unit under his direction might get some footage that would enhance the movie, especially one scene involving a huge wagon train under attack by Indians. One of the reasons we were shooting in Mexico was that we could hire more extras for less money, and the wagon scenes involved a lot of settlers and Indians. Ford, with his flair for the dramatic, set up a stunt that damn near killed me. Here I was in the back of a wagon with no top, and as we raced down a trail, Indians were running by the wagon whooping and shooting at us while we returned fire. The Indian players, mostly local guys, really got into it and had a hell of a good time. Often, when Farrow yelled "cut!" they'd just continue on. It was hard to get them to stop.

So now the cameras were rolling and dust was swirling around as the wagon bounced all over the place. I'd pop up and shoot a couple of rounds, then duck, reload, pop up again and start firing. Ford told me he wanted to get a cut of me during this action. When I ducked down, he said, he'd have an arrow fired that would hit the front seat behind me before I popped up again. This would look great, he explained, because just as I lowered my head, *boom!* In would come this arrow!

I liked the idea, and Ford went on to say that I wasn't to worry about getting hit with the arrow, since he was using the archery champion of Mexico. He introduced me to the guy, who had on huge, thick glasses. Ford laughed at my initial reaction, but I didn't worry too much about the guy, since Ford was known for his practical jokes. Probably the glasses were one of these, I imagined.

As we began the scene, Ford directed me through the sequence. "All right pop up, fire a couple of rounds. You see the guy coming at you, now duck, all right stay down there, all right I'm going to have the arrow shot. All right now you pop up and fire another shot." As I popped up, an arrow zoomed right past my nose and hit the back of the seat, missing me by no more than four or five inches!

Of course, this had all been preplanned, and I was really miffed. Ford told me I was a hell of an actor. There wasn't much I could do: he got the shot he wanted, and that was typical of the way Ford worked.

On another occasion, he complained about the way some of Duke's stunt men were doing a scene. He said he was going to try some of the locals, since the professionals were expensive and eating up the film's budget. So he called over some of the guys on horses, riding bareback. Through an interpreter, he asked about a dozen of them to ride up in front of the camera, full speed, and when they saw a flag waving in front of them they should pull up and fall off their horses. He had the guys charge at the camera, all revved up because the assistant director said if they did the scene right, they'd be paid a little extra.

When they saw the flag waving, they pulled back and went sailing off their horses and hit the ground. They didn't know anything about stunts and didn't

Island in the Sky starring John Wayne and Lloyd Nolan. This movie, directed by Wild Bill Wellman, is the only Wayne movie I know of that has not been released for TV or made available on video. I'm pictured here flying a search plane sent out to find "Duke" and his crew who had crash-landed in the Arctic. We did our search from a studio set that ran screen shots of ominous skies, snow and ice terrain around us so it would look like the real thing. It did! (Arness Collection.)

seem to be any the worse for wear, since they were probably used to such falls. Ford told them they were terrific, then turned to our stunt men and said, "I don't know about you guys, but I can get these boys to do your work for two dollars a stunt." Then everyone realized that he had done the whole thing as a gag. They all broke up laughing, including several of the locals who understood English and overheard Ford's words. He was always pulling off stuff like that.

I went back home after we finished *Hondo*, but it wasn't long before they had me doing *Island in the Sky*, a movie based on a true story. During World War II, cargo was flown between the United States and England, and one of the planes had to crash-land over Greenland. William Wellman directed the film, and John Wayne's costars were Lloyd Nolan, Andy Devine, Walter Abel, and Allyn Joslyn. I played a pilot flying a C-47, searching for Wayne and his crew who were stranded on an ice cap. My part was shot in a mockup cockpit at a studio. I looked down from my cockpit window, while film footage of ice floes

I co-starred with James Whitmore in the sci-fi thriller *Them!*, which was filmed in the desert outside of Lancaster, California. This was the biggest part I had so far in a movie. The film later became a classic. Here, Joan Weldon and I are facing down the enemy: a giant ant. (Arness Collection.)

and cloudy skies was run behind the mockup. I had several good scenes in this movie.

Wayne-Fellows loaned me out for a major role in a Warner Brothers sci-fi movie, *Them!* It had an excellent script (by Ted Sherdeman) and first-rate cast: Jimmy Whitmore; Edmund Gwenn, a very sweet man who later played Santa Claus in the original movie version of *Miracle on 34th Street*; Joan Weldon; and Onslow Stevens. Fess Parker had a small role, and Leonard Nimoy appeared sitting at a teletype machine. Whitmore and I played two investigators tasked with tracking down ants who'd mutated into monstrous killing machines because of their exposure to atomic waste. We had a lot of scenes in a morgue, where we looked at mangled bodies to determine by their wounds and smell if the ants had been the culprits. Someone would pull back a sheet and the director, Gordon Douglas, told Jimmy and me to give each other that "knowing" look, indicating "My God, the ants did this!"

After several of these morgue scenes, we started cracking up every time a sheet was pulled back. Whitmore was a very serious guy, and this was the first time something like this had happened to him. He just walked away from the camera, composed himself, and returned with a serious look on his face. Then the sheet was pulled back again, and boom, off we went!

The director got so frustrated that he called upstairs for one of the big production managers to come to the set and straighten us out. We were soon face to face with an angry executive, who warned us that if we didn't do the scene right, we'd never work in the film industry again!

The problem was finally solved by separating us for the morgue shots. They did a two-shot take right up to the point where a guy lifted the sheet, then cut and showed only Jimmy with a "knowing" look, while I stayed offstage. After that they did the same with me, while Jimmy was off-camera.

To this day, *Them!* is considered one of the better sci-fi movies of the '50s.

Duke's next picture, a true story, was *The Sea Chase*, filmed on the big island of Hawaii. His costar was Lana Turner, and I had a part in the film along with a lot of Wayne's regulars, including Claude Akins. Duke played the part of German sea captain Karl Ehrlich, whose ship, *Ergenstrasse*, was to be interned at the start of the war in Sydney, Australia.

The real Ehrlich was a former member of the Imperial German Navy, and when he would have nothing to do with the Nazi regime, he was demoted to a freighter command. As World War II erupted, he was faced with a terrible choice: accept internment of his old freighter by the British or escape to Germany, where his men would be at home. He made a run for it.

He broke out into the Pacific and eluded pursuing British warships until he made port at Valparaiso, Chile. A British warship patrolling offshore appeared to have him hemmed in, but was called off station to join other combatants that had trapped the German pocket battleship *Graf Spee* in the harbor at Montevideo, Uruguay.

Ehrlich was able to depart Valparaiso unchallenged, and he continued his journey homeward sailing around the tip of South America. Then he headed north, into Atlantic waters. As the *Ergenstrasse* entered the North Sea, British warships attacked and set it afire. Ehrlich got his crew safely into lifeboats, and once they were making their way toward the enemy ships for rescue, he maneuvered his burning *Ergenstrasse* into a position to ram the lead British ship. The freighter was quickly taken under fire and was sunk.

Ehrlich and Lana Turner's character, Nazi spy Elsa Keller (who had elected to accompany him even though she could have returned to Germany under diplomatic auspices, had she stayed in Chile), were not among the survivors, nor were they seen again. But the British skipper who sank the vessel, an old friend of Ehrlich's, suspected that Ehrlich and Keller had somehow escaped to a nearby Norwegian landfall.

Left to right: Tab Hunter, me, Lyle Bettger and an unidentified cast member arriving in Hawaii to start shooting the movie *The Sea Chase*, which starred John Wayne and Lana Turner. (Arness Collection.)

Appearing in that movie was a lot of fun, and working with guys I'd worked with before made it like old-home week. We played crewmen, and I had a pretty good part in it, at times verbally sparring with Duke. He married his third (and last) wife, Pilar, during shooting.

When we weren't acting, several of us, including Claude Akins, headed a few miles south of Kailua to White Sands Beach to surf. Lana Turner was beautiful, and very friendly with all of us. The movie was completed on schedule, without a hitch.

Back home, I learned that Republic was about to do another picture, and they thought they had a part for me. I signed on for a major role in *Flame of the Islands*, starring Howard Duff and Yvonne De Carlo. Before the deal was finalized, though, I had to meet with the president of Republic. I would be one of the leading players, and he wanted to be sure I was right for the part. After I passed muster with him, we shot the movie in the Bahamas.

Just before I left, Charles Marquis Warren called to let me know that CBS was going to make a television show out of the radio hit program *Gunsmoke*. I'd worked with Warren in *Hellgate*, which he had written, produced, and directed. I'd read about the *Gunsmoke* venture in the trades, but Warren added the information that they were bringing in actors who'd previously appeared in westerns

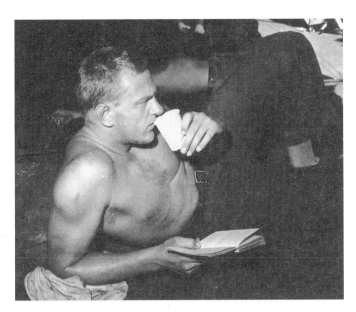

Relaxing between takes on *The Sea Chase* set. Because of my experience working as a logger in '42, they had me chopping logs in a scene. Seems no one else in the cast really knew how to handle an axe. (Arness Collection.)

to read for the role of Marshal Matt Dillon. At some point, he said, he was going to bring me in.

I went on down to the Bahamas as scheduled, to begin making *Flame of the Islands.* Soon I was getting calls from CBS executives, wondering when I would be back. I said I didn't have the foggiest idea, and they would have to talk to the producer. The director of the film was Eddie Ludwig who had directed *Big Jim McLain* and wanted me for this picture. I finally told the CBS people that I'd be back when I was finished and would talk to them at that point. Well, they started calling daily. They were in a bind, they said. They had interviewed all the other candidates, and I was the last one on their list, and they wanted to interview me before they made a decision. They said I'd be back on the set within ten days.

I talked it over with Eddie. He cautioned me that I might make a mistake, moving over to television. What if the series flopped? I might be giving up a promising movie career. I respected Eddie's opinion, and I was hesitant anyway about signing up for a television series. We finished shooting on location and came back to the studio for the last few days of the movie. CBS was still pushing hard for me to test for the Dillon part, but Eddie advised me point-blank not to do it.

Then, on the last day of shooting, I got a phone call from Bill Dozier, one of the top execs at CBS. He said they wanted me to come over the following night to make the test. I thanked him for the call, and said I was still considering whether I should do it. He pushed on, and finally I told him I was going to pass on it.

There was a moment of silence. Then Dozier asked me what I'd done before becoming an actor. I said I'd been in the Army, gone back home, attended college and did some radio announcing for a while. He interrupted me and said, "It doesn't matter: whatever you were doing before this, if you don't show up for the test tomorrow night, you might as well go back to it!" There sure wasn't anything subtle about his words and tone of voice!

Anyway, I decided, what the hell, I'd better show up the next night and make the test, perhaps I might get a better feeling about the whole thing. I got to their studio on Beverly Boulevard about eight o'clock that evening, and they had a set upstairs which was the marshal's office. Bill Warren was there, ready to direct the scene. Dennis Weaver was to play Chester, and a third party played the heavy in the test episode, which included a shoot-out. We did the test, and it seemed to go okay.

The next morning, CBS offered me the part of Marshal Matt Dillon. They got Leon's approval, and as I was about to sign the contract I hesitated again, thinking maybe I really shouldn't do this. Television was not the big business it is today, and once you became known as a TV actor it could be difficult to get back into movies. So this was not a decision to take lightly.

I called CBS and explained my misgivings, after which I got a call from John Wayne. He asked me to come over and see him. Duke had been in contact with CBS, and he strongly suggested that I take the part. He said his film company wouldn't be able to keep me any longer anyway; they had a couple of pictures lined up, but there wasn't a part in them for me. But more importantly, he said, the series was going to be a tremendous break for me. "You know," he said, "I started out doing little acting parts like you've been doing, and it took me a long time to get noticed and begin getting roles that meant something. If you do this you'll get a tremendous amount of experience, and most importantly, you'll learn how to work in front of a camera."

At this point I was thinking, my God, here's this guy who's been great to me, someone I've always thought the world of, telling me I ought to do this. I decided the hell with it, I'll do it! I signed immediately after that visit, and within a few weeks, we were shooting the pilot film at the Gene Autry ranch.

Part V

Gunsmoke

Gunsmoke was the first adult western to be shown on television. Before it, there were black-and-white westerns starring Gene Autry, Hopalong Cassidy, and Roy Rogers, and mostly these appealed to a much younger audience. We were fortunate in that the radio version of *Gunsmoke* had been on the air for six years already, and some of the best scripts were adapted for our initial episodes, half-hour programs.

Leon met with the CBS executives and negotiated a contract calling for me to receive $1,200 per show, just $200 more than Wayne-Fellows had paid me. Then, in January 1955, we shot "Matt Gets It." In that first show, I'm wounded by a gunslinger played by Paul Richards. After recovering, at the end of the episode I bested him in a shoot-out. We also made a backup episode, "Hack Prime," so the producers would have another choice for the critical pilot program. Often that makes or breaks a show. They chose the more dramatic "Matt Gets It."

Favorable viewer reaction was immediate, and the guys up front wiped the sweat from their brows. They'd made the right choice. Still CBS was undecided about going ahead, but finally they scheduled *Gunsmoke* for a 1955 fall debut. Unbeknownst to us, they asked John Wayne to do an opening introduction.

The cast assembled to watch the show at our home, and we were all caught by surprise and thrilled by the Duke's words. In essence, he created the initial momentum and horsepower that got the show noticed. The press immediately got behind it, things started happening, and very quickly CBS picked up the show for a full season. I can still remember John Wayne's inimitable style that night. He said:

> Good evening. My name's Wayne. Some of you may have seen me before. I hope so. I've been kicking around Hollywood a long time. I've made a lot of pictures out here, all kinds. And some of them have been westerns, and that's what I'm here to tell you about tonight, a western. A new television show called *Gunsmoke*. No, I'm not in it. I wish I were though, because I think it's the best thing of its kind that's come along. And I hope you'll agree with me. It's honest, it's adult, it's realistic. When I first heard about the show *Gunsmoke*, I knew there was only one man to play in it, James Arness. He's a young fella and may be new to some of you. But I've worked with him and I predict he'll be a big star. So you might as well get used to him, like you've had to get used to me. And now I'm proud to present my friend, Jim Arness, in *Gunsmoke*.

Our debut got good reviews. It seemed as if the show might actually catch on and become a hit! Little did we know then that it would become the longest-running series in TV history.

CBS had wanted a smoking gun as the opening scene, but Charles Marquis Warren, the lead producer and director, insisted that Matt stand on Boot Hill overlooking Dodge while making a few philosophical comments about the challenges he faced. This opener stayed on the air for the first several years.

Later the writers changed it to a shoot-out on Main Street between Matt and a faceless man-in-black. The producers decided to reshoot the scene to make it more realistic, and they used a new man-in-black, since the actor they'd been using was getting too expensive. One of our own directors, a kind of nervous perfectionist, Vincent McEveety, was given the task of directing that scene. All the rehearsals went off as scheduled, and when the scene was shot, who should fall flat on his face but Marshal Matt Dillon.

McEveety was dumbstruck! He raced over to me as I lay sprawled face downward in the mud. What McEveety didn't realize at the time was that it was all a staged gag. The blood capsules that exploded under my shirt were harmless props, and everyone started laughing. Finally McEveety caught on. We were always pulling hilarious stunts on the set. It loosened everyone up, and we just had fun playing our parts. Just as in my radio and movie days, I'd get into a fit of laughter over something during a scene, and they'd have to suspend shooting until I could gather myself. Our guest actors often told me how much they enjoyed working on the show, and asked to come again.

As we started into the series, I realized that we were scheduled to do a number of shows in quick succession, yet I had more to do on the first one than ever in all my previous shows and movies. I had the central role, and, back in those early episodes, I was in every scene. I had page after page, scene after scene, and at first I felt comfortable with it. I thought, hell, I can handle this.

In the beginning, I worked hard on learning my lines and becoming accustomed to playing Marshal Matt Dillon. Our schedule was very professionally organized, and the shows went off quite smoothly. Our weekly program was shot in three days after a half day of rehearsal, usually on Monday afternoons. The cast sat in a large office around a table and read through the script. Comments were offered to enhance a scene here and there, and then we'd have a final read-through and be on the set the next morning to shoot the episode.

A great deal of the show was done outside at nearby locations, like Thousand Oaks or out at Gene Autry's ranch in Newhall. Eventually we expanded outside California.

U.S. Marshal Matt Dillon in action. (Courtesy of CBS, Inc.)

As the weeks went by and each show was produced, I started to feel like I was falling behind a little in the routine. I had no concept, at first, of how much work was involved in getting a solid grasp on the character I played. The pressure of the undertaking began to build: I'd arrive in the morning to discover I had eight pages of dialogue for an interior-set scene, followed by a six-page scene out on the street. Then I had to adjust to working with different actors from the usual cowboys I was accustomed to. The producers began to bring in actors from the East Coast, people with vast acting experience on the stage and on live telecasts. Their intent was to introduce new faces to Hollywood casting directors.

In *Gunsmoke* I soon found myself facing not the heavies who got off the train in Dodge City, but those who got off a plane in L.A. By and large they were top-quality actors, and many appeared in more than one episode during the show's 20-year run. Milburn Stone played the gruff Doc Adams; in person he was

Having fun on the *Gunsmoke* set. (Arness Collection.)

a genial gentleman, a wonderful character actor who'd already enjoyed a long theatrical career. He was born in Burton, Kansas, in July 1904, and toured with repertory groups before making his screen debut in 1935. He appeared in more than 150 films during his illustrious career. In 1968, much to the delight of us all, he won an Emmy for Best Supporting Actor in a Drama for his work on the show. The Kansas Medical Society paid further tribute by giving him honorary membership for the authenticity of his performance. Milburn Stone was one of only five laymen to be so recognized in the society's 100-year history.

He and Ken Curtis (who played Festus Haggen as of 1964) visited the Kennedy Space Center in the summer of 1968, while preparations were underway for Apollo 8. The launch of our country's first attempt to orbit the moon was scheduled for later that year. During their visit, Milburn and Ken met astronauts Frank Borman (mission commander), James A. Lovell, Jr., and William A. Anders. They invited the space men to visit the set—and they came! The astronauts offered to take a memento from *Gunsmoke* into space with them. We gave them four powderless/capless bullets from my gun.

Apollo 8 was launched on 21 December 1968 and orbited the moon 10 times before returning to earth. Soon thereafter, Milburn got a package in the mail, with the four bullets and a nice note. He got each bullet encased in a plastic table mount with a plate on its back, commemorating the event. Keeping one for himself, he gave the others to Amanda, Ken, and me. I still treasure this wonderful piece of history. Milburn and I were good friends, and it was a personal as well as a professional loss when he passed away in 1980, at age 75.

Amanda Blake, who played Kitty Russell, proprietress of the Long Branch Saloon, was an example of the superb casting that made the program such a success. Amanda's desire for the part was fierce, and she got it through persistence and tenaciousness. At first she couldn't even get into Warren's office to read for

I'm enjoying a laugh in the Long Branch Saloon in Dodge City with (left to right) Amanda Blake, Buck Taylor (as Newly) in the background, Ken Curtis, and Milburn Stone. Buck was a new addition to the cast and he became a great asset to the show. (Courtesy of CBS, Inc.)

the part. Finally she just marched over to CBS and sat there until he agreed to see her. Titian-haired Amanda had the right look, and after auditioning she was hired on the spot.

Her real name was Beverly Louise Neill. Born in Buffalo, New York, of English and Scottish descent, she moved with her family to California, where she attended Claremont High School and Pomona College. But she quit college after one year to pursue a career in acting. She once said that her past, present, and future were all the same—she'd never thought about anything but being an actress. She found work in summer stock, Little Theater, radio, and eventually motion pictures. MGM signed her in 1950 and promoted her as a young Greer Garson. But she said the films she made for MGM and Columbia were miserable. It was *Gunsmoke* that finally made her a star, and she stayed on for 19 years. By then she was tired of both the part and the commute from her home in Phoenix. Amanda Blake kept acting occasionally in movies and TV, until her death in 1989.

Over the years, fans have often asked me about my character Matt Dillon's relationship with Kitty, and why it never seemed to progress beyond the air of the romantic between us. That was the producers' decision, since going a step

With Amanda, a wonderful actress and great friend. Many of the lady fans wanted Matt and Kitty to marry. The writers felt that it would be better for the storyline to keep the relationship a question in the minds of the fans. (Arness Collection.)

further would complicate matters and might even lessen the show's popularity. Our relationship was downplayed because they thought it was more titillating to leave matters to the viewers' imagination.

They never even kissed. But Matt Dillon did get a kiss in one episode—with actress Michael Learned (of *The Waltons* fame, 1972–1981). That was in "Matt's Love Story," which aired September 24, 1973. And by the way, Matt had amnesia during that episode. Other actresses tried to kiss him: Anne Francis and Beverly Garland were cast as women who made serious runs at Matt. But he never wavered. His focus was on his job. He was a bigger-than-life law man, obsessed with fighting evil in Dodge. His interactions with the other principal players in the show made *Gunsmoke* one of the most popular programs in the history of television, and I'm proud to have been a part of it.

One of the most talented and popular stars of the series was Dennis Weaver, the first principal actor to be signed for *Gunsmoke*. His portrayal of Matt's sidekick, deputy Chester Goode, was superb. I often found myself playing second fiddle to him when he would appear limping along beside me or enacting his famous twangy call, "Mr. Dillon." Dennis later told me he had a heck of a time losing his limp after he left the show. On other shows when a director yelled "action," he'd automatically start to limp. It took him several months to walk normal when on camera. *Gunsmoke* may be the first western in which one of the principal characters was a handicapped man.

Dennis Weaver had been relatively unknown until he appeared on *Gunsmoke*, but I guess that could be said of all of us at the time. He'd appeared in 19 movies and ended up staying with the show for nine seasons, winning an

Emmy in 1959 for Best Supporting Actor. His enormous popularity carried over to the appearances we made around the country at rodeos and state fairs.

Dennis left the show because he wanted to prove his versatility on the stage and in movies. Eventually he came back to television, though, in two short-lived series: *Kentucky Jones* (1965) and *Gentle Ben* (1967–69). Finally he found a role that was ideally suited for him—that of *McCloud* (1970–77), a western deputy marshal who, transplanted to New York, ends up becoming a big city detective.

I was particularly sorry to see Dennis leave us, since he'd become such an integral part of our seamless

Gunsmoke **principal characters Doc (Milburn Stone) and Chester (Dennis Weaver). Particularly notable were the scenes where Doc and Chester endlessly argued and hassled each other. The fans loved it. (Courtesy of CBS, Inc.)**

theatrical family. As a team, we'd realized near instantaneous success, and I worried about how the rest of the cast would react to Dennis' decision. I clearly understood his desire to move on, though, and it turned out to be a wise choice on his part.

After Dennis, our producer, Norman MacDonnell, came up with a terrific new character: Festus Haggen. For the part, MacDonnell and our director, Andy McLaglen, picked Ken Curtis. A gifted character actor, he possessed a musical talent few people knew about. He was born in July 1916 in southeastern Colorado and grew up in Lamar. His father was sheriff of Bent County. Ken left Colorado College to become a songwriter, and eventually he wound up in Hollywood as a staff singer on NBC radio.

When Frank Sinatra went out on his own, Tommy Dorsey hired Ken to replace him. He also sang with the Sons of the Pioneers, and with Johnny Mercer and the Pied Pipers. And he could act. We all realized what a stroke of luck we'd had in finding him—he portrayed a thoroughly believable crusty, often disagreeable, unkempt deputy. He became a regular in 1964.

A fifth main character was added to the show in 1962: Burt Reynolds. For his dark good looks, he was cast as Quint Asper, Dodge City's blacksmith. This was Burt's first major role, and he made the most of it, drawing an immediate reaction from our viewers. He bared his chest during his first appearance, and CBS got 4,000 fan letters for Burt that week.

Before that, most of the mail had been directed to me. We'd all sit around a table and read the letters to each other. But after Burt arrived, we'd just listen to his letters, since they outnumbered all the others. Many included photos of women.

Burt stayed with us until 1965, and he loved the show. "It was the happiest years of my life," he said in an interview for the book *Gunsmoke* (McFarland, 1990), "in terms of just the working relationship with those people. I was crazy about Jim and Amanda—what's not to love? And Milburn Stone was like a father to me ... and Kenny Curtis ... it was a delightful time. It was just a wonderful time."

We were all sorry to see Burt leave the show. He fit right into our close-knit group from the first day he stepped on the set. He acted with ease, was unflappable and always in good humor. We often played cards together and shared many good laughs. Knowing he was going to be a major star, we wished him well as he departed.

In the early days, as I began to act with these people, I got the feeling that my inexperience really showed. They knew how to play a scene with all the nuances of a pro, while I had all I could do just to keep up with them. I carried this feeling of insecurity throughout our first season.

We had just two sponsors, Remington Razors and L&M Cigarettes. Each firm had its ad men on the set, and they'd look at the daily rushes. One of the reps was Sid Marshall, a heck of a nice guy who'd come over and chat with me about the show. One day he said he had the feeling that maybe I was a little uncomfortable with some of the scenes. "But if you'd like," he said, "I might be able to find someone to help you out." His boss had given the okay for him to check around and find me a first-rate private acting coach.

Boy, was I appreciative. It was like someone was suddenly extending a hand to a drowning man. Aside from my lack of experience, I was also growing concerned about the people in the front office. After all, many of those who'd produced the original radio show hadn't picked me as their first choice. If they couldn't get Wayne, they wanted Joel McCrea or Denver Pyle. When I look back on those times, I sometimes wonder how they settled on me to play the lead role. Even the director, Charles Warren, with whom I'd worked in *Hellgate*, wasn't too sure if I was the right actor for the part. I could sense the uneasiness of some of these people as we continued to produce the series.

At the start of the second year, Sid Marshall said he'd found a lady coach who was really top drawer at this kind of thing. She'd worked with a number of movie actors, he said. Her name was Elsa Schreiber, and she'd seen the show and agreed to see me. I went to her house, out above Sunset Strip. Elsa, a short elderly woman with a German accent, greeted me at the door and welcomed me into her home. She never mentioned her other pupils, but I later discovered that Gregory Peck never did a show without her. After just ten minutes of conversation, I knew she was the ideal coach for me.

I started going to her home every Saturday, and most of the time I sent her an advance copy of the script for the next show. Elsa would quickly focus on each scene and tell me what I had to do and how to present this character, essentially a man who had to dominate every situation. She told me to forget the actors from New York. I was to control each scene.

I studied with her for about 20 to 25 weekends, and during that time I got to feel much more comfortable. Elsa gave me the confidence that I could play the role and hold my own with anyone. At a certain point she said she wanted me to stop coming and continue on my own, using the techniques she'd taught me. She'd given me everything I needed, she said, and she was right. I never went back and was completely comfortable in my work. Elsa was a tremendous help.

By now I'd starting getting offers to do personal appearances at rodeos and fairs. I signed with the William Morris Agency to organize and schedule these promotions, and I wound up making more money on these weekend events than doing a weekly *Gunsmoke* episode.

My first appearance was for a close friend of mine, Big John Hamilton. He was a great big, wonderful, good-natured Texan with a mile-wide grin, just a terrific guy. He owned a restaurant in San Antonio, Big John's Steakhouse. The appearance was at a football game between 10-year-olds who were going to play in what was called the Milk Bowl. John said it was a charity event, so I flew down there and rode a horse into the stadium waving my hat, to the cheers of players and folks in the stands. It was great fun, and the people were wonderful. They were big *Gunsmoke* fans and crowded around me asking for autographs and pictures.

John remained a close pal for many years, and later I got him a part in a couple of our shows. I still like to tell people that my first public appearance during the *Gunsmoke* days was at the Milk Bowl in Texas, just to see their perplexed looks.

My second, arranged by the Morris Agency, was in Philadelphia. A Catholic priest was raising money for his church by putting on a rodeo, so I flew in. The

Public appearance in Tampa, Florida, 1958. I did many shows like this during the early years of *Gunsmoke*, **traveling all over the country visiting fairs, rodeos, circuses, military bases and prisons. (Arness Collection.)**

priest met the agency's representative and me at the airport, and he took us right back to the church to look over the situation. Standing behind a microphone, I was to put on a little skit that the agency comedy writers had dreamed up. They had some of the best writers in the business at that time, developing material for the likes of George Burns and Milton Berle.

I had to do three shows over a weekend, for a fee of $5,000. Well, things kind of bombed. First off my comedy gig fell flat, and I knew immediately that the audience didn't want to hear Matt Dillon do comedy. Then the rodeo, which was really an amateur affair, didn't draw much enthusiasm from the crowd. After each performance, though, I was mobbed by fans, which said a lot for the popularity of *Gunsmoke*.

After the affair was over, the priest invited us back to the rectory. There he told me that their monetary goals had fallen far short. Would I consider not taking a fee for my performances? God would bless me, and the sisters of the school would offer up their prayers in my behalf. I agreed, much to the chagrin of the agency rep. He just sat there shaking his head. But soon his mood was to improve, if not his financial situation: We had a few hours before the plane took off, so the priest asked if we'd like to go down to a local night club and see a terrific entertainer who did a fast-draw routine. We agreed, and lo and behold, the star of the show was Sammy Davis, Jr. Sammy was told I was in the audience before he went on, and when he made his appearance, he said, "We have a great guy with us tonight that you all know and love. He's got a great western on television, *Gunsmoke*. We've got Matt Dillon here!"

He invited me up to the stage, where he continued his complimentary remarks and then said we'd take a quick break while he changed costumes. Within minutes we were back on stage, Sammy dressed in black as a frontier gunfighter. He went into his fast-draw act and was really fast-firing off a few blank cartridges, much to the delight of the audience. I stood with him during his dazzling display, and told him he was indeed the fastest gunman alive.

We had a great time joking around, and the crowd loved it. He asked about appearing on *Gunsmoke* at some future date and I, of course, said anytime. Sammy wasn't at his theatrical peak yet, but he was an incredible performer who would soon become a major, multi-talented star.

During the first three years of *Gunsmoke*, I did many appearances around the country. The show was so popular that often I didn't need to be directly connected to an event. Just showing up was enough to draw huge crowds of fans. Dennis Weaver appeared with me during some of the promotions, and he often drew a bigger audience response than I did, since his character was so beloved. By this time I was making 10 to 15 thousand dollars a weekend; the money just flowed in.

However, there were times when we'd get scammed by someone who ran off with a show's receipts before we got paid. There was one particular promoter who got to us on several occasions. Our first encounter with this guy was when he offered to pay us big money if we would appear at a rodeo in Shreveport, Louisiana. Dennis and I arrived in town and were met by a group of civic leaders, many of them Shriners. They explained that the promoter had arrived with a very skimpy show of carnival acts but no grand rodeo, which he'd promised, and which had been heavily advertised all over town. He'd given them the excuse that his rodeo performers hadn't shown up. Of course, they'd paid him a lot of money in advance, and expectations were high in town regarding the show. At the same time, the promoter had disappeared. These folks found themselves in a very embarrassing situation and were concerned that we were somehow a part of the scam.

We convinced them we knew nothing about the situation, and together we worked out a solution. Unfortunately, they explained, due to the mix-up they wouldn't be able to pay us, but we felt so bad for them that we agreed. The Shriners gathered riding clubs from all over the city, including their own riding

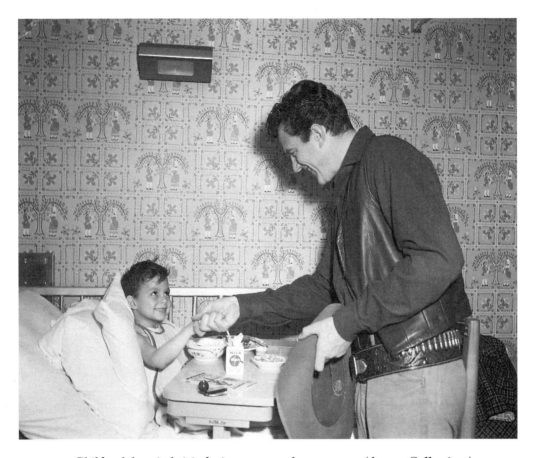

Children's hospital visit during a personal appearance. (Arness Collection.)

ensemble, and put on a first-rate show in a closed arena, to packed audiences. Dennis and I performed a skit that we'd rehearsed, and after our last appearance they asked if we would visit the Shriners' hospital and meet all the kids. We were delighted to do this; that visit became the highlight of our trip.

They even paid us, because, to their surprise, they earned enough money from the show. You'd think we'd have learned after this first time, but the promoter was such a likable guy and super salesman that we fell for his b.s. more than once. Finally, though, I'd had enough of his shenanigans and demanded to be paid up front, which seemed to solve the problem.

In terms of popularity, Dennis and I made quite a team. The same thing happened every time we stepped off a plane to do a public-appearance gig: we were mobbed by fans. They followed us to our hotel, and they waited out front to chat and get autographs as we left to do a show. Among television viewers, *Gunsmoke* was immensely popular. The show continued to climb in weekly ratings, and we were overwhelmed to see firsthand the public's reaction to our innovative Western drama.

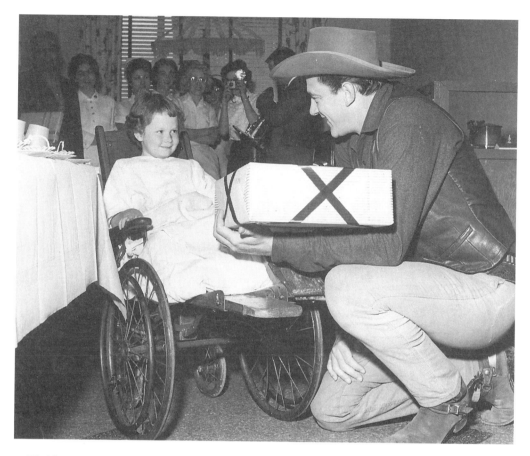

Children's hospital visit during a personal appearance in St. Louis. One of the things that made my role as Matt Dillon so pleasant was seeing the expressions on the children's faces as I visited different hospitals. (Arness Collection.)

In a skit that we'd worked out, I entered the arena first, on horseback. Matt Dillon was expected to ride nothing less than a mighty steed, and I'd get this horse that, they assured me, was tame as a cat. Well, I'd get on these damn stallions, and man, would they take off. Once they got running, I couldn't get them stopped. I'd go charging around the arena, trying to hold on to my hat and keep from falling off. Finally I'd manage to slow the horse down and get off, and then I had to walk up to this mike they had set up in the middle of the arena.

I went into a monologue about the show, talking about Miss Kitty and Doc, and then Dennis came out through a tunnel calling, "Mister Dillon!" The crowd hushed, and as he came limping across the arena, the place erupted in cheers. Dennis was a very skilled actor, born and raised in the little town of Joplin, Missouri. His personal experience really helped him play his character. He was always a smash hit at the shows, and often he got more applause than I did.

A wonderful sidekick on the show, Dennis Weaver often became the main attraction when we made public appearances together. (Courtesy of CBS, Inc.)

Of course, a few funny things happened too. While performing at a rodeo in Ohio, I was standing at a microphone doing my monologue when suddenly, the crowd's attention turned to one end of the arena. The scene before me seemed to play in slow motion as a bucking bull with its rider hanging on for dear life charged straight at me. They'd started the bull-riding competition while I was still in the ring!

I stood at the center of the arena, frozen in place and unable to predict which way the animal would go. Then the rider was thrown off. The bull started looking around, and a couple of clowns raced out to distract him so the cowboy could get on his feet and out of the ring. But the bull spotted me. He started toward me, and the only way I could see to escape was if I could make it to a high board fence behind me.

I ran toward the fence. I was no longer Matt Dillon, just an actor running for his life. Jumping up, I caught the top of the fence and lifted my legs just as the bull arrived beneath me.

After that, some of the rodeo promoters referred to me as a "paper tiger," which was certainly true. I couldn't do any of the events the riding cowboys did at rodeos, and I greatly respected their skill and courage.

Another type of performer with great talent and bravery was the stuntman. During a St. Louis policeman's circus, I worked with one of the greats: Bob Morgan, a western veteran and regular in Duke Wayne films. He and I worked up an act in which he was way up in one of the top rows in the arena, while I was down in the center talking to a woman who looked and dressed like Miss Kitty. Some locals had built a replica of the Long Branch saloon, and we were in there surrounded by men dressed in cowboy outfits sitting at tables and standing along the bar drinking and talking. During our act, I got into an argument with someone seated at a table, and I said something like, "I'm the marshal and there's nobody that can whip me."

With that, Bob yelled from his perch, "Oh yeah, well I can whip you, Dillon." A spotlight was turned on him, and I dared him to come down and fight me. He jumped on a high wire and streaked down, in a spectacular sight that drew gasps from the crowd.

Well, then Bob and I got into a rousing good fight, tore up the place, and sent everyone scurrying from the saloon. It was a terrific act. The crowd loved it.

On the way out of the arena, we were mobbed by fans. After signing what seemed like hundreds of autographs, we made it to a police car that was to take us to our hotel. On the way, I remarked to Bob that he smelled bad. "It wasn't me," he said, "You're the one stinking up the car."

The policeman thought it smelled like animal poop, and then we realized that a lion act had preceded ours. Mixed in with the deep layer of sawdust on the saloon floor was a little something the lions had left behind. During our mock fight, we'd rolled around in the stuff, and now were covered with it. We all had a good laugh over this, and it's a wonder our fans didn't shy away as we signed autographs.

Sadly, during Bob's stunts for the movie *How the West Was Won*, he was thrown under a moving train and suffered career-ending injuries.

Back on *Gunsmoke*, the network found an actor who could do stand-in scenes

A pint-sized child runs out into the street to get my autograph during the Grand Marshal parade in San Francisco, 1960. I was honored to be named Grand Marshal for the affair. (Arness Collection.)

for me, Tiny Nichols. He was a big, solid guy who stood 6' 5". Tiny was warm and friendly, and over the years we became pals. He accompanied me on some of the out-of-town jaunts, hawking *Gunsmoke* photos up and down the aisles to pick up a little extra money for himself.

One event we went to together was the Houston Fat Stock Show, an institution in that city. Ranchers brought in their prize cattle from all over the West, and there was competition for best-of-show by cattle load lots and individual stock. The show took place in a regular arena that seated around 20,000 people. I was offered a really large sum of money to perform in 27 appearances.

Per my usual routine, I came hell bent for leather out of a tunnel and rode around the arena waving my hat. The crowd roared their approval. When I got off the horse in the middle of the arena and approached a microphone, there was a western musical group waiting for me. I opened, singing Gene Autry's classic, "Back in the Saddle Again." After acknowledging the crowd's applause, I followed

Public appearance at Los Angeles Coliseum. During this appearance I was made an honorary Deputy L.A. County Sheriff. (Arness Collection.)

with a recitation of "The Cowboy's Prayer," a beautiful story about a cowboy out on the range at night. As he looks up at the moon and stars, he knows God is watching over him. The group hummed "The Sweet Bye and Bye" behind me as I recited, making for a solemn few moments.

I went on to describe a wagon train heading West, carrying settlers toward their new destinies. I painted a picture of the wagons circling for the evening, and families sitting around campfires. Then, dramatically changing the tone of my voice, I boomed out that an Indian call was suddenly heard. As the house lights dimmed, I told of an Indian attack out of the darkness.

With the sound of war whoops and thundering horses' hoofs filling the arena, I looked up to see a full-blooded Comanche Indian streaking toward me. With spotlights on us both, I fired off three shots at this fierce-looking warrior, and his horse went down in a tremendous fall.

My attacker was one of the great stunt men of Westerns in those days, Chuck Roberson. He raised himself from his fallen horse, pulling out a long knife and charging at me. I tried to fire my pistol again, but the gun jammed. Chuck jumped on me, and I threw away the gun and we got into a heck of a fight, rolling around the arena floor and throwing fake punches at each other.

Finally I was able to wrestle the knife from him and drive it into his chest. I stabbed him several times as the lights faded and we were engulfed in darkness.

The audience cheered as the lights came up and I introduced them to Chuck. I must admit that the scene was so realistic that we got really engaged in the action. I think our intensity became such that we stunned many in the audience.

In several of these shows, we'd hear of some guy claiming to be a faster draw than Matt Dillon. He was going to challenge me to a shoot-out, he boasted. Fortunately we never experienced a confrontation, since local security was always on the lookout for these types, most of whom were drunk.

All of these appearances occurred during the first three years of the show. By that time, I'd left the William Morris Agency and was signed with the law firm O'Melveny and Myers. Our new legal and promotion team got us a contract to do a show with the Ringling Brothers and Barnum and Bailey organization down at their winter quarters in Florida. Not only did we get paid a handsome fee, but as part of the deal I was given a 40-foot sloop built by Kettenberg in San Diego. This was a boat I'd always dreamed of owning.

Dennis and I had a marvelous week with the circus folks, and since we had only one major show to do, we spent a lot of time watching the performers and wondering at their skills, especially those who worked the trapeze routines. Dennis was a good athlete and tried his hand, but he fell into the net a few times and decided to call it quits. They wanted me to join them too, but I just couldn't imagine a person of my size doing their routines without serious injury ... and besides, I didn't have the foggiest idea what to do on one of those perches.

On the morning we were to leave, there was a touching moment I'll never forget. The hotel manager asked if we would come downstairs and greet the guests at the pool. They were mostly wealthy folks from the garment district in New York. I frankly couldn't imagine what interest they would have in our *Gunsmoke,* but they'd seen us around the hotel, the manager explained. They would be forever grateful, he said, if we would spend a few minutes with them. His closing words have stuck in my mind all these years: "You don't understand what your show means to people."

He asked us to just walk through the crowd and greet them and sign a few autographs. There must have been a couple hundred people there waiting for us. They stood up and cheered and clapped and swarmed around us. Their warm reception was overwhelming.

Occurrences like this made me understand that people from all walks of life were fans of the show. We knew we'd struck a chord with the average American;

Gunsmoke meant so many different things to so many people. More than once we were humbled by personal comments, but I guess the ultimate honor came when we learned that families across the country were naming their male off-spring Matt. *Gunsmoke* had become a television phenomenon, and I was booked almost every weekend for its first three years.

On one occasion I had to go to Washington to attend an affair. I believe at the request of one of the show's sponsors. I had previously met our California senator at a social affair and he told me to look him up if I ever came to

Personal appearance at the San Diego naval base with naval escort. (Arness Collection.)

Washington. When my son Craig and I got there I called his office and his secretary told me that he was away on a trip. She went on to say that she knew we were coming and offered to show us around Washington. This sounded like a real treat for us so the next day we went with her to the senator's office, then she took us up to the Gallery of the Senate where we sat and listened to the senators on the floor discuss some issue. The senator making a speech at the time we sat down was Texas senator Lyndon Johnson. After awhile she took us over to the White House where she wanted to show us the Oval Office. We had to go by the press corps offices and when they saw us they left their desks and crowded around us. I told them that this was my son Craig, and introduced them to the senator's secretary. The press folks, a nice bunch of people and all fans of *Gunsmoke* were enthralled with our unexpected appearance. We went into the Oval Office and a lady came in and told us that President Eisenhower was in the building and she wanted to track him down because she knew that he would want to meet us. "After all," she said, "He's from Kansas, born and raised in Abilene and if he knows Matt Dillon is here he'll want to see you." Leaving the room she said, "I know he's around here somewhere."

She finally returned and said that Ike was tied up in a meeting and he said to give you his best wishes and all but he just couldn't break away. As we left the Oval Office the press corps was waiting to talk to us. One of them asked, "Did you meet the President?" I said, "No, he's in a meeting but sent us his best regards." One of the reporters quickly clarified the excuse. "Meeting, hell, he's out on the back lawn hitting golf balls." So the next day one of the Washington papers carried an item on the front page that ran, "President Eisenhower didn't have time yesterday to meet Matt Dillon, the legendary Kansas lawman and his son, 'cause he was too busy hitting golf balls on the back lawn." I held on to that clipping for a long time.

During the week I was immersed in rehearsing and shooting, and by the time I got home it was late and I was very tired. I was away practically all the time meeting professional commitments, and in the end it affected our marriage, as was the case for many Hollywood couples. Virginia and I drifted apart—more and more, she lived a separate life from mine. I was completely involved in the personal-appearance routine at this point, since it was so lucrative. And it garnered more viewers for *Gunsmoke*.

There were already plenty of these: following one appearance in Lafayette, Louisiana, an official told me that on Saturday night when *Gunsmoke* aired at 10:00 P.M., every television set within range of the local station was tuned in. In fact, a survey taken at that time of most-watched TV shows estimated that 40,000,000 tuned in each week.

While doing an episode in the late '50s, I was approached by an assistant director, Bob Rosen, who said that he had read in a magazine interview I did that I was at Anzio during World War II. Evidently his mother wanted to know if I knew a Jim Rosen, who was also at Anzio. She had received letters from him written at the time that mentioned my name. I answered that I was there and that I had a friend, Jim Rosen, who was killed the same night I was wounded. I went on to say that Jim had been point man for his squad which was next to ours. As it turned out, Jim was Bob's brother. I briefly described to him the battle action that took place that night and hopefully gave him some comfort in knowing that his brother died bravely.

One of our biggest fans was Lady Bird Johnson. If she missed an episode, the Army Signal Corps would tape it for her later viewing. It was said that Matt Dillon reminded her of the young Lyndon Johnson, and that she was anxious to meet me. However, once she found out I was a Republican, she was crestfallen and was heard to remark, "How could he?" We never met.

When *Gunsmoke* first began we were living in Santa Monica Canyon in a house that was newly built. It was a nice home, just the right size for our family.

Across from us and down in the canyon on Brooktree Road was a beautiful ranch style home which had been designed by Cliff May, a famous architect in Los Angeles at the time. After we were there about a year the owner retired from business and sold it to G.L. Harrington, who was a psychiatrist. He and his wife, Willie, hailed from Topeka, Kansas. G.L. had been in the Navy in the Pacific during World War II and worked with pilots who were burned out or suffering from battle fatigue. When he was discharged from the Navy he joined the Veterans Administration and was assigned to the VA offices in Los Angeles. We became very good friends. We just liked them and enjoyed a good rapport with them. G.L. loved sailing, and one of the first things he did upon moving to Los Angeles was

My son Craig Aurness, 1980. Craig became very successful in the world of photography, and has given us two grandchildren. (Arness Collection.)

buy a boat, a 25 foot sailing sloop. After settling in their new home, G.L. and I made numerous sailing trips around the harbor and eventually decided to go across to Catalina Island some 30 miles off shore. We sailed across to the island on smooth waters on a warm sunny day with just the hint of a breeze. However, as we neared Catalina we noted that the wind had picked up off our stern. When we arrived at the island there were no sailboats around; usually there were 50 or so tied up, so we went to a boat club, The Toyan Boat Club. We were the only ones in the club besides the help and they informed us that there was supposed to be a tremendous off shore blow coming. Luckily the storm didn't materialize and we sailed back the following day feeling like real sailors 'cause we had (unknowingly) gone out into the teeth of the storm. I was stoked up about the whole thing and a year later bought my own boat. After that we were on the water continuously and our kids just loved it. We named our boat "Sea Smoke" which was a nautical term referring to mists cast from the tops of churning waves. It got so that we'd spend whole weekends on the water and those years were filled with sunshine, happy kids and a warm friendship with the delightful Harringtons.

With Bob Wilke (right) in *Gun the Man Down*. We made this movie while we were off from *Gunsmoke*. Andy McLaglen, Burt Kennedy and I did the movie together, backed by John Wayne. Bob Wilke is probably best remembered as one of the heavies sent to gun down Gary Cooper in *High Noon*. (Arness Collection.)

As *Gunsmoke* continued to be rated among the top TV programs being aired, I got to be good friends with one of our attorneys, Jack O'Melveny, and I stayed with his firm until I left the show. They successfully negotiated my contracts, and I seemed to always walk away better off financially than before. By 1961 the show was expanded in length to one hour. The story line had to be broadened, no longer just focusing on the principal actors, which meant I didn't have to appear in every program. The scripts were labeled Light Matt (meaning the show was carried by another principal or guest actors), Medium Matt (I'd make a few appearances), and Heavy Matt, which meant I carried the show. That arrangement plus the six weeks off during the summer kept me from burning out.

It also gave me wanted freedom to hit the beaches and travel. Virginia and I had been divorced in 1958, and I was awarded custody of the children. She continued to live in Los Angeles, never remarried, and passed away in 1975.

All through the 1960s I took the kids to the beach, where I taught them swimming and my favorite sport, surfing. At the time we lived in Pacific Palisades, and since we were at the beach much of the time I built another house at San Clemente, about a ten-minute ride to San Onofre. The same group that I'd surfed with there had since gotten married and were there with their families, and it was like an ongoing reunion. Craig was 12, Jennie 10, and Rolf 8, and all the other kids in our crowd were about the same age.

We surfed until we dropped, enjoyed warm and humorous chats around a crackling fire, marveled at the beautiful sunsets, and enjoyed unbelievable barbecues. Every time I go to a barbecue these days, I'm still reminded of those marvelous years.

Around the time of the divorce, I decided it was time I went to search for my Norwegian roots. A Norwegian relative had sent my father a postcard in 1909, and he'd saved it. Then, always curious about our lineage, I saved it. When the postcard was fifty years old, I began a search for Norwegian relatives during a break in our *Gunsmoke* production schedule. I had only that card and my knowledge that the family was from Sykkylven, along the northern coast of the Stor Fjord.

In 1958 Tiny Nichols and I flew to Oslo, then took a train across Norway to the coast. There we boarded a steamer that took us to the fishing port of Alesund, Stor Fjord. Flagging down a taxicab, I showed the driver my postcard. Despite our language barrier he understood that Sykkylven was our destination, and soon we were aboard a car ferry heading up the fjord.

We disembarked at Sykkylven, where the driver stopped at several shops in the tiny village. The whole area was poor, and most of the families lived modestly. Our driver showed the postcard to people until someone recognized the name and pointed to a road that wound up a hill at the base of a mountain. Apparently there was a house along the road where we might find an Aursnes family. The house, small and old, sat astride a rise overlooking the fjord. It was a beautiful setting; the deep blue waters of the fjord merged with surrounding mist-covered mountains, where waterfalls cascaded from rocky crevices. The cloudless sky was breathtaking.

The driver knocked on the door, and an elderly woman came out. They talked for a few moments, then the lady waved us in. She greeted us warmly as we entered her small living room. The furnishings were sparse, but several framed photographs on a wall caught my attention. To my astonishment, one was similar to a photograph we had back home. I pointed to it: "My grandfather!"

We needed no language in common as she understood me, and, beaming, led us next door to a little log cabin. She brought the picture of my grandfather. By pointing to it and the cabin, bare except for an ancient spinning loom, she explained that this had been the home of the young Peter Aursnes.

Her name was Anne Petrine Fauske, and she was herself one of my distant relatives. Back in her house she called her son, who spoke English and who worked at the village bank. He came over immediately to talk to us. He and Anne were both thrilled, he told us: this was their first contact with the American relatives. Within a half hour we were surrounded by people from the village, all greeting us enthusiastically. We stayed for the entire afternoon, enjoying a hearty Norwegian lunch.

When we took our leave, we promised to return one day. Anne wanted us to take the spinning wheel, but we didn't want to add to our baggage. We said we would pick it up on our next visit.

Since Tiny was of Swedish descent we decided to go to Stockholm where he hoped to contact a relative. En route we spent a few days in Copenhagen and just cruised around seeing some of the sights. It was great being able to walk down a street and not be mobbed. This was when *Gunsmoke* was almost at the peak of its popularity and there weren't many places in the States where I could go and not be recognized. I loved our fans but sometimes it was overwhelming. Nobody knew me in Copenhagen and I enjoyed the anonymity. When we got to Stockholm Tiny had no luck in contacting his relative so we toured around the city. As we went by a travel agency we noted that they were advertising "over the Pole" flights from Stockholm to Tokyo, Japan, and we decided "what the heck" let's buy a ticket and do it. We'd fly over the North Pole, see Japan and go on down to Hong Kong while we're at it. We boarded a Scandinavian Airline DC-7, made a stop at Anchorage, Alaska, and then took off for Japan. Tiny and I were sitting in the first class section which seated about 20 passengers. As we flew along, the pilot would come up on the public address system periodically and talk about where we were and what we were flying over. He was kind of a kidder; he'd like to see if he could make a joke out of things as we flew along. At a given point he said, "Well folks in a few minutes we're going to be passing over the island of Attu. This, of course, is where the Japanese landed shortly after Pearl Harbor." Then he made a crack about it, something like they thought they were going to get somewhere but they didn't. (Except for 28 prisoners the entire Japanese garrison of over 2000 soldiers was wiped out by American troops at Attu.) Who should be sitting around us but Japanese businessmen. I don't know what was going through their minds as the Captain talked but I'm sure they didn't appreciate his remarks.

We stayed a few days in Tokyo but whenever we tried to go somewhere the streets were jammed with traffic and people were everywhere. It was all rather suffocating. We headed for Hong Kong where we had learned from a stuntman who used to work on the show that Hong Kong was the place to go in the Orient. He had appeared in the movie *Love Is a Many-Splendored Thing* which starred William Holden and Jennifer Jones and said they all had a great time while shooting in the city. When we bought our tickets in Stockholm I think in the back of our minds we knew Hong Kong was our real destination; Tokyo was just a quick interlude. When we arrived in Hong Kong we checked into a hotel in Kowloon, a teeming city on the mainland. Trying to get some sleep during night hours was almost impossible. Even with our windows wide open the heat was insufferable. In addition it seemed that people jammed the streets 24 hours a day and there was always some sort of ungodly discordant music. The next evening we were in the bar of the hotel having a drink when I noticed two men staring at me. This was the first time during the trip that I sensed that I was recognized. Finally, one of them approached us and said to me, "Aren't you Matt Dillon in *Gunsmoke*?" His friend soon joined us and we sat around, chatting. They were from the British Embassy, and asked us to join them on a trip which would take them into China. We thought it would be an interesting experience and agreed to go along. The next morning they took us to a gate at the border and told us that we could get a pass there and hop a train with them that would take us inland to a town where we could buy souvenirs and then we'd catch a train together back to the border gate. This was not too long after the end of the Korean War and not many Westerners were traveling around in China in those days. When we arrived at the gate we began to have second thoughts about the whole idea. The border site was an imposing place. There was a huge gate with a number of Chinese men running around in uniforms. Tiny and I took one look at what was happening at the gate and we decided that doing what our newfound friends suggested wasn't for us. We told them thanks but no thanks and we all returned to the city. However, they offered to show us the city the next day, so the following morning we met them and they took us down to a police station and because of their diplomatic status (Hong Kong was still a British colony at the time) three or four policemen acted as our escorts as we toured the city. They took us down to the harbor which was packed with little boats called sampans. We walked out onto a few of these boats and the people were very friendly. Our escorts told us that many of these people spent their whole life on the water and never set foot on land. We enjoyed the tour as we walked down the crowded streets but felt a little spooked being packed into all that humanity. We saw a few bodies lying along the curbs that hadn't been picked up yet, and the people just threw anything and everything in the way of garbage out their windows. Tiny was a bit blown away by the whole experience and in fact became sick that night. He wanted to leave as soon as possible. We took a flight out the next morning and returned to Los Angeles. It had been a really enjoyable hiatus and I felt refreshed and ready to go back to work.

I've always regretted not returning to Sykkylven, but my son Rolf visited in the late 1960s, when some 200 Norwegian relatives gave him the royal treatment. By then *Gunsmoke* was well known, and they were proud that one of their own had become a recognized actor. When Rolf arrived, about ten years after my visit, the village was thriving. Everyone seemed to be well off. Oil had been discovered, and, according to Norwegian law, each person within the vicinity of the "find" received a share of the income realized from the revenues. Today, with a population of about 8,000, Sykkylven is the major center of Norway's furniture industry.

In 1959, on the advice of our law firm, I began looking for real estate as an investment. We found a beautiful thousand-acre place in Simi Valley. The land was rolling hills, pastures, and oak groves. I loved it right away and didn't hesitate to buy it. My father, who'd returned from Alaska many years ago, had been working for Howard Hughes Aircraft in El Segundo, California. In 1960 he retired and we moved him to the ranch. He fell in love with the place and became its custodian. To the day he died, 20 years later, he said how grateful he was to be able to live there. I think those were the happiest years of his life.

The ranch's southern border dipped into the Santa Susana mountains. Farther south, the North American Rocketdyne Company had an installation in a valley. At that time, in the early 1960s, rocket fuels were being tested that would eventually power our big rockets to the moon. We often drove up into the mountains at night to watch. Huge, bright flames roared from the stationary rocket vehicles. It was an awesome sight, like something from another world. As I remember it, the testing went on for several years.

Just above the ranch was the Brandeis Institute, which was used as a summer camp for Jewish youngsters from all over the world. My father became great friends with its director, Dr. Schlomo Bardin. Born and raised in Israel, he'd been a cabinet minister in one of that country's early administrations.

We had many gatherings out at Simi Valley. My brother and his family were regulars, as were several friends. We had horses, a herd of Charloise cattle, chickens, dogs, and cats. Stables and barns were scattered around the main house, and the ranch was always alive with activity. There was nothing to want.

We even bought a few motorcycles, and some of our family members and stuntmen from the studios would race around the property. We could have lived there forever.

We ran the ranch as a business, even though we also enjoyed the place to the fullest. Local hands grew and tended crops of hay and oat hay on a couple hundred acres. I believe our annual harvest yielded about 150 tons, and each year a breeding farm for thoroughbred horses bought the entire crop. Eventually we purchased a fine stallion of our own and ran a small breeding operation.

Surfing was still our first love, of course. When the kids had been just tots, I'd rented a home on the Makaha coast in Hawaii. We kept it for fifteen years, living there during the big surf months and then enjoying the company of our California friends at San Onofre and Simi Valley.

At age eight, Rolf suffered a terrible accident at our Santa Monica canyon home. He fell out of a tree and cracked his skull. I was out on location at the time, and when I got word of his accident I jumped in my car and raced to our doctor's office in the Palisades. Rolf couldn't talk and was in shock. The doctor and his staff were trying to locate a neurosurgeon who was noted for his work on this type of injury. An operation was required immediately, before the brain had a chance to swell. Everyone was on the phones trying to find the surgeon. It was just a nightmare. We almost lost Rolf.

Finally they found the doctor. We raced Rolf to a hospital where the surgeon was waiting for him, and within a few hours of the fall he was on the operating table. While he was in recovery, the doctor told us a piece of bone was missing, the size of a quarter. It covered the speech area of the brain, and we wouldn't know if Rolf could speak until he came out of the anesthesia. Of course we were thrilled when we heard Rolf's first words. Bone eventually grew back, covering the small hole in his skull.

Prior to his accident Rolf had been surfing with his friends at San Onofre beach and wanted to continue with the sport. I was very worried about letting him return to the water and when the doctor suggested that Rolf wear a baseball helmet to school I wondered if perhaps we could rig something up that would similarly protect him while surfing. The sport meant a great deal to him and I was determined to find a way to enable him to safely enjoy the sport again. We found that by wrapping duct tape over his helmet and under his chin the helmet held steady and his head was well protected. With our doctor's O.K. we let him rejoin his friends at the beach and the helmet worked fine. In fact, in no time he was keeping up with the other kids.

Impromptu surfing contests were held all year round up and down the California coast. I encouraged him to participate in these events and we'd travel between San Diego and Santa Cruz, competing and often winning. Rolf worked extremely hard at it and each day he'd practice an hour before school started and a few hours later in the day. I could see his steady improvement and in the early '60s we went to Makaha which was the mecca of big wave surfing and stayed in our rented house whenever we could get over to Oahu. Rolf did quite well riding the big surf and ended up being seeded high enough to be invited to compete in a World Surfing contest in Puerto Rico. He didn't win that event but the experience was invaluable and gave him confidence that he could compete with some of the world's best.

When he was 18 he was again invited to participate in the World Surfing Competition held in Melbourne, Australia. He won that event and became the youngest surfer to win the competition and the first to bring the title to the United States. When he returned he became somewhat of a heroic figure back here in the Palisades. After graduating from high school, I decided not to push surfing so much and let him just have fun with his friends and think about his future. He, himself, was ready to push back and relax. He needed a hiatus from surfing. A few years later he was out surfing again at Makaha and I couldn't join him because of my work. That year Hawaii experienced a horrendous winter with the biggest waves seen in years. A friend of mine called me one evening and said, "I'm happy to tell you now that Rolf's O.K. He was out there with my son riding some huge waves and we all thought they were going to drown. We called in fire trucks and other emergency vehicles and prepared ourselves for the worst but the boys made it to shore and everything's fine." I thanked him and talked to Rolf. I didn't have to tell him of the dangers one could encounter riding such turbulent waves. By this time he was practically a pro and knew how to handle himself on the water under the worst of circumstances.

Skiing at Sun Valley with friend Rick Hambro (left), Jennie and Rolf, 1964. During my early *Gunsmoke* days, when I had time off, I used to take my kids every winter to Mammoth Lakes Ski Resort up in the High Sierras. Mammoth was not widely known then as one of the great ski hills in America, with one of the longest seasons. If they had a good winter with a lot of snow, good skiing conditions could last until May. I bought a little log cabin up there and we made that our wintertime home for skiing. We would usually take one ten-day trip every winter up to Sun Valley and then spend another week at Aspen. Additionally, we skied at Snowbird and Alta in Salt Lake City. At Alta I met a great Norwegian skier, Alf Engen, one of the best jumpers and powder skiers in the world. I was lucky enough to spend some time with him on the slopes, and under his direction I became a pretty good skier. (Arness Collection.)

We used the ranch less and less as the children grew older and began to make their own way, and finally we all agreed to donate it to the Brandeis Institute. The Institute wanted to expand their program for children, and they had been such wonderful friends over the years. We worked out an arrangement whereby we were permitted to live on the ranch for the rest of Dad's life, which would be thirteen more years. Dr. Bardin was so grateful for our gift that he wanted to establish a center for higher education and call it the Arness College.

I was flattered by this kind gesture, but the Institute had other priorities and the college was never founded. Bardin had also dreamed for years of building a temple on top of one of the surrounding mountains. With the help of his board of directors, which included such luminaries as Jack Warner, he built his temple, now known as the House of the Book.

When I look back, I'm most grateful that I was able to spend so much cherished time with my kids, live in splendor, and work steadily on a show I truly loved.

I remember back in the early days of *Gunsmoke* I was asked to appear on an afternoon show with a new personality at CBS, Johnny Carson. I don't remember at that point whether it was weekly or daily but Carson was just getting started and I agreed to make the appearance. Johnny was glib and very entertaining and I felt then that he would someday become a talk show star. The way things turned out for him I guess my hunch was on the mark.

Later, I was asked to appear with Bob Hope at a matinee in Cleveland, Ohio, his hometown. A little skit

My son Rolf winning the World Surfing Championship off Melbourne, Australia, 1970. (Arness Collection.)

had been worked out between Bob and me. When Bob introduced me and I walked on stage, the audience stood, clapping and cheering. *Gunsmoke* was very big in Cleveland. I was supposed to do a fast draw routine in the skit but as the fans kept cheering, Hope told me to forget the skit and just wave my hat. Afterward he told me, "Geez, I never had it this big in my own hometown!" He was a terrific guy but to be upstaged in his own hometown was a bit much for him. He had no idea that our show was so popular.

There was a publicity trip that still stands out in my mind. It was decided by the networks to get all the western TV stars together (and there were a lot of them in the early days) for a publicity junket at Dodge City. Steve McQueen, David Janssen, Robert Culp, and a bunch of other western stars and "Miss Kitty" (Amanda Blake) flew out to Dodge in a chartered plane. When we arrived, the city was all dolled up and we were greeted by a crowd of people who were thrilled to see us. Bands were playing and the town was really into the festivities. There were lots of group pictures taken and many of the stars posed with the townsfolk. They renamed a street, "Gunsmoke Street." We all had a wonderful time

With actor Chill Wills, a very special guy. Chill and I became good friends over the years. (Courtesy of CBS, Inc.)

and I still get letters from Dodge City fans recalling that visit.

Shortly after the Dodge City affair, my good friend Red Skelton, whom I had known for a number of years, lost his son to leukemia. The young man was the pride of Red's life and the tragedy struck him hard. He had a show to do the night his son died and he just couldn't do it. At the last minute his friends put a show together with Milton Berle as the host. I was working on location in Newhall at the Gene Autry Ranch when I got a call, asking if I could appear on the show. They told me that all I had to do was to come on stage, stay a few moments and Miltie would ask me a few questions and talk about Red. I said that I would, but was concerned about how I would get to the studio because of the traffic. They got me a chopper and flew me right into the CBS studio lot there on Beverly and Fairfax. Having just come from a western street set I still had my stuff on and was somewhat unkempt. I went on the show and did a little thing with Milton Berle and he was great, a marvelous guy, one of a kind. He managed to instill humor and entertainment into the show at that trying time. It was a very emotional process, but we all managed to get through it.

Gunsmoke was in its eighth season in 1963, and some of our actors and writers were getting pretty worn out. The downturn showed in our slipping TV ratings; things began to look tenuous. One day a network executive stopped by the set to let me know what the thinking was in the front office. He left it up to me: if I wanted to go ahead with the show, they were with me. I told him I loved it and had no intention of leaving *Gunsmoke*. He passed my words on to the other execs, and they gave the okay to continue.

But they wanted the show to be produced, directed, and written by a whole new set of folks. They gave two main reasons: they were going to switch to color, and, though we'd made it through one-hour time slots for the past few seasons with the old crew, they wanted to freshen up the program with new writers and directors and more noted guest actors. Only the principal cast would remain the same.

The producers at this time were the originators of *Gunsmoke* back in the radio days, Norman MacDonnell and John Meston. I felt sorry for them, the creators of the concept who'd realized such tremendous success with it. But they were drained, creatively; Meston made no bones about it. He was a real nice guy—we met every once in a while for a couple of drinks and a chat. I remember him shaking his head and saying, "Jim, I just don't have any more *Gunsmoke* stories in me." He said he couldn't continue in good conscience. Meston was a superb producer and writer, as well as a heck of a human

William Boyd in costume as "Hopalong Cassidy," visiting the set. That's Dennis Weaver in the middle. (Courtesy of CBS, Inc.)

being. He moved to Spain, and MacDonnell left the show too.

In 1966 John Mantley was hired as our new producer and one of the writers, and he stayed for the show's final twelve years. He'd cut his teeth on *The Untouchables,* starring Robert Stack as special agent Elliot Ness. Mantley's assistant was an Englishman, Phillip Leacock.

It was as if we were starting all over again. Mantley spent most of his time in the front office, while Leacock stayed on the set and relayed the producers' decisions. The CBS executives switched us from Saturday night to Monday, not the best night for a new season.

Finally Mantley, Leacock, and I began meeting in private, to discuss the forthcoming season. No execs were present, and we usually met over drinks and dinner. Mantley wanted all my inputs about the show—how it was going, where I thought it should go, and what new ingredients would get us back on top.

At first Mantley wanted to orient the show around the four principal actors, but then Dennis left us and Ken Curtis had not yet developed his mastery of Festus. Everyone had loved Dennis, and to this day he's still remembered as Chester.

Mantley's revised concept was to shift the emphasis from our "family" of central characters to an interweaving of these veterans with top-quality actors and actresses who would come and go each week, thus allowing *Gunsmoke* to transition into a more anthology-type series. He said he couldn't go on doing hour-long shows that focused mainly on the same four actors.

I agreed with these thoughts about making the shows more diverse, and the front office bought it too. Soon we were drawing the likes of Bette Davis, Charles Bronson, Richard Dreyfuss, Jodie Foster, Ron Howard, Ellen Burstyn, Gloria de Haven, Bruce Dern, June Lockhart, Carroll O'Connor, Harrison Ford, and many, many others. Harrison Ford fell on his gun during shooting, and he knocked out several of his teeth. Superb dental work fixed that problem, of course, before he became a major star. But we can always claim that the first real wounding of the action actor was on *Gunsmoke*!

One of the finest performances by a guest star was Bette Davis'. One day Amanda was called up to the front office for a chat with the producers, and she really thought she was going to be fired. Instead, they told her she was going to be a main player in a forthcoming show, "The Jailer." And as a casual aside they added, "You'll be playing opposite Bette Davis."

Later, in an interview for the book *Gunsmoke*, Amanda said she must have turned purple. She told of practically being carried out on a gurney; she was a basket case. She could hardly walk, she was so scared. But Bette was wonderful. When they met, she said she too was nervous about the show, and she threw out a few

Bette Davis, Bruce Dern and Amanda Blake in one of our most highly acclaimed *Gunsmoke* episodes. (Courtesy of CBS, Inc.)

Celebrating our tenth season of *Gunsmoke*. Left to right: Milburn Stone (Doc), Ken Curtis (Festus), Amanda Blake (Kitty), Burt Reynolds (Quint) and "The Marshal." Burt came on the show for two seasons. He did a wonderful job, and we all felt he was destined to do great things. (Courtesy of CBS, Inc.)

salty remarks about acting. The two got along great, and together they produced a memorable show.

In the 28 June 1997 issue, *TV Guide* included it in their 100 greatest episodes of television history. "No. 28: *Gunsmoke*, October 1, 1966" declared that "Guest stars on TV shows are usually window dressing. Only once in a very great while do they put their indelible stamp on an episode and make it theirs, and almost never does their one appearance elevate the entire series to a whole new level of excellence…. Davis takes a simple role and plays it like Medea, turning an ordinary horse opera into something akin to a Greek tragedy."

Even so, we had several scares regarding unexpected cancellations of the show. In February 1967, the CBS vice president in charge of programming announced that *Gunsmoke* would be canceled due to "program fatigue"—our ratings had been declining. It was probably no accident that the announcement was made while the president of the network, William Paley, a great fan, was vacationing in the Bahamas. People all over the U.S. protested furiously, with calls and letters pouring in. CBS and the perpetrators of the decision were astounded, but the network stood firm: the show would be canceled.

We, of course, were stunned. No one in the front office had mentioned anything, and it was Mantley who was tasked with giving us the bad news. He even arranged a farewell party and asked me to come. I got into my car five different times to attend, and once I got as far as six blocks. But I just couldn't face saying good-bye to those people I loved so much. I never did show up.

Fortunately, I didn't have to bid farewell after all: midwest affiliates refused to carry CBS programs unless *Gunsmoke* was reinstated. In another lucky development one day after the farewell party that I missed, Paley learned of the announced cancellation of his beloved program and the national uproar. He reversed the decision of his program council, and the next day *Gunsmoke* was back in business.

Many of the executives at CBS still believed in the original decision, but John Wayne stood up for us. He'd understood the show's appeal since the beginning. "They always get back on top of the heap. They represent our folklore," he's quoted as saying in a 1958 *TV Guide* (Dwight Whitney, "Why *Gunsmoke* Keeps Blazing Away").

I took my first flying lessons in 1968. When I used to be with my surfing friends at San Onofre beach, there was always talk about the terrific surf down in Baja, Mexico. However the area was extremely remote and it was almost impossible to get there by car or truck. One of the surfers said that he and a buddy had flown down there and found that the beaches were wide and the sand along the water's edge so hard packed that that they were able to land. They were overwhelmed by the many beautiful surfing points, and returned with glowing stories of the beaches and so many awesome rolling waves that the area appeared to be a surfer's paradise. Those stories really got my attention, so we went to a small airport at Oceanside and found a Cessna agency there that offered charter flights. We asked the agent if one of his pilots would fly us to Baja. In no time John Horn, who was a friend of mine and an inveterate surfer who had surfed with us for many years out at Makaha in Hawaii, Rolf with a small surfing board, and I were en route in a Cessna 206 to the beaches of Mexico. We flew down to the very region the other guys described, and sure enough, the place looked incredible. There were seven points (we called them the "Seven Sisters") with bays that came in just one after the other. What a sight, and not a living soul could be seen for miles. Prior to flying down we had attempted to drive there and struggled to get down to the beach over a two rutted dirt road. It proved to be impossible and we almost didn't get our car out of there. In contrast, flying down there was a breeze. The flight took about 90 minutes from the border, and we could see from the air that the beach nearest the water was a darker color and appeared to be hardened sand, capable of holding up for an aircraft landing. We dropped into one of these points and the surf was beautiful. We didn't have room in the plane for our big boards, but Rolf had his small board and he went out and rode about six-foot surf. It was like surfing on the moon; we were totally alone on the beach and it was like discovering new territory. I doubted that anyone had ever been to the beach we found. So that experience started the wheels rolling in my mind that I was going to learn how to fly, come to the "Seven Sisters," and enjoy the best surfing of my life. Surfing had become such a big part of my family's life that it really became the major factor that got me into flying.

I started taking lessons immediately. I was living in L.A. and doing *Gunsmoke* at this time, 1968. There was a good flight school in Burbank, Pacific Air Motive, that came highly recommended so I signed up. My first lessons were in a Cessna 172, a little four seater, and I flew every morning before I went to work. I'd get to the field at about 6:00 A.M. and we'd go up, even though the valley was socked in with a low overcast that came in from the ocean. The instructor would file an instrument flight plan and we'd take off and fly up through the overcast under the control of air traffic controllers until we'd pop up out of the overcast at about 3,000 feet into clear skies filled with bright morning sunlight. We'd head up to the desert where there were several fields around Palmdale and Lancaster. We preferred to use Fox Field at Lancaster which had a long paved runway good for landing and take off practice. It wasn't long before I fell in love with flying.

When we moved to San Clemente, Oceanside Airport was only a 30 minute drive, so I left the Burbank program and continued my lessons at Oceanside. Later, I took additional training at Van Nuys and it was there that I finally took my check ride for my private license and completed the required written tests, which I found to be quite difficult. I believe that I had about a hundred hours of flight time when I got my private license. Prior to getting my license I bought a Cessna 210 and had taken some of my training hops and my check ride in the aircraft so when I got my license I felt quite comfortable in the familiar setting of my own plane.

Shortly thereafter one of the instructors approached me and suggested that I would probably want to move up to a twin engine plane with greater speed and range, since, aside from flying to different events, I would be using the plane to go to shooting locations for *Gunsmoke*. This would require an aircraft with some range to it. When a twin engine Beechcraft "Baron" came up for sale, I took a ride in it and bought the plane. I went through the necessary training to be certified to fly multi-engine aircraft and completed about 100 hours of instrument training hops "under the hood" to become qualified for an instrument rating using the "Baron." By this time we had nicknamed the plane "The Red Baron."

I really never flew long hops in instrument weather; the main reason for getting my instrument ticket was to leave Van Nuys early in the morning, climb through the morning overcast and get to Baja and then be able to make an instrument approach if necessary when I returned. However, as it turned out when I took my instrument check ride I flew a round robin flight between Van Nuys and Long Beach airport in a tremendous storm. We took off from Van Nuys in a fierce rainstorm and made our way to Long Beach through turbulent weather. I was doing everything by the book and the check pilot just remained silent. As we let down and I was flying toward the runway using an Instrument Landing System (ILS) taking off power and letting my flaps down, the pilot leaned over to me and said, "Jim, don't you think you ought to let the gear down." I guess I was a little excited.

After landing we got clearance for proceeding to Van Nuys, and though the weather hadn't changed the flight back was uneventful. This time I made sure I let the gear down in plenty of time to ensure a picture perfect approach and landing. I felt so proud of myself for completing the entire program since most weekend flyers never went as far as getting instrument rated and passing the various written tests, especially the instrument phase which was extremely difficult for me since I had never been much of a scholar.

It just so happened at the time that there were many *Gunsmoke* episodes requiring little set time on my part. Usually, I'd mount my horse, place my rifle in the saddle boot and say to Festus that he was in charge while I was out of town and the scene would end with me riding out of town. And then right after that they would shoot me coming back into town, riding down the street to my office, and tying my horse to the hitching post. Festus would come outside and I'd ask him how things had gone. He would usually say, "Matthew, you wouldn't believe it if I told you." The crew could shoot these two scenes in a couple of hours in the morning. I'd usually try to arrange this type of show on a Friday morning and then I wouldn't have to work the next week while they completed the episode. I'd jump on the first plane to Hawaii and be down there surfing on weekends. There were days when I would just take off for anywhere on the spur of the moment. Sometimes I flew up to see my mother who was living in Carmel; then I would fly over to the Grand Canyon or to one of many destinations where I would land, have lunch and return at my leisure. Flying gave me a great sense of freedom and once in the air I forgot about what went on far below me; yes, even *Gunsmoke* left my mind.

Owning my own aircraft like the Beechcraft "Baron" allowed me to fly to our various *Gunsmoke* shooting locations as well as take the family to many parts of the country. (Arness Collection.)

As I mentioned, the whole flying thing began because of my desire to surf down at Baja. I made one flight down there to see if the beach could accommodate the "Baron," which was heavier and had smaller wheels. I took John Mantley and Tiny Nichols with me and because of his size I put Tiny up front with me. We landed without incident and shut down. After strolling along the beach for an hour or so we returned to the plane to find that the wheels had sunk into the sand. I got in the plane alone, fired it up, gave it full power and the plane jumped forward out of the sand. John and Tiny got into the plane and we took off for L.A. I decided to look for another airplane more suited to the Baja beach conditions. I bought a Cessna 207 which had a stretched fuselage so we could get our surfboards in it. The plane had a bigger engine and was a much beefier airplane. I had it modified for short field take offs and landings and put huge tires on it. It worked great! We subsequently flew down to Baja many times, set up camp and just surfed. I guess you could say that we were "Baja flyers." I later heard about an aircraft which at the time was considered the ultimate "bush" plane, the de Havilland "Beaver." We contacted the de Havilland company and they informed us of a "Beaver" that was up for sale on Long Island, New York. A good friend of ours, who was a former Vietnam chopper pilot and highly proficient flying the "Beaver," went to New York and flew the plane out to us. We took it to Baja and found that it was the perfect aircraft for operating on and off the beaches down there.

The de Havilland "Beaver"—what a wonderful, rugged plane. We used to land it on remote beaches in California and Mexico. Here we're enjoying camping and surfing at Baja California. (Arness Collection.)

My flying fit easily into life at Hollister as well. The ranch next to Hollister, covering more than 20,000 acres, was owned by the Bixbys, prominent oil people. They gave me permission to build an air strip right at the end of their property, adjacent to ours. All that had to be done was scratch the sagebrush off about 500 feet of ground up on a bluff and I could take off and land from that make-shift runway. They built a square barbed wire fence enclosure so that I could taxi the "Beaver" in there and then close the gate because they had cattle grazing there that might bump up against the plane and damage it. When I flew up I'd fly low over my house and rev the engine a few times so my ranch hand knew it was me. He'd jump in our truck and by the time I was taxiing into our protected enclosure he would be there waiting to take me to our place.

In June of 1972, I got an invitation from the U.S. Marshals Service to come back to Washington and give the opening speech at their annual convention. Marshals from across the country convened in the capital city each year to listen to a variety of presentations. I felt I could not turn down such an invitation so I went to John Mantley, our *Gunsmoke* producer for many years, and told him of the invitation. John was a superb writer on top of producing and I asked him if he would write a speech for me. He readily agreed to do it, saying that it would be an honor to a write the opener for me, adding that it would be a glowing

I bought our Hollister Ranch west of Santa Barbara in 1964. It was 15 miles of dirt road to get to the house, but it provided a lot of privacy. It was like living in paradise. The land, hills and mountains surrounding the house were beautiful. Surfing at Point Conception became a daily ritual, and it was awesome to watch wildlife such as mountain lions, bear, lynx, wild boar and deer in their natural habitat. (Arness Collection.)

acknowledgment of the U.S. Marshals Service. After he had written the speech I asked him to accompany me to Washington for the affair, which delighted him. We arrived in Washington on a Saturday afternoon. On Sunday we attended an informal reception and I stood in line meeting many of the marshals and their wives. At the time *Gunsmoke* was still a highly rated television show and they would come up to me and give me the full shot. "Oh my God, Matt Dillon, hey this is a great pleasure ... you do a great job of portraying the marshals and your show is great!" Standing next to me in the reception line was Attorney General Richard Kleindienst, who was taking in the many comments of the marshals as I greeted them. After awhile he said, "My God, man, you could be elected to office; these guys would all vote for you!" He said these were tough guys and when you get this kind of reaction that means you're still really going strong. He seemed to be quite impressed. I was, of course, thrilled with the reaction from these men since this was my first encounter with the marshals in a formal way. I'm sure that through the years I had met many of them, a couple here and

Being notified of one of my three Emmy nominations by Ed Sullivan, president of the National Academy of TV Arts and Sciences. Later, I appeared on Ed's show and did a fight scene from *Gunsmoke* with stuntman Bob Morgan. (Arness Collection.)

there. But this was the entire Marshals Service and I was honored. The marshals and their wives were very gracious, just wonderful people.

The next morning, Monday morning, was supposed to be the formal opening of the convention. I think Attorney General Kleindienst was supposed to start the event, introduce people, and then the head of the Marshals Service was to welcome everyone, say a few words and then introduce me. What happened was that after the reception Kleindienst called me up and asked if I could meet with him for a few minutes. So Mantley and I went up to his room and he said, "Jim, there's some things happening here which I can't tell you about right now. We have an unusual situation that's developed and depending on what happens within the next few hours we might have to alter our plans somewhat for tomorrow." He told me to just hang loose until he could see what was going on. He told me to plan to go down to the auditorium tomorrow morning and be ready to participate in the opening ceremonies as scheduled. He seemed reluctant to provide any further explanation and frankly, I didn't know what he was talking about.

John and I arrived in the auditorium the next morning. Kleindienst opened the convention with a few quick words and then was gone, as was the head of the Marshals Service. That left the next guy in line to step in and take over, and he wasn't prepared. He walked up to the speakers' platform and you could tell he was quite nervous about what had just been thrust upon him. Things seemed to be in disarray. I didn't find out until later that a break-in of the Democratic Headquarters Office at the Watergate building complex had occurred and all hell was about to break loose.

I obviously didn't know any details about the situation at the time but I do remember very well that series of events because that Sunday afternoon at the reception everybody was happy and having a good time. And so probably none of the marshals had any inkling that something this major was going on. By the next morning they sure did! I got to make my remarks and later that day Attorney

General Kleindienst took a few minutes to thank me and present me with a U.S. Marshals appreciation plaque and we posed for a picture of the presentation. I still have that picture today.

Years later the U.S. Marshals called me again; the agent who called was Duke Smith. This happened after we did *Big Jim McLain*. I subsequently got to know Duke Smith quite well and he turned out to be a terrific guy. He told me he was coming to Los Angeles and asked if I would have time to meet with him and one of his associates. We met and they explained that they wanted to make a short recruiting film, which would not be shown on public television, but be

Attorney General Richard Kleindienst presents me with an Honorary U.S. Marshal Award, 1972. (Arness Collection.)

used only by the Service to bring in new members into their ranks. It would be a 30 minute film and they asked if I would help them with the project. I said, "Well by God that's the least I could do for the great life that I had playing a U.S. Marshal!" So they got to work and put together a production and we met in Tucson where we had shot so many *Gunsmoke* episodes. My role was a speaking part where I talked about real marshals, how they worked and what they did. I mentioned how the U.S. Marshals Service was the oldest law enforcement agency in the U.S., its first marshals appointed by George Washington in 1789. In addition to the outside locales in Tucson we shot part of the film in a Federal court room. They cut in a lot of footage of other aspects of the service and it turned out to be a fine production. After we were finished we all went out to the airport to catch our planes. As we arrived a huge U.S. Marshals' jet passenger plane landed. It was loaded with prisoners and as they offloaded and came in our direction they were staring at me. It was probably because I was in this western outfit with a big white hat on, wearing a suede jacket and leather boots. The film crew took some shots of the prisoners leaving the plane and spliced some of these takes with old clips of western carriages with bars on the windows, which was how they used to transport prisoners years ago.

The Marshals Service won a government award for the film and Duke Smith and many other marshals came to Hollywood. They held a ceremony after showing the film and made me an honorary U.S. Marshal complete with a marshal's badge. Afterward we went over to Disney Studios and had the place to ourselves for the evening. Later, we got together again when they formed the United States Marshals Foundation, headquartered in Oklahoma City, to honor fallen marshals. In fact, the site was directly across the street from the Cowboy Hall of Fame. I was elected to the Board of the Foundation. As a government agency the Marshals couldn't be involved in the Foundation; its members were all civilians. The Board had numerous luminaries on it: one of the Rockefellers, the governor of New Jersey, Gene Autry, and hotel magnate J.W. Marriott (who was a big *Gunsmoke* fan). There was a huge dinner held in Washington by the Foundation and I was asked to say a few words. As the speakers rose to give short presentations the house lights were dimmed and from the corner of my eye I saw a man slip into the room and sit down quickly at our table. After the speeches the lights went up and they went around the tables introducing the attendees. The mysterious guy who had joined us was Senator Warner, married to Elizabeth Taylor at the time. When they introduced him he went up to the podium, made a few remarks, came back to our table waving at everyone as they applauded. He was quite animated. As soon as the house lights went down again, he was gone. I told Duke Smith, "That's the way I'd like to get to where I could do stuff like that, just slip in and out real quick."

I've always looked at the whole of my life as providential, feeling that God's hand somehow has guided me along an unsought path. I've never reached out for anything. Things just seemed to happen, changing my life in so many ways. The unexpected happened to me again in 1974, when I met Janet Surtees, who became my second wife.

I'd remained single since my divorce in 1958. Although I had dated a lot of women in that time, I'd purposely kept the relationships casual in order to spend more time with my family. Then I met Janet. She was from Chicago, Illinois, and her family had moved to California when she was a young girl. Her mother worked at Lockheed Corporation, and her father at Pathé Film Processing Laboratories in Hollywood. Janet worked at a boutique in the Valley owned by June Alden, wife of my 20-year makeup man, Glen. It was they who introduced us.

I still owned the "Red Baron" and on my first date with Janet we flew to the Mammoth Lakes Ski Resort and had a wonderful time riding horses, picnicking and just enjoying ourselves. After that outing I was beginning to think that Janet would make a good co-pilot and companion.

Janet and I took other trips and soon became inseparable; we had so many things in common that I knew this was the right woman for me to spend the rest of my life with. Divorced several years before we met, she had one son, Jim. She was a very special lady and I knew that our relationship was going to go somewhere. And it did!

By now I had the whole family near me, including my mother. She and her second husband, John Salisbury, had visited often over the years, and later they moved to a nearby retirement community. When John passed away, Mom relocated to a condo in Montecito, Santa Barbara. Life was good.

Our good fortune turned suddenly, however, with the loss of my daughter, Jennie. She'd been into the rock scene for a number of years, and we'd tried to get her away from the negative elements of that

Top: Janet and my stepson, Jim Surtees, in 1978. (Arness Collection.) *Bottom:* With Janet in 1986, just kicking back and enjoying life. (Arness Collection.)

life. But she got into drugs and traveled with some of the rock groups. Finally, on 16 May 1975, I got a call from Janet in Studio City while I was on location. Jennie had died of an overdose of prescription drugs.

I was devastated. I wanted to quit the show, get away from everyone, and just kind of hole up. I often thought of the solace I'd found as a youngster on our island summer home on Ox Lake in Minnesota. I needed time to heal, and it was very, very tough. It was Janet who saved me from myself. She nursed me through those terrible days, and it was through her warm, tender care and love that I survived.

My daughter Jennie Lee. (Arness Collection.)

We were married on 16 December 1978, and it was the best thing I've done in my life. Today, after more than 20 years of marriage, we are as one—soulmates, living each day in happiness and contentment.

Prior to owning and piloting my own planes, I took four military jet rides, the first one at the Miramar Naval Air Station. I was making an appearance there all dressed up in my costume and someone asked if I'd like to have a jet ride so of course I jumped at the invitation. A few days later I went back to the air station and went through ejection seat training, in-flight operations and safety procedure briefings, the works. Navy Captain Ed Pawka took me up for a ride in an F9F-8T Cougar jet and it was a blast. Ed and I kept in touch for years after that. He was a hell of a pilot and a terrific guy. My next flight was in an Air Force supersonic F-102 "Delta Dagger" which was a delta wing jet made by Convair. The Navy made all the arrangements to have the plane flown to Miramar and I went for a ride in it. The difference this time was that I had to wear a pressure suit to handle the "G" forces that we'd encounter in flight. We took off and headed out over the desert where we blasted through the sound barrier. What a thrill! We must have flown for a thousand miles. A few years later I was up in Vegas and met a few Air Force guys who were big *Gunsmoke* fans and they asked if I'd like to take a jet ride. I accepted the offer and the next day was strapped in an F-100 Super Sabre jet. We departed Nellis Air Force Base and headed out over the Grand Canyon. Flying out over the desert we went through the sound barrier and then the pilot nosed the plane straight up and left the earth behind us. I needed the G-suit for that maneuver. It was another great experience. My last military flight was arranged by our old friend G.L. Harrington. His son was a naval aviator and had flown in Vietnam. He remained in the Naval Reserves after the war and arranged a ride for me in one of the Navy's "Blue Angels" A4D "Skyhawks." Like the other military flights it was a thrilling ride. All of the military pilots were real professionals and their skill in the air, personal pride and dedicated demeanor would make any American proud.

Back seat ride in a Navy "Cougar" jet at the Miramar Naval Air Station. (Arness Collection.)

My next flying venture was just about my last extended flying excursion and eventually I lost interest in flying. John Mantley, G. L. Harrington, Jim Mock, a TWA captain, and I decided to fly up to Plummer's Lodge at Great Bear Lake in the Northwest Territory of Canada. We flew from Van Nuys to Edmonton, Canada, stayed overnight and took off the next morning. We flew over the Great Slave Lake to the town of Yellowknife, which was located on the north end of the lake. Yellowknife was an airline hub which serviced air liners that regularly flew polar routes to various countries and cities. We had a quick lunch at Yellowknife and took off for Great Bear Lake which was about 400 miles further north. We got an outbound heading on a "variable Omni Range" (VOR) station and flew northward until we lost its signal about 125 miles out. From there on it was dead reckoning with Jim Mock doing the navigating. He was a master at this type of thing and we made every check point almost to the minute. We finally reached the lake, which was huge, and found our destination, where we landed on a stone runway near the lodge. We noticed when we flew over the lake that it was still pretty much iced over though it was July, and only a few hundred yards of water was showing around the shoreline. We were greeted by the owners of the lodge who told us that they had delayed the other visitors for a week due to the ice on the water, thus we found ourselves

Boarding an Air Force F-105 for a supersonic ride at the Miramar Naval Air Station. (Arness Collection.)

the only ones at the lodge. They had an old twin Beech float plane which they told us they used to fly groups up to the Arctic Sea 400 miles further north where they had another small lodge. The main attraction up there was fishing for Arctic char, fish that could be found only in the Arctic. They offered to take us up to the other lodge and we piled into the float plane and headed north. The plane held seats for about ten and our fellow passengers were Eskimos going back north to their homes. We landed on the Tree River near the town of Coppermine. Blacks River, which was just a short distance away, was where the remains of the last survivors of the ill fated Sir John Franklin Polar Expedition (1845–1848) were found. Setting out to find the Northwest Passage, the crew had to abandon their ship which had been locked in an ice pack in the Beaufort Sea and attempt an overland march to Fort Providence at Great Slave Lake. It wasn't until 1859, five years after the crew and ship had been removed from the Royal Navy's List of Ships, that explorers found the crew's remains near Blacks River. The mystery of how England's largest, best equipped expedition the country ever sent in search of the Northwest Passage resulted in such a disaster has never been solved.

We taxied up the Tree River until we reached a small village where some 50 Eskimos met us and we went up into the small lodge and prepared our gear for char fishing. We got into boats and traveled further up river and came to a lake that was just churning with char, but for some ungodly reason none of us could hook on to one. Right across the lake watching us was a big herd of muskox.

We stayed there for three days and gave up and flew back to the lodge. We then took off and headed north for Inuvik, just a short distance from the Beaufort Sea. We landed there and found that it was an oil town; a lot of drilling was underway. Several of the people we met up there recognized me from the show and were delighted to have "Matt Dillon" in their town. One man came up to me and said, "Matt Dillon, you're one hell of a guy, ya know it would be a real honor to go a few rounds with you. What do ya think about that, can we just go a couple of rounds and mix it up a bit?" Strangely enough he said all this in a friendly manner and thought it would be a great honor. I said as politely as I could that we were about to leave and he seemed disappointed. Probably if he had laid one on me he could boast about it for the rest of his life. We went into a store which had all kinds of ivory carvings, fur coats and hats, about everything you'd expect to find in a store that far north. They had a wolf skin jacket which was beautifully tailored and it fit me perfectly. Thinking that I might be able to buy it for a good bargain price considering where we were, I asked the clerk how much it was, and he responded, $4,000! So much for the jacket. They must have seen us coming. But visiting a thriving, remote town like Inuvik at the edge of the Beaufort Sea in the Arctic, not far from where early explorers had sailed and died trying to find a Northwest Passage, was an awesome experience.

We left Inuvik and flew to our next planned destination, Fort Yukon, Alaska, which was a few hundred miles west. Fort Yukon was an old town established during the early fur trading days. Traders settled in the town about the time of Lewis and Clark. The town had all log buildings. We checked into a hotel and stayed the night. When we took off the following morning the sky was cloudless and the sun was bright and warm. We were in a great mood and full of enthusiasm. We flew south along a beautiful river at a low altitude and just took in the sights. There were moose foraging below us; some wolves were on the shore drinking from the river; and the land on either side of the river was covered with what they called fireweed, which was a thick blanket of rich, red, flower-like brush. We continued to head south and could see a range of mountains ahead of us, the Alaska Range, and hoped to catch a glimpse of Mt. McKinley. We began to climb to get over the mountains and as we did some puffy white clouds appeared. Then within a matter of 30 minutes we found ourselves in a heavily clouded sky. We climbed up to about 12,000 feet to clear the clouds but they continued to rise as we proceeded and soon we were in dense clouds. The "Baron" didn't have any oxygen on board and our performance ceiling for the aircraft was limited to about 15,000 feet altitude. Alaska is noted for having the quickest forming weather fronts and we were suddenly in one. Jim Mock contacted an air controller and he said he could get us to the town of Yakatut, Alaska, but we'd have to climb to 20,000 feet before he could make radar contact with us and bring us in. Well, there was no way we could get up to the 20,000 feet. I was getting somewhat nervous because we had nothing but Alaskan wilderness below us and at that point we didn't know exactly where we were. As Jim Mock was studying some charts and I was trying to get some more altitude, I looked down and found a hole that opened up in the clouds. I could see the ground and a road. In a split second I made the decision to go down through that hole and we leveled out underneath the clouds at about 2,000 feet, in the clear. All the way down Jim Mock was yelling for me not to do it since if the hole closed up we'd be in real trouble. However, the road turned out to be the Alcan highway and we followed it to the town of Whitehorse, Canada. We stayed overnight and had a few drinks and relived the day. We all knew that we had had a close call. The next day we headed for San Francisco, stayed the night and then flew into L.A. the following morning. When we got back from that trip I had had enough flying for awhile. I sold the "Beaver" and eventually sold the "Baron" so I was without a plane for some time. I was busy doing *How the West Was Won* and after the end of that show I began to miss flying and bought a Beech Bonanza and flew that for several years. We sold the "Bonanza" in the late 1980s and that was when I quit flying and haven't flown since. In 20 years of flying I accumulated about 3,000 flight hours. I was getting older and the yen to fly had diminished. In looking back over those years of flying I can say that we had some wonderful experiences even though we pushed the edge somewhat, especially on the Canadian trip. That experience taught me that flying for the most part could be enjoyable, but there were always hazards when one took to the air. I think that one exhausting and near perilous trip forever etched in my mind the saying that "there are old pilots and there are bold pilots, but there are no old, bold pilots!"

Because of my *Gunsmoke* prominence, I had been the recipient of many awards, but on occasion the tables were turned. In 1984 the William Morris Agency asked me to present CBS network president Bill Paley, who had earlier saved *Gunsmoke* from cancellation, as he was named to the Television Hall of Fame. Even though I was greatly honored I declined, feeling that there were many more important people in the business to bestow this prestigious award. But the Morris people said Mr. Paley insisted that I be the one to present the award.

We had some hurdles to overcome during our *Gunsmoke* years. Early on, Congressional hearings propelled an antiviolence movement across the country that linked crime with the media, especially movies and TV. The movement gained momentum after the assassinations of John F. Kennedy and Dr. Martin Luther King.

Gunsmoke, less violent than other television westerns, survived the ordeal only by adhering to restrictions imposed on the industry. We changed the storylines to more dramatic confrontations, rather than violent ones. Episodes now dealt with important social issues such as racism ("The Scavengers," 1972, won

Janet and I and an unidentified guest at the TV Hall of Fame awards ceremony in 1984, where I presented Bill Paley with his award. (Arness Collection.)

the prestigious Black Image Award), mental retardation, and other thought-provoking problems. Mantley had saved *Gunsmoke* for the time being, but it wouldn't be long before the Long Branch Saloon would close its doors for good.

The end of *Gunsmoke* came with a jolt! Mantley was informed on 25 April 1975 that the network had decided to kill it. Of course, none of the people working on the show were informed of the cancellation. The first we heard of it was when we read it in the monthly trade paper, *The Hollywood Reporter*. Mantley was livid, as were many others. Eulogies in the press were numerous, and scathing of CBS's decision. Columnist Cecil Smith wrote in the *Los Angeles Times*, "The first moon colony we establish will be watching *I Love Lucy*. And probably *Gunsmoke*" ("Legend Goes Down the Tubes," 1 September 1975). Some would later date this as the beginning of CBS's fall from its position of uncontested prominence.

But I had a different take on it. It was a wonderful show that lasted more than any other TV series—20 years. That record still stands: we filmed 635 episodes. It was probably the most watched television show in the history of the

On the *Gunsmoke* set: Dennis Weaver and I (white hat) with an unidentified actor in the "Long Branch." It was a great set. After *Gunsmoke* ended, CBS sold the whole street to a private party. (Courtesy of CBS, Inc.)

business, and it's still alive today. After being off the air for 25 years, I still get about 50 to 100 fan letters a month. Letters like this one, which I received in August 2000, illustrate how *Gunsmoke*'s characters reached into the hearts of Americans:

> When I was seven years old, Mom got me a *Gunsmoke* toy rifle, canteen, and, of course, a U.S. Marshal embossed star. I don't remember how many times

I saw your show while I was dressed up like Matt Dillon, but it was a lot! I and my pals would play Cowboys and Indians, but I never wanted to be the cowboy so I could kill Indians; I wanted to be the Marshal so I could preserve Law and Order; I wanted to be like Matt, strong, fair, respected; and of course quick on the draw! I once paid my sister a dollar to cut off her long blond hair so I could use it as a pretend-horse's tail on my bicycle! Fortunately, our mother came in and stopped us.

I guess the point of this is to tell you that I still carry with me to this day all that Marshal Dillon stood for. I didn't have a dad while growing up so I [gleaned] from several different heroes of mine the ethics and sense of duty and justice that have carried me through life.

To have met one of the men who have helped to mold me into what I am and what I shall be was an honor indeed. The writers and producers of that show gave us an hour of entertainment; but you, dear sir, gave us more, you brought Marshal Dillon to life, and he lives forever not just in TV land, but where it really counts: in the heart.

Thank you, and may the Lord Bless you and keep you always!

James Paul Zernk, Jr.

Part VI

And Beyond

Not long after I left *Gunsmoke*, ABC asked me to play in the made-for-TV miniseries *How the West Was Won*, based on a 1962 film directed by John Ford. That MGM blockbuster won Oscars for best story, screenplay, and editing. It was a star-studded epic, with John Wayne, Henry Fonda, Jimmy Stewart, Robert Preston, and Eli Wallach; and Spencer Tracy narrated it.

Our show, initially called *The Macahans*, aired in January 1976. I played a rugged mountain man who'd spent ten years in the Northwest Territories before returning to Virginia to lead his brother's family on a hazardous journey west. A six-hour sequel was shot in 1977, and this time the title was changed to *How the West Was Won*. Twenty more hours were aired the following year, and the series ended with the survivors of the trek homesteading a ranch in the Teton Mountains in Wyoming. During the course of this saga, the Macahans faced hardships caused by Indians, renegades, and the untamed West. I loved my role—the series was shot in spectacular settings in Utah, Colorado, Arizona, and Southern California. I was particularly pleased with my performance in *How the West Was Won* because I got to play a character who was the complete opposite of Matt Dillon. Jeb Macahan was somewhat of a wild man, unlike the steady lawman I'd played for 20 years on *Gunsmoke*. Macahan tested my skills, and the plaudits I received for my acting in the miniseries brought me great satisfaction.

The last episode was broadcast on 23 April 1979. The producers wanted to continue, but by that time my right leg, which had been wounded during the

151

With Ricardo Montalban (right) in *How the West Was Won*. Ricardo won an Emmy for playing the role of an Indian chief. (Courtesy of ABC.)

With Jack Elam (left) in *How the West Was Won*. (Arness Collection.)

war, had really begun to bother me. In fact, in the final show I limped quite a bit. The leg needed repair surgery, which I had done.

Within a few years after that I was back on TV, playing the lead in *McClain's Law* in 1981–82. In that show I was again in the law-enforcement business, in a very different setting. I played a San Pedro, California, cop who'd retired from the force because of a leg injury. My MGM producers, familiar with the surgery I'd undergone, wrote the impediment into the script in case I limped during shooting. In the storyline, my character, McClain, fights to be reinstated on the force after a close friend is murdered. McClain feels he's the only one who can solve the case.

He did finally solve it as the series came to an end, in 1982. It was a great show, and I enjoyed working with that group of young professionals.

That same year I got an invitation to go to Oklahoma City to be inducted into the National Cowboy Hall of Fame, a beautiful museum and an organization dedicated to preserving the values, interest and history of the old West. Most of the museum, of course, is taken up with the real history of the old West, artifacts from early days and wonderful Remingtons and Russells. And they, of course, honor artists and writers and real cowboys, rodeo riders and people from the authentic western culture. They have a section that is devoted to western

McClain's Law, **TV series, 1981–82. I took quite a chance going from an early western lawman to a modern day policeman. Instead of keeping law and order in a small town like Dodge, I worked the city streets of L.A. (Arness Collection.)**

actors who did either western movies or television. So that's how we happened to get invited out there for induction. Janet and I, my dad and Dennis Weaver and his wife were picked up in Los Angeles by a Kerr McGee corporate jet and whisked to Oklahoma City in three hours. My dad, who was in his eighties, was quite excited because a favorite of his, Joel McCrea, was also going to be inducted. Joel was one of the founders of the Hall of Fame and was involved in many of its activities. He was not only a western actor in movies, but he also was a real rancher. He had two ranches in California on which he raised cattle. One of his ranches was out in Moor Park, which was close to our Simi Valley ranch. As I mentioned before, we raised cattle ourselves and we used to have a round-up every year where we would rope and brand calves, sort out cattle on horseback and in general have a good old western time of it. We made it kind of a social occasion for nearby ranchers and local people who lived around the valley. Back in those days, in the early 60s, the entire area was ranch country. Over on the north side of the valley there was a huge ten to fifteen thousand acre ranch. I think it was owned by J. Paul Getty, the oil magnate. Joel McCrea used to come over to our place and help out during the round-ups. He was a wonderful guy, a quiet, well spoken gentleman. I performed in two movies with him, *Stars in My Crown* and *Wyoming Mail*, both released in 1950. As I remember it, he had three sons, and one of them was around my daughter Jennie's age. They got to know each other at the ranch and dated for a while.

The Hall of Fame affair was quite an event. There were ranchers, cowboys and prominent people from all over the west who always showed up for the induction ceremonies. It was a great evening and Dennis and I were inducted into the Cowboy Hall of Fame. During the evening we visited the section for western actors. They had portraits of each inductee. When I returned to Oklahoma

City last year I went back to the room and one huge wall had been dedicated to the *Gunsmoke* cast. Our portrait was the largest and right next to me was a beautiful oil of Amanda (Miss Kitty). On the other side of me was Doc and, right below that, Dennis and Festus. The room itself was incredible. They had paintings of Ronald Reagan, John Wayne, Joel McCrea, Gary Cooper, Randy Scott, William S. Hart, and, of course, Gene Autry and Roy Rogers and Dale Evans together. The museum has been expanded since I was inducted and it's a marvelous tribute to our western heritage.

Early in 1986 I got a call from Stockton Briggle, a producer who wanted to do a TV movie on the battle of the Alamo. He'd had a lifelong passion to make this movie, regardless of what had previously been filmed. He'd convinced NBC that his production would be a ratings winner and was gathering a group of well-known actors to star in it. He asked if I would be interested in playing the lead, Jim Bowie. His offer was appealing, and, since he'd already signed up Brian Keith, Raul Julia, Alec Baldwin, Lorne Greene, and several other stars, I agreed to join the cast. *The Alamo: 13 Days to Glory* was shot in Brackettville, Texas, on the same site as the 1960 movie starring Duke Wayne. I enjoyed making the new *Alamo*, except for the intense heat. We endured daily temperatures of over 100 degrees throughout the shooting.

Shortly after that, CBS asked me to appear in a television movie version of the 1948 classic *Red River*. I was somewhat taken aback, since I considered it to be one of the greatest westerns ever made. The original cast included an incredible array of talent—Duke Wayne, Montgomery Clift in his first movie appearance, Walter Brennan, Joanne Dru, John Ireland, and many others. Our shooting was to begin in three weeks, and I was to be cast in the same role Duke had played. After some soul searching, I accepted. We shot the movie in Tucson. Our television remake was generally well received, but I still don't believe any production could have matched the original version.

In 1985, CBS wondered if I would consider doing a made-for-TV *Gunsmoke* movie. I agreed, and we did *Gunsmoke: Return to Dodge* with only myself and Amanda from the original cast. The show was shot in Alberta, Canada, and I was amazed that the producers had constructed a set that was a near-perfect reproduction of Dodge City, the Long Branch Saloon, the buildings and streets, all inside a large warehouse. When Amanda first saw what they'd done, she started crying. It brought back so many wonderful memories. It had been 12 years since the end of our series.

After our indoor scenes, we shot the rest of the show among the magnificent landscapes of the Canadian countryside. I must admit I was a little shaky about getting back into character after having been away for so many years. But I donned my costume and badge, and as I began to work in the Dodge City setting, it was like old times. John Mantley produced the movie, which got good ratings.

With Michael Learned in the 1990 *Gunsmoke* **sequel** *The Last Apache*. **In twenty years of the original** *Gunsmoke* **series, she was the only woman I kissed on the show. (Courtesy of CBS, Inc.)**

CBS decided to produce a sequel, *Gunsmoke: The Last Apache*, which was shot in Santa Fe under the direction of Norman Powell, son of the late actor Dick Powell. Our ratings were quite good. We went on to make three more *Gunsmoke* TV movies.

Gunsmoke: To the Last Man was shot in Tucson, Arizona, in 1991. There was great trepidation on the part of some of our producers about this third movie, since we were slotted to run against Burt Lancaster in *The Phantom of the Opera*. That story was very big at the time, what with the huge success of the musical. Nevertheless, we beat Burt in the ratings!

We felt that with a guest star like James Brolin for the fourth, we'd realize another winner. But to our surprise, *Gunsmoke: The Long Ride*, shot in Tucson in 1992, lost out to another made-for-TV movie that ran opposite us, starring Raquel Welch. She must have had something we didn't!

After the fifth film, *Gunsmoke: One Man's Justice* (made in 1993 in Del Rio, Texas), CBS lost interest in continuing. I didn't retire, but the calls offering me more work were less frequent. Even if I had received more offers, my physical condition was such that I just didn't have the energy to put in a full day's work on the set, let alone mounting a horse. Over the years I'd had a series of operations on my leg, and I knew that some additional repair work would be necessary to avoid walking without severe pain. More surgery did improve my condition, but I already knew that I'd always have a problem with my right leg. Over the years, bullet fragments had infused the bone. Following the operation

Dad, Peter and me. "The Happy Vikings"! (Arness Collection.)

and recovery from a staph infection in my knee, the doctors told me that my more athletic days were over. Skiing was out as was surfing, which I sorely missed.

When I look back on my life, I'd have to say that I've been one of the luckiest men among the many who came to Hollywood seeking fame and fortune. I truly believe that some divine hand was guiding me along the way. Certainly my survival of World War II was a near-miracle, since my outfit got so badly battered at Anzio. To this day I feel that had I not been wounded and evacuated, I wouldn't have survived those days of fierce fighting.

So many around me fell to enemy fire. Riflemen suffer tremendous casualties during war. They're the ones who join in fierce fighting day and night with determined enemy forces. Death comes suddenly in the form of rifle, machinegun, mortar, and artillery fire, and hand-to-hand combat. Riflemen face strafing from the air, and hidden land mines as they move across the earth to meet the enemy and gain their objectives. I often think of those young soldiers with whom I went ashore at Anzio and wonder how many made it safely through the war. The real heroes of that war, or any war, are the ones who died for their country and are buried on foreign soil. In a way, I feel lucky that I survived the war but saddened when I think of the cost.

I went to Hollywood on a whim, and within weeks I met several movie executives whose names were foreign to me. Cast in my first film only because

I could speak with a Scandinavian accent, I went on to enjoy a wonderful career surrounded by friends. Ed Hampel brought me back into the business after a year of surfing; Duke Wayne liked me and signed me with his company; and then came *Gunsmoke*.

Janet has been my best friend of all—she's seen me through some rough times and has been my champion throughout the 20-plus years we've been together. She remains my bedrock and soulmate, and every day I thank the Lord for the gift of her.

Throughout my life, another close friend has been the sea. From my childhood forays on the lakes surrounding Minneapolis and my early voyage on a freighter in the Caribbean to my many years of surfing, sailing off the California and Hawaiian shores, the water has been my second home.

When I started sailing with friends shortly after *Gunsmoke* aired, I became so enthralled with the sport that I bought boats of my own, over time. "Sea Smoke" was the first of three that I owned. I had heard of a San Diego company, Paul Kettenberg Boats, that built quality boats. They had an excellent reputation and I visited their sales office in San Pedro where I met their representative, Peggy Slater. Peggy told me that Paul was coming out with a new boat that was somewhat bigger than mine. It was a 50 footer with accommodations that were twice as big as my 40 foot "Sea Smoke." It had two private staterooms and two heads. It sounded just great. She told me that when it came on the market or when it was ready for presentation, she'd take me out for a spin. So when the time came, G.L., John Horn and I went down to San Pedro and took a ride on it. That was it! I had to have that boat. So I traded "Sea Smoke" in on the magnificent 50 footer. It seems that once you get hooked on owning a boat you start to look for a bigger one and then a bigger one. The boat was just a beauty and we named it "Sea Smoke II." And yes, eventually there would be the biggest and best of them all, "Sea Smoke III."

We made some wonderful trips on "II" and during the summer I would bring it up to Santa Barbara and tie it up at a slip in the harbor. By this time we'd gotten heavily into sailing and I did some racing with the boat, but this was all with Peggy Slater on board. She was the skipper of the vessel who always had an experienced crew that could really run the boat. With her at the helm and her crew working the sails, we won a number of competitive races. I was always embarrassed because we'd win a race and we'd sail to a small anchorage, Emerald Bay, where the L.A. Yacht Club was located. We'd go ashore for the presentations and they'd say, "And Number One Prize goes to James Arness in 'Sea Smoke II.'" And I'd have to go up to a podium and accept the trophy and guys in the audience would look at me and say, "Hey, why don't you leave Peggy on the shore some day and come out and race with us and let's see how you'd do." It was all in good humor and everything, but they knew and I knew that Peggy had really won the race.

Catamaran "Sea Smoke III" shown passing Diamond Head. The craft measured 59 feet bow to stern and we could make 30 knots under full sail. (Arness Collection.)

Peggy was a terrific gal and we learned a lot about sailing from her and enjoyed being with her. She was a very unusual lady. She at one time was named "Woman of the Year" by the *L.A. Times*. She was about 5' 8"or 5' 9" and sturdily built, all solid muscle. When she'd get out on the boat in a race, she was commanding a whole crew of ten guys, telling them exactly what to do. She was running the ship. She had that capability like a man but she wasn't like that in private life. She was very pleasant and somewhat shy. She was born in San Pedro and she got into sailing when she was a little kid. I think maybe her father had been a sailor and sailing became the main thing in her life. Those were wonderful times and we did quite a bit of racing. We did one where we raced from San Pedro up toward the farthest Channel Islands. It was a very difficult upwind trip. We'd then sail around the west end of San Miguel Island, which was about 100 miles off the coast. Then we'd sail from San Miguel to a point around the end of San Clemente Island, which is way down off San Diego. This was a five day trip through rough weather and turbulent seas. I only made one of these trips and it was an unforgettable sea voyage. The nights were bitter cold and while standing the night watch it seemed we were always wet, standing in the cockpit with the wind blowing on us. I just loved the experience and felt like a real, crusty old sailor.

Around 1968 we met some people from a catamaran group of sailors. They were totally separate from the orthodox boat people, and after talking to them I got enthusiastic about the idea of catamaran sailing, which is a much faster way to go. It's also more dangerous because you don't have the protection of a lead keel that will pull you upright. So the more I thought about it and talked to the guys, I really wanted to experience that type of sailing. At the time there was a standard catamaran race to Hawaii in alternate years; every other year they had a regular sailboat race to the islands. It was a long standing traditional race that had been going on for years. The catamaran race was relatively new. Only a few boats were usually entered in the race since there weren't too many catamarans around in those days. The sailboat crowd looked down on these new craft and didn't consider them legitimate sailing vessels. I went out for a few catamaran rides and loved it. They were fast, in fact, two or three times faster than the standard sailboat.

I got to thinking about building a big catamaran and entering the race to Honolulu. I got together with a couple of Hawaiians, Rudy Choy and Alfred Kumali, and Warren Seeman, who owned a catamaran building company (CKS). Warren was an inveterate catamaran sailor and had been sailing these craft for many years. Choy was the business man besides being an expert catamaran sailor and Warren was THE man when it came to sailing the boat. Initially we talked about building a boat which would break the existing record, and that was the kind of a catamaran we designed, a 60 foot "cat." There was one other around at the time that was a little larger but had not been built for "cat" racing. One of the things with a catamaran is that you have to keep the weight down to the absolute minimum. You want it to be the lightest boat that you can build. The designers and builders did some preliminary sketches for my approval. After various discussions about the design and some technical matters, we decided to go ahead with the building of the boat. We rented an old storage warehouse down in Inglewood which was almost as big as an aircraft hangar. The three guys proceeded to build the boat from scratch. They were marvelous craftsmen. Building a boat like that was like building custom furniture. It was similar to other catamarans in the sense of top craftsmanship, but its size and design gave it an entirely different look.

A catamaran is a two hull boat with no keels, which gives the craft its speed. It has to be built out of very light materials, as in our case marine grade plywood, which was structurally very strong. I really got excited about what lay before us, racing our hand-constructed boat some 2,500 miles across Pacific waters which at times would be unpredictable, as would be the weather and the all important wind factor. For even the most experienced seamen the trip would be a challenge. But I became more and more confident in our builders with every passing day. The men not only knew how to build this boat but they knew that they were the guys who would ultimately sail it.

It took several months to complete the basic boat and we took it to Marina Del Rey, transporting it by night down streets and side roads. We held a big ceremony when we launched "Sea Smoke III." The Harringtons and many of our friends celebrated the event and it turned out to be a very exciting day. Of course we still had many months of work ahead of us to finish the boat and prepare it for the race, but to see that beautiful craft now in the water was a thrill for me. When we finally were ready to test sail the boat the crew couldn't wait to see how she handled and took her out for several trial runs. Her name was appropriate because this baby could really "smoke." Our crew for the coming race would consist of Choy, Seeman, Kumali, eight experienced catamaran seamen and two semi-passengers, my son Rolf and me. We sailed it down to San Pedro to a place called Hurricane Gulch which was known for its high westerly winds, and because of a breakwater, a smooth lake-like sea, we were able to measure the speed of the boat. Numerous speed trials were conducted, and we were finally ready to see what "Sea Smoke III" could do in a racing competition. When the day came for the start of the competition, seven or eight catamarans were docked at the L.A. Yacht Club in San Pedro. Buddy Ebsen had a boat entered in the race, in fact his boat had also been built by CKS. The night before we left, a big dinner was thrown by all of the crews at a restaurant in Long Beach. Toasts were made and there was an air of excitement.

The next morning we were all off our marks on time, surrounded by many power boats and yachts. Milburn Stone and Ken Curtis were in one of the power boats, cheering us on. The first goal of the contestants was to get around the western tip of Catalina Island and out into the open sea. The day was beautiful, with bright sunshine and good visibility. Warren quickly set up a routine establishing night watches and directing daytime sailing procedures. All of the crew were highly experienced and didn't have to be told what to do as the boat sped across the water westward. One night we encountered mist and fog and the visibility was down to two or three miles. All eyes kept watch for any ship that might suddenly break out of the fog. Sure enough one did. A giant aircraft carrier appeared about a mile ahead. We only saw one other large ship during the entire trip.

By the third day the sea was clear around us, and no other catamarans were in sight. When we were about 350 miles off the coast of California, we expected to pick up the northeast trade winds that blow from northeast to southeast, which would carry a ship right toward the islands. Unfortunately, the trade winds failed to materialize. So, for a number days we sailed along at a slow pace and came to the conclusion that it would be impossible to break the record, which had been our goal. When we were about 300 miles north of the island of

Molokai, the trade winds kicked up and the boat began doing what it was designed to do, which was to go sea-smoking through the water at 20 to 25 knots.

That night we suddenly found ourselves in a squall doing about 30 to 40 knots in gusty winds and rolling seas. It was tremendously exciting but frightening at the same time. I looked back at Warren at the helm and, man, he really had ahold of that helm. I'll never forget his face. It was lit with fanatical excitement, for this is what he had yearned for his entire life, to be in command of a catamaran this size being challenged by fierce weather in an unpredictable sea. Our situation was further complicated in that we had a huge light-air spinnaker up and couldn't get it down before we hit the squall line. But Warren was a master at the controls during the storm. He kept his head looking straight forward, listening for wind changes so he would adjust the course of the boat within seconds. He was actually sailing the boat by his ears, since he could feel the wind shifts by listening and feeling the wind swirling around his head.

The next morning we passed the towering mountains of Molokai, and as we headed for Cocoa Head on Oahu, we all got decked out in our crew uniforms—hats and shirts with "Sea Smoke III" emblems on them, the whole works. It was getting dark so we lowered the sails and motored into Alea Wai Yacht Club. As we tied up, people arrived in hordes. The press and television cameras were there and everyone seemed to be excited to see us arrive. Hawaiian girls came on board and put so many colorful leis around our necks that I could barely see over the top of them. Mai Tais were passed around and we had just a great party that evening. We were wined and dined for the next few days in Honolulu, and then one evening a big celebration ceremony was held at the Waikiki Yacht Club. By this time all the boats had arrived and during the dinner party we all got up and received our trophies and then went out on the town.

I finally returned to Los Angeles about a week later after having taken a bunch of people on a tour around the island of Kauai. The boat was eventually brought back to Marina Del Rey and just kind of stayed there for a few months because not just any crew could take it out. It demanded skilled catamaran seamen to operate it. By the time it had returned I was back at work and involved in other activities. I had sold "Sea Smoke II" awhile ago and I eventually donated the catamaran to the Sea Scouts. Its ownership passed through several hands until it ended up back in Hawaii. It's used as a touring boat today and is identified to its passengers as a boat once owned by Jim Arness.

I can't enjoy the sea these days, but an excerpt from Lord Byron's *Childe Harold's Pilgrimage* helps me to revisit it:

> There is a rapture on the lonely shore,
> There is society, where none intrudes,
> By the deep Sea, and the music in its roar:
> I love not Man the less, But Nature more,

Jim and Janet Arness with Jim Wise in January 1999. (Arness Collection.)

From these our interviews, in which I steal
From all I may be, or have been before,
To mingle with the Universe, and feel
What I can ne'er express, yet cannot all conceal.

And I have loved thee, Ocean! And my joy
Of youthful sports was on thy breast to be
Borne, like thy bubbles, onward: from a boy
I wanton'd with thy breakers—they to me
Were a delight; and if the freshening sea
Made them a terror—'twas a pleasing fear,
For I was as it were a child of thee,
And trusted to thy billows far and near,
And laid my hand upon thy mane—as I do here.

My life has been like an ocean voyage. I've experienced my share of heavy
weather, but mostly it's been smooth sailing, with fair winds and following seas!

Others Remember

There are few members of the original *Gunsmoke* cast alive today. Milburn Stone (Doc), Amanda Blake (Kitty), Ken Curtis (Festus), Glenn Strange (Sam, the barkeep at the Long Branch Saloon), and James Nusser (Louie Pheeters, Dodge City's resident drunk) have all passed away. Burt Reynolds, who played the city's blacksmith (Quint Asper), and wrote the Foreword to our book, is still making movies and going strong, and Dennis Weaver (Chester) is presently living in Ridgeway, Colorado.

In our search to find cast members and others who might add their personal remembrances about everyday happenings on the *Gunsmoke* and *How the West Was Won* sets, some of my old pals came to mind: Buck Taylor, who played Newly O'Brien, deputy marshal and gunsmith; John Stephens, who was a producer during the last year of *Gunsmoke* and subsequently produced the *How the West Was Won* television miniseries; Ben Bates, who was my stand-in for many years; Morgan Woodward, who appeared on more *Gunsmoke* episodes than anyone else; and Bruce Boxleitner, who appeared on *Gunsmoke* and *How the West Was Won*. I contacted them and they were happy to pass along some anecdotes that I believe our readers will find interesting and amusing.

Buck Taylor

(Buck was born on a small ranch in the San Fernando Valley. His mother was an acrobatic dancer with the Dean Sisters and his father was the well-known character actor Dub "Cannonball" Taylor. He was a star athlete in high school and tried out for the U.S. Olympic gymnastic team in 1960 and 1964. However, his athletic career was cut short when he was injured while riding a horse as a stuntman. Buck aspired to be an artist and at USC studied art, cinema and theater. He served in the Navy for two years and when he returned to civilian life decided to become an actor. Today, Buck and his wife, Goldie, live in Louisiana. He continues to be active in theatrical pursuits and is also a nationally recognized watercolor artist.)

BUCK SAYS: Being a part of *Gunsmoke* was a great experience for me because here I was a guy still in high school when the show started in 1955. And years later, in 1967, I joined the cast and found myself sitting in the Long Branch with Jim, Kitty, Doc and Festus, having a wonderful time with a family of folks I grew to love. To grow up watching *Gunsmoke* and then be a part of it was something unbelievable for me. I always had to pinch myself. Jim at 6' 7" was quite an imposing figure and a real hero of a man. I was in awe of the guy.

Jim liked his privacy and came to work, got his job done and that was it. You never saw him again. I think in the eight years I was on the show I rarely socialized with him, maybe two or three times. I didn't even speak to him a lot. I gave him a lot of space. I think that's why I lasted as long as I did. It was also probably because I didn't crowd anyone's space. We worked hard together and when we finished shooting for the

day we went our separate ways. I had my family and they all had theirs.

I remember that in 1973 or '74 they had a press promotion to bring the cast of *Gunsmoke* to Dodge City and then on to the White House to meet President Nixon. It was a big promotional thing for the network and the PR guy came by and asked me, "Would you be willing to do this?" And I said, "Well, sure, it'd be great!" And Ken, Amanda and Doc and all of us agreed on it, and then we got to thinking, wait a minute, is Jim going to do this? Because it was a little unusual for Jim to want to do something like that. So I said, I don't know, maybe we better talk to him. So Jim called us into his dressing room and we all sat down and he said, "You know, I know how you all were planning this big trip to the White House and Nixon and Dodge City, and all this kind of stuff." But he said, "You know for twenty years now I've created this Greta Garbo and Howard Hughes image," and he said, "I just can't break it. Now if you all want to go that's fine but," he said, "you know, I just can't do that kind of thing. It's just too hard for me." And we all agreed that if Jim didn't go, we wouldn't go, so none of us went. Our decision was out of respect for Jim.

I currently travel all over the country with my artwork and meet hundreds of thousands of people every year, shake hands and chat with them. And they're all interested in Jim and how he's doing and what he's doing. So I'm starting to spread the word right now that he's working on an autobiography and I think people will love it.

I always found it extremely difficult to work with Jim, mainly because I couldn't look him in the eye and not start to laugh. I think Jim thought, this is my feeling, that Hollywood and making movies and all that went with it was a lot of fun but it's a silly kind of business. You know here's these grown men playing cowboys and Indians. I think Jim's sense of humor was the funniest of anyone I've ever met. I believe that it was hard for him to get serious about this stuff and if you started laughing or made some funny comment, then that was it for the day; he was ruined. Of course, he didn't have to do much to get me laughing. He just had to look at me. But I was always a serious guy. I'd rehearse by myself and then when we'd rehearse a scene together I'd give it 100 percent. A lot of actors don't. They come in and kind of go through the motions and then they get better as they go along and get more serious. But I didn't want to mess up, so I came in dead serious and ready to go! Often my role would consist of running into Jim's office and saying, "Marshal, there's a fight in the Long Branch!" And I'd be out of breath, I mean I'd be serious about this. Well, he'd look up at me and go, "Oh, my God, yeah?" And he'd start laughing and then during the re-shoots I could hardly come in the door. I couldn't even look at him, 'cause he just got silly. The whole thing got to be silly. So we actually had to

As Zeb Macahan in *How the West Was Won*. This was a great role for me after *Gunsmoke* when westerns were pretty much fading from TV. The show revived the public's interest in our western heritage, and it has been ranked number five as an all-time favorite among TV miniseries. (Courtesy of ABC.)

get a master shot done and then he would have to leave the set and I would say my lines to the script supervisor and then I'd have to leave the set and he'd say his lines to the script supervisor. This got to be an expensive way to shoot a scene. Of course the producers got on us and told us to get serious. Jim would then get serious but I just couldn't. I loved working with him. There were times when he would deliberately mess me up when he had his back to the camera. I remember we were loading luggage on a stagecoach one day. Well, I'm on top of the stagecoach looking down at Jim while he's handing me these bags. Doc and Festus have a scene going on, kind of below us. While I'm grabbing the bags from Jim, he was giving me all these funny faces. I started laughing, ruining the scene for everyone down below. And I wasn't even involved in the scene with any words or dialogue. I was strictly an extra in the background loading luggage. But I blew this shot four or five times and the director was getting on my case, saying, "Buck, what is it? What's so funny? What's the deal?" Of course, I couldn't tell him it was Jim because that would get him in trouble. Jim thought it was just great fun and he kept doing it. Jim had a great laugh. It was loud and infectious. Once he started, the entire set would start laughing. The Matt Dillon that people see on the screen is a serious guy but Jim was really, after he got to know you, and felt comfortable around you, a funny son of a gun.

At the height of the popularity of *Gunsmoke*, I believe it was during the early 1970s, I was in Kanab, Utah, doing an episode with Buddy Ebsen and Ben Johnson. Ben had just won an Academy Award and was real happy. And we were happy to have him join us on the show. We had chartered a plane that was going to fly us back to Los Angeles. Passengers slated for the trip were myself, Buddy, Ben, Ralph McCutcheon, who was an animal trainer, and a Rottweiler named "Rote." Anyway, the pilot was kind of a nervous guy and he forgot the key to the luggage compartment in the nose of the plane and we had to load everything in the aisle of the passenger section. In hindsight this was a mistake and we all knew it then but we were anxious to get back to L.A. So we climbed aboard in street clothes and the pilot started the engine and revved

it up. Looking out we could see Jim and the crew shooting a scene down near the runway. Jim was there in his Matt Dillon outfit with his badge and everything. There weren't many people in the United States at that time that didn't recognize Matt Dillon. As we started down the runway the pilot was talking to us and as we went by the set there's Jim, all 6' 9" of him in his boots, kneeling beside the runway and crossing himself. We all looked at him and started laughing. And the pilot turned around to us and said, "Hey, who's that guy?" Well, that was a tip-off. I knew then that we were in trouble. The plane took off and we flew into a dust storm. Oh, man, the plane was dipping and diving and I could see the pilot up there by himself with his hand over his mouth looking like he was going to throw up. So I climbed over the luggage to get in the co-pilot's seat and I turned to the pilot and said, "How do you fly this thing? Can I help?" He mumbled something and then threw up in one of those up-chuck bags. I turned back and looked at Ben Johnson and he looked away from me. He was scared to death. The dog was trying to find a way out of the plane, Ralph McCutcheon was having a drink and smiling. It appeared that only Ben and I, and the dog, now frantically crawling over the luggage, were upset. We barely made it into Las Vegas. And, you know, it was a frightening experience, but for this pilot to turn around and look at us and say "Who is that guy?" has always stuck with me, cause everybody knew who Jim was at that time. As I said before, after the pilot made that comment we knew we had a dimwit at the controls.

I remember that when my five year contract was up I wanted a bit more money. I asked Ken Curtis if I should get my agent to ask CBS to give me more money. "Yeah," he said, "you can do that," but he said why don't you ask Bob Emme, I believe that was his name, he was Jim's business manager. If you needed anything from Jim, you ran it through Bob first. You really didn't ask Jim. I mean I wouldn't go up to Jim and say "Jim, I need more money on *Gunsmoke*," you know. So I asked Bob Emme. I said "Bob, do you think I have, you know, a legitimate cause to ask for a little more money per episode, a little better deal?" Bob answered, "Yes, I think you do. I think what you're asking is reasonable, very reasonable." He went on, "Let me talk to Jim about it." I said, "Well, that'd be great. I don't want to bother Jim." When I got back home after work that day I got a call from Bob and he said, "Buck, call your agent and tell him to tell CBS to make a deal with you and that Jim doesn't want any problems with it because he doesn't want to have to interrupt his trip and fly back from Hawaii and go to CBS and raise Hell!" I said, "Wow! OK," and I called my agent and told him what Bob said and I guess he called CBS and everything was fine. The deal worked out just great. We shut down on a hiatus at that point and the next time I saw Jim was the following September. I hesitated about going up to Jim to thank him for helping me out. I just wasn't that kind of

guy and I think it would have embarrassed him, but he made the overture to me. He said, "Buck, everything work out all right with CBS?" I answered, "Yeah, Jim, it sure did and I appreciate it." And that's all he had to say because Jim wasn't one for accolades and pats on the back. I understood that about him. Jim was always there for me if ever I or any of the cast needed him to confront CBS on a legitimate issue. He was a man of very few words, but what a fantastic, magnetic personality.

Later we were back at Kanab, Utah, shooting another episode, and I went fishing at Lake Mead by myself. I caught some nice sized bass and came back in. While I was putting my rented boat away, the guy who I had rented the boat from said, "Hey, Matt Dillon is staying at that hotel," pointing to a nearby building. I said, "Is that right?" I knew that Jim was at the hotel and he usually stayed in a different place than the cast where he could spread out. He was a big man and needed his space. However, this time there were no rooms of any size. In fact, his was kind of small. It was a weekend on a Sunday and I thought I'd just go by his room and maybe say hello. As I got close to his room I could hear him talking. He and *Gunsmoke* regular Ted Jordan and Jim's make-up man for over 20 years, Glen Alden, were in there and they were having margaritas or something. So I knocked on the door and he opened it and said, "Oh, my God, Buck, come on in." I walked in and he said, "Have a drink. What are you having?" I answered, "Well, whatever you guys are having." Ever generous, Jim picked up the phone and immediately ordered 12 more margaritas! We had great fun that afternoon talking and telling jokes. Jim drove fairly fast. His cars were always late models and he had fast airplanes. He was always careful not to drink while driving or flying. He had a Beechcraft "Baron" that he used to fly to locations and buzz the set when he left. His "Red Baron" was really neat looking.

After the show was discontinued I lost touch with Jim. I knew of his desire for privacy, which I deeply respected. About three years ago after I had been remarried for several years, my wife said, "You know, you never talk to Jim Arness." And I answered, "Well I love him, but he's a real private kind of guy and I respect that, and besides, maybe he wouldn't want to talk to me." I didn't know. She pressed a little, "Well you ought to call him." And I said, "I guess you're right," 'cause I hadn't spoken to him in about 10 or 12 years. So I called up Bruce Boxleitner figuring that he'd have Jim's number, which he did. I called Jim and it's one of the neatest things I ever did in my life because his response to me was so warm and friendly; I just had a great conversation with him, and his lovely wife, Janet. I told him about my artwork, what I was doing, that I was still making movies … but my artwork was really going great. It had become a business for me, thanks to *Gunsmoke* and all the other shows I'd done. My 40 years in movies had greatly helped me realize my avocation. I sent some samples of my work to Jim and he

called back and said the work was "fantastic." He was almost overwhelming in his praise. He ended the conversation by asking me to drop by his home whenever I got into L.A. and we'd have dinner together. So for another year or so we conversed by phone and then sure enough, Burt Kennedy and my wife and I and Jim and his wife met at Trader Joe's in Beverly Hills and had a great dinner. We spent the evening talking over old times, laughing and joking. How wonderful it was to make contact with an old friend after all these years. I did a show with Burt Reynolds a couple of years ago and all we did was talk about Jim and how much we respected and loved him.

There've been a few stars of his stature and magnitude, but men like Jim Arness come along only once in a great while. I think John Wayne was, you know, in that category. And I know that my friends Sam Elliot, Katherine Ross and my contemporaries that I work with just revere Jim. I think one of the greatest moments I ever saw on television was when Jim was giving John Wayne an award for something, I can't remember what it was for, but it was on television. I was watching the show and Jim introduced Wayne for this award. Jim said, "So now I'd like to introduce you to my friend, John Wayne." Well, the Duke walks on stage, tuxedo and all, looked at Jim and said, "You're bigger than I am." There was a split second pause and then Jim responded, "Taller, maybe." That was Jim. That's one of the greatest lines I ever heard. I don't know if someone wrote it for him or whatever,

With Alec Baldwin (center) and Brian Keith (right) on the set of *The Alamo*, a made-for-television movie. The picture was filmed on the original set used for the John Wayne movie *The Alamo!* (Arness Collection.)

but what a great response to John Wayne, 'cause I don't think anyone was bigger than John Wayne.

The member of our cast that was really the patriarch of the show, and Jim would readily agree, was Milburn Stone. Doc was the one man that got Jim's rapt attention. Well respected for his professionalism, guidance and wisdom, Milburn offered me some good advice when I joined the cast. He said, "You know, when you're ready to deal with networks and so forth, make sure you're in a position of power. Don't go shooting your mouth off if you don't have the right cards."

In 1986 I was cast with Jim in the made-for-television movie *The Alamo: Thirteen Days to Glory*, and I'll be danged if I didn't have a potential laughing scene with him in that movie. I was playing a guy named Colorado John Smith and he was Jim Bowie. The script called for me to come into his office which was in his home and deliver an urgent message. I thought to myself as I was about to enter the room, "Oh God, I don't even know if I can get this out!" I knew this would probably be déjà vu. When I went into his office we just looked at each other. We certainly looked strange to each other and just our outfits alone could have started the laughter. Jim had on these sideburns like Jim Bowie wore and was dressed in an officer's uniform. I had on a handlebar mustache and for a moment I thought "God Almighty."

I was really dreading the scene. Burt Kennedy was directing the scene and we did it with both of us keeping a straight face. But it was really tough.

Jim seemed to have a photographic memory. I don't think he ever read the *Gunsmoke* scripts. He would come on the set and the prop man, why the prop man I don't know, would hand him the four or five pages to a scene and Jim would look them over one by one, which took him about a minute. And then the director would kind of tell him the story of what this episode was all about, then Jim would look the pages over again, then he would look up and say something like, "Yeah, O.K.," and crumple the pages up and toss them into a waste basket that was about 15 feet away. Usually he'd score a basket, then turn around and the director would say, "OK, let's shoot it." The actors he would be working with had already rehearsed the scene with the script supervisor and after watching Jim give a quick reading of his lines they were sure he wouldn't remember them. However, it usually turned out that they, not Jim, would blow the scene. Once Jim got the scene right in his mind, the words just came out as they were scripted. It was fascinating to watch. Jim was a quick study and had a brilliant mind. How he memorized his lines so quickly I don't know but I think when you do a show for so long it's a question of knowing what the character would do. There's only so many situations that you can be in and he'd been in every one of them many times and there are only so many things you can say, I guess. But a lot of

it was the language, the scenes were expository scenes where you had to say, "We went over there and we fished in the lake," and so forth and so on. "Then we went to Jim's place and Joe's place and picked up the mules, hitched them up to the wagon," and all that kind of stuff. So that dialogue was a little trickier. What I ended up doing was, when I had a scene to do with Jim, if there were a lot of words in it, I'd memorize the whole scene. Because inevitably Jim would look at it and say, "You know, I just can't say all this stuff. It's not something that Matt Dillon would do, I don't think he'd say all this kind of stuff. It's too much talk. You know, I can be a man of few words." So he would look at me and he'd say, "Buck, why don't you say this stuff?" (words that seemed to fit my character more). After we did this a few times it was easy from then on because I had everything memorized. He'd say, "Buck, what do you think?" And I'd answer, "I've already got it Jim." He'd respond, "That's it. Buck, c'mon, let's do it." So he would give me all these extra lines. Now a lot of actors love lines, they like their face up there speaking and talking. But not Jim, his presence and his lack of having to say much added to his characterization of Matt Dillon. You know Gary Cooper used the same technique and Jim knew that. He knew his character so well that he sensed what the marshal would say under certain circumstances. Newley, my character, talked a lot. So I always took the liberty of memorizing the whole scene verbatim and then Jim would say, "Well, I can't say this," and I'd say,

"Well, I can do it if you want, Jim." And I usually did. Jim was such an unselfish actor. He didn't want all the attention nor did he wish to be in the spotlight all the time.

I learned many things from Jim which stood me in good stead after I left *Gunsmoke* and began to perform in later western movies. Actors have a hard time with close-ups or shots from the waist up. They'll stand there and their hands will fidget, you know, even though their face is very calm. Well, I watched Jim and he'd always take his hands and stick 'em in the top of his gun belt, take a deep breath (whoosh) and then just relax and look right into the camera and talk. It really worked. I've been doing that ever since but it's something I learned from him. I also picked up a number of acting tips from him 'cause he was a master at what he did. He got better and better as the show went along and by the time I joined the cast he had his character down cold.

Jim had a very compassionate side to him. During his life Jim had tragically lost his daughter and I knew that that was a shattering experience for him. Unfortunately, my son was killed in a motorcycle accident six years ago. He was twenty-seven years old and a first assistant director. His name was Adam Taylor. When I got back with Jim and called him a few years ago, I told him what had happened and he understood my feelings and what I was going through. It takes enormous courage for parents to go through such ordeals, and having both been faced with such a tragedy, I found great

warmth in Jim's consoling words. Jim and I continue to stay in touch and of course we always talk about *Gunsmoke*. While discussing the cable reruns of the show Jim once said to me, "Buck, you know we did some pretty dad gum good shows back then." And I said, "Yeah we sure did." He said, "Some of these I hadn't seen before." It wasn't unusual for Jim not to watch an episode on TV after it was shot.

At one time *Gunsmoke* had cigarette sponsors but Jim didn't smoke. He was always a health-minded guy. He loved to ski and surf. He was a Viking from Minnesota and took to skis naturally and loved surfing because he found a kind of personal freedom in both sports. He had a rented house in Hawaii, a log cabin at Mammoth and two or three other houses. I thought we had the best working conditions of all the television series. We had three months off in the summer and three months off in the winter. We worked in the fall and we worked in the spring. That was so Jim could go surfing in the summer and skiing in the winter. But I think it went further than that because it gave all of us a chance to be with our families during the important times of the year and enjoy outings in the summer and the joy that winter brings with its traditional holidays. I think Jim had that in mind when he set our schedule.

After all of these years I'm still in awe of the guy. He was always a gentleman around the ladies and very manly around men. I just look at him and he's Matt Dillon and I and thousands of his fans will always see him in that light. I named my middle son Matt, Matthew, who is a stuntman right now. I named him after Jim Arness, that's for sure, and Matt Dillon. I had another son I named Cooper Glenn Taylor and he's named after Gary Cooper and Glenn Strange, the Bartender on the show who was my dear friend that I toured with. We were the "B Team." Festus and Doc were the "A Team" going to rodeos and fairs. Glenn and I would go out on the arena floor and I would sing and play the guitar while Glenn played the fiddle. Eventually we took a singing group, Johnny and the Frontiersmen, with us and they made us sound better than we were. So we toured in the summer months, affording us another chance to make some more money. During the fair and rodeo seasons we toured all over the United States and kind of kept *Gunsmoke* alive that way by reaching out to people and being in touch with them. Jim didn't do much of that after the early years of the show but encouraged us to keep it up saying, "You're what's keeping us on the air." So we were always kind of representing him. Of course Festus had several jokes that he would tell that only he could get away with, you know, like "Matt Dillon is so high that he could hug geese with a rake." It's not very funny when you say it, but believe me when Festus said it, the people would howl.

What a great time in my life! In 1971 I moved my family from Los Angeles to Ennis, Montana. I'm sure that the move was influenced by Jim's example. Like him I wanted to be away from the city somewhere in the moun-tains where I could raise my kids on a ranch with horses and farm animals, a place of beauty with a big sky. I commuted the last four years on *Gunsmoke* and after the shooting of our final episode there were many tearful farewells. The *Gunsmoke* family broke up after a long and memorable journey. A 20 year television journey that might never again be duplicated in quality and possess a cast that so touched the heart of America.

John Stephens

(John and I worked together on the last season of *Gunsmoke* and all three years on *How the West Was Won*. He was a top notch line producer, a respected professional and a really good guy with a great sense of humor. He started in the business with Don Fedderson as a production manager and line producer for shows such as *My Three Sons*, *Family Affair*, *To Rome with Love*, *The Smith Family*, and the last two seasons of *The Millionaire*, and produced numerous movies of the week such as *Tramp Ship*, *The Chairman*, *Stan's Waitin*, *The Golden Monkey*, and *Marciano*. He produced *The Brian Keith Show* in Hawaii, the original pilot of *Wonder Woman*, and was the first to produce the single camera show for Mary Tyler Moore, a show called *Three for the Road*. While with Universal he did *Buck Rogers*, all eight years of *Simon and Simon* and was the creator of the show *Major Dad*. For the past seven years he has been teaching at UCLA and giving guest lectures.)

JOHN SAYS: As far as I'm concerned Jim Arness, along with Fred Mac-Murray, is the most enjoyable actor/star I ever worked with. I say that mainly because Jim and Fred were down to earth people who happened to be actors. You could talk to Jim about any subject and he was not totally absorbed talking about show business or who went to this premiere or that premiere. He was a pleasure to work with and we had a lot of fun together working on *Gunsmoke* and *How the West Was Won*.

One of the funniest things I remember during one of the *Gunsmoke* episodes happened with a new director. He met Jim and Jim proceeded to rehearse the scene we were going to shoot while Ken Curtis was in a jail cell. Following that we went

John Stephens (right) with director Burt Kennedy.

for a take. It was a five page scene and we shot the take and afterward the new director said, "Cut. I'd like to do another one. I think we can do it a little better, Jim." Jim kind of stopped and said, "Better? That's the best I can do. You want better, get Laurence Olivier." Well the director was just stunned. He turned to me and said, "What should I do?" I said, "Say, 'Cut, Print.'" And he said "Cut, Print." After

that the two of them got along fine. I think the main thing a lot of the younger directors never realized was that no one knew Matt Dillon's character better than Jim Arness. Jim on the *Gunsmoke* set WAS Matt Dillon. And when he knew he had done something right, he knew far better than any director that would ever come on and do it. That's so true in really any part where an actor has been doing it for a

Cast of *How the West Was Won*. (Courtesy of ABC.)

long period of time and especially in the case of Jim, who had been doing the part for 19 years.

We had another funny incident that would occur often on *Gunsmoke*. Jim would come on the set and there'd be a fellow, say in jail. Jim would look at the director and me and say, "Do I like that guy?" And he'd give you a look and that meant that he really wasn't comfortable with the actor. I found that the only actors Jim wasn't comfortable with were those that came out of the Actors Studio, the method actors. He got along with them and treated them in a very professional manner but he'd prefer that he was against them in

Gunsmoke episodes. It enabled him to play his part a bit better. If we told him that the actor had saved his life in the episode and that he liked him, then Jim's eyes would light up and though he might not care to work with the actor, he'd go ahead and do the scene.

Jim was always totally professional both on and off the set. There were never problems such as producers and directors encounter with actors today. We had 8:00 A.M. shootings on *Gunsmoke* and Jim was always there ready to go at 8:00. Today, if there's an 8:00 A.M. shoot, actors usually arrive on the set at 9:30 in their bathrobes, discuss the scene and then they'd be ready to shoot at 10:00. Then at 5:00 that afternoon they'll usually question why they're still on the set at that time.

We prided ourselves that shooting a *Gunsmoke* episode never went over six days. We did what we called "bottle shows" in five days. We did a few shows in what we called back-to-back bottle shows, where we did two shows in 11 days. We'd do like 11 pages in a jail cell to finish one show, and maybe 9 or 11 pages in the same cell to start the next show. We just seemed to whiz through the dialogue; it was all rather simple. The bottle shows were very tight shows, small casts and all the shooting done on our standard sets. I remember one difficult episode called "Hard Labor." It was supposed to finish on a Tuesday. On Monday, Jim had a very, very heavy day. When he came in at 8:00 he looked at me and said, "Well, John, you know I'm gone at 4:00 this afternoon." I said, "What! What do you mean you're gone at 4:00?" He said, "Yeah, you'd better talk to your boss, Mantley. He's taking me to a football game. I thought you knew that." Well, I didn't know it, of course, so I went to talk to Mantley and John said, "Well, yes, of course, Jim wanted to go to the game, so we're going." With those marching orders we quickly went down to the set, and of course you always did this, changed things around, shot a lot of Jim's close ups out of continuity which we would have done another time and Jim was gone at 4:00. One thing about Jim though, he most always would let us know when he was leaving as he came on the set in the morning. He wouldn't let you know at 4:30 that he was going to be leaving at 5:00 that day. Jim's basic way of filming which we all loved was to get in early and lump all the stuff together. He didn't like to lay around the set wasting time and he'd usually get out of there around 2:00 or 2:30.

Jim had a deep sense of loyalty about his people. He had certain friends that he carried with him his whole time. It was not a group of sycophants or an entourage, just two or three people that always worked on *Gunsmoke*. I always admired that trait in Jim. When he became a star, which happened very early on, he never, ever forgot those people, which was to me really impressive.

After *Gunsmoke* we went on to do *How the West Was Won*. I think the main job I had on that series, other than producing the show, was to find Jim a house, a cook, and a driver. The main thing was that Jim could walk down the streets of Los Angeles and New York and never be bothered. But when we shot westerns in Kanab, Utah; La Junta, Alamosa, and Canyon City, Colorado, places like that where Jim's biggest fans lived, he couldn't go anywhere without drawing a crowd. So we would always find him a house and get him a cook and go from there. I always had a deal with the people whose houses we rented—whatever you do, just tell the folks in town that you're renting your house to a member of the set crew and never say who was going to live in it during a shooting. We'd pay the people then to go to a hotel. No one was ever told that Jim was going to be the occupant of a particular house ... except on one occasion.

Riding with Eva Marie Saint in a covered wagon on location for *How the West Was Won*. (Courtesy of ABC.)

The only thing about that was Jim would get in his plane, wave goodbye and he and his pilot would take off. But instead of heading straight home, being the great practical joker that he was, he'd buzz the set for two hours, rendering our sound totally useless. Finally, the pilot would dip down where we could all see Jim waving goodbye and he was off for Los Angeles. We could then resume shooting.

A lot of people who didn't know Jim were naturally a little bit afraid of him and even though they shouldn't have been, they were. We had a huge, huge scene in Kanab at the fort once and I would say that with the extras, cavalry and Indians and all that, there were at least 200 people. All I wanted to do was get the master scene before lunch. There was no dialogue in it, Jim was all set, no problem at all. I said, "O.K., now everything's fine, the camera's all ready," we'd done a rehearsal and then I left since I had a small matter to take care of. When I came back about 10 minutes later and saw the whole crew leaving for lunch, I thought well great, they've gotten the shot, that's good. I saw the assistant director in the group and said, "Michael, great, you got the shot." He

Someone told and Jim was besieged that night. He came in the next morning and asked me, "What happened?" So we changed houses.

While on location there were certain rules that you abided by with Jim which made perfect sense. Who wanted to lay around Kanab, Utah, for a couple of days with nothing to do? So we had a deal with him whereby he would shoot everyday he was on location. No off days. Then on Saturdays he had to be gone by noon. That was the rule and we always adhered to it.

answered, "No, we didn't get the shot, we broke for lunch." I said, "You broke for lunch? Why?" He said, "Well, I just looked over at Jim and he happened to say, 'I'm hungry,' and I said, 'Oh you're hungry, OK, lunch, one-half hour.'" I told the director that he didn't understand Jim, Jim didn't mean you had to break the crew, he was just making a statement that he was hungry. I went and talked with Jim and he laughed and said, "Well, when the assistant director tells me it's lunch, it's lunch, right?" "Yes, yes, right," I said. But that was Jim.

Jim always would pretend that he didn't really read the scripts or didn't know the scenes that well, but he really did. We were shooting day for night (shooting bright sunlight through trees using a camera lens that would give a moonlight effect) on *West* once and the light had to be exactly so or you can't do day for night. I remember at 9:00 we'd lost the day-for-night light so we decided to spend the rest of the day shooting a nine page scene with Jim and Bruce Boxleitner. I knew that they hadn't read the script and they were not prepared to do it. I went to the two of them and said, "Look, if I let the crew just hang around until 1:00 and then call an hour for lunch from 1:00 to 2:00, do you think we can give that scene a go? If you don't think so, we'll go with some little scene but I'd kind of like to get that done." They both agreed to give it try but Jim added, "I don't know about this. I'll see what I can do. I'll let you know at 2:00." So, fine, I schedule a lunch call for 1:00. At 11:30, two and a half hours later, Jim

walked out of his motor home and said "Let's do the scene now. I'm ready. Ask Bruce." Bruce came out and was kind of stunned. He took an extra 20 or 30 minutes. We actually did that scene, a nine page scene that they had never actually studied up on, in I'd say at the most two hours, which was somewhat incredible. I would say that along with Brian Keith and Mickey Rooney, Jim was probably the fastest study that I had ever worked with. He was just amazing in that way. The only problem I ever had with Jim was that he was always for saying less. He always thought less was better, more was too much. And it got to the point where we'd be going over scenes on *West* and Jim would say, "Well I don't have to say THAT. Why doesn't HE say that. Why don't we cut THIS page here. Do we really need THAT page there?" I'd say, "Jim, would you like to ADD something?" "Well, no, I don't want to ADD anything!" "Well, Jim, we're doing a two hour show, you know, and the way we're going we'll wind up with a 45 minute show instead of a two hour show." So the only battle I would say in the years that I worked with Jim was convincing him that if we were going to take a line out, we'd have to add a line in. If he didn't feel comfortable doing a line then we'd give the line to someone else. But we couldn't just keep cutting scripts down and down. So he'd agree, but it was always a struggle. It was kind of like a game between the two of us and it was a lot of fun. Also when we had a difficult show to shoot, we'd try to use a certain stable of actors and actresses that we

On the set of *How the West Was Won*. (Taken by Janet Arness.)

I know, but we never wanted to take a chance with our major star doing any tough stuff. In the scene we were shooting we had a canoe coming into shore. So we planned to have a little fellow, a professional canoeist, start paddling the canoe toward the shore quite a ways back and stop at a certain point. Then we wanted to have Jim's stunt double, Ben Bates, pick up the canoe and bring it all the way up to the shore, lift Vera Miles out of the canoe and then we'd put Jim into the shot and have him carry Vera a few feet, kneel down with her, and start to talk with her. Well, when we got up there, Ben Bates informed me that he was scared to death of water. He couldn't swim. Who would think that the "Marlboro Man" was afraid of water and couldn't swim! So we had to find someone to do the middle part of it after the regular canoeist got finished. We found a prop man who'd been with Gunsmoke and then *West* for years. He was close to Jim in size and we'd be far enough away so that he wouldn't be recognizable. So we used the prop man to do the paddling up until you could make out his build then we put Ben Bates in the canoe and he paddled up to shore, lifted Vera out and then we put Jim in

knew Jim really liked and enjoyed working with. The episode always worked out well when we used these people. Belinda Montgomery, Jack Elam, people like that made Jim comfortable and he usually did his best acting when surrounded by these folks.

Jim loved to have certain people like Ben Bates, his double and stuntman, and Dick Lundin, the wrangler, around. I remember that we were going to Bend, Oregon, to do a very, very difficult white water show. And naturally, in the scenes we used doubles whenever we could. Jim did a lot of his stuff in the early years of *Gunsmoke*, to do the final scene. So that meant that we had one, two, three, four people, including Jim to do the shot. But everything went off like clockwork and the scene was flawless.

One thing I most admired about Jim was, and people would be surprised how many stars get into this, that he never tried to tell us how to do our job. Jim put total faith in us, never said, "I don't like this location," or "I don't like that camera person," or "Can we hire this person for that or that person for this?" It's so much easier for the producer and from my point of view mostly handling the production end of producing, I know that John Mantley would feel the same way. We'd get these stories to Jim on *West* and there was seldom if ever a problem; if one did arise it would be discussed with John Mantley and by the time we went to script there was never any discussion about, "I wouldn't do this, I won't do that." As I said earlier, all Jim liked to do was to make things as short as possible. But most stars today seem to know not only their jobs but ours as well. Which can make it a little difficult and sometimes you start to think about maybe they really DO know our job better. But not Jim. He was just great. He was such a big star and yet you never felt intimidated in his presence. He was just a real, real down to earth guy. I've never told this before but prior to becoming a production manager, I was a casting director. I met Jim a few times for a couple of shows and lucky for Jim he didn't get them. I remember seeing the first episode of *Gunsmoke* and I said, "Oh, boy,

that's really a show!" So I was well aware of what a great show I was walking into. I was unable to work on the pilot of *How the West Was Won* but did produce the other shows. On the first season of *West* we did a six hour miniseries that was shot half in Kanab and half at the Hunter ranch. The second year we did a 20-hour mini-series, which was basically a serial, going back-to-back with only two directors, Vince and Bernie McEveety. The third season we did ten two-hour episodes, back-to-back, with only an eight day break in the whole schedule. Now I daresay that there's no other show that works like that. One of the reasons was that the cast and crew were able to work so well together. And to get such results everything starts from the top. With Jim and John Mantley, everybody had a job to do and did it. No one questioned how anyone was doing their job, it was all done. We were prepared. That was the big thing. On *West* we didn't even have a location manager. The director and I would go up, actually the production manager and I would go up first, pick the locations, then John Mantley would come up and OK them with the director. And they were always OK'd. Later when we were at Universal, John Mantley and I were called up to find out if we had any suggestions. We handed them the crew sheet of *How the West Was Won*, which I attributed all to the top people and that would be Jim and, of course, John. On the *West* episodes John Mantley was the executive producer and I was the producer. We had a story editor, Cal Clemens, one helper, one unit manager and two first assistant directors. That was it. When we got to Universal, we wound up with nine and ten producers, who were all basically writers, writing one scene here and two scenes there, but never, ever contributed to the production effort as we did.

Today when I hear Jim's booming voice over the phone I remember those wonderful years that we worked together. There's no question that he's an icon that will live forever in the hearts and minds of those he worked with and the millions of *Gunsmoke* fans that still remember "The Marshal."

Ben Bates

(Ben Bates was my photographic double and stuntman during the last few years of *Gunsmoke* and all three years of *How the West Was Won*. Ben was a super rough guy who had been raised on a ranch and early on joined the rodeo circuit doing steer wrestling. He still appears in the ring doing team roping. Ben looked a lot like me, was tall and had a build similar to mine. During shoots when he doubled for me he could come fairly close to the camera before I was put into the scene for close up work and dialogue. Ben was one of the two original "Marlboro Men," and did television Marlboro commercials, appeared on billboards and ads for the company for eight years. This eventually led to work at the studios and roles in various films and television. During our time together we became great friends and he re-

mains one of my closest buddies to this day.)

BEN SAYS: I went to work for Jim along about 1972 and right away I could tell that he was a happy go lucky guy who liked a good joke. One day we were sittin' on the porch outside the old Marshal's Office in Dodge City and I was telling him a joke. The director at the time was Gunnar Hellstrom who was an actor and through Jim was given the opportunity to direct one of the episodes. So I was sitting with Jim telling him this joke and I wasn't paying any attention to what was going on inside the office. I hit the punch line about the time Gunnar yelled "Action!" and Jim went into a fit of laughter. If you ever heard Jim laugh, he laughs from his toes to the top of his head when something strikes him funny. And this time he just couldn't stop laughing. Gunnar hollered, "Cut. Cut. Cut. Get that SOB off my set!" not knowing it was Jim out there laughing. It was really funny. Jim just casually got up and walked off. And, of course, there were five or six others out there who were laughing too. We immediately shut up. But Jim just couldn't stop and had to leave the set.

On another occasion we were shooting out at Tapo Canyon. We shot a lot of *Gunsmoke* episodes out there. It was over in Simi Valley, California, not too far from Jim's ranch where he kept his plane. Jim really loved to fly and one day he had it set up with Johnny Flynn, our camera operator, to film him buzzing the set. All of a sudden here comes this plane flying at tree top level down the valley and everyone ran for cover. Of course, Johnny got it all on film, though everyone pretty much knew that it was Jim up to his old tricks. Jim came sauntering onto the set the next morning, acting very casual and nonchalant. However, when Johnny showed the film to the crew which had caught them scurrying in every direction, Jim and the gang got a big laugh out of the prank.

After a period of time where I was doubling for Jim and doing his stunt work, I was going to quit because of a hassle I was having with the assistant director, basically over my pay and some other matters. It got to be something that I just didn't want to deal

On the set of *How the West Was Won*. **(Taken by Janet Arness.)**

with anymore. I discussed my intention with my good friend, Johnny Flynn, who told Kenny Curtis and it wasn't long before Jim knew about my situation. He subsequently asked me how things were going. I asked him if I could be honest with him and he said "Yes" and I proceeded to tell him of the problems I was encountering. After I finished he said, "Don't quit. Let me see what I can get done." Well, after lunch here comes Larry Kaaspins who was one of the producers of *Gunsmoke* at the time. And we hashed out a deal

where I didn't have to walk any streets or stand-in for anyone else or do anything. I was only to rehearse script lines with Jim, double for him and whenever they needed a stunt man for him, I would be given the job. So I was totally there for Jim, which made it better for both of us. We became close friends over the years and I always appreciated his loyalty. Each year he would make them pay me more money and the outstanding way he treated me is something that I'll never forget. But that was the kind of person he was and

Eva Marie Saint on the set of *How the West Was Won*. (Arness Collection.)

raring to go. He just had this knack of bringing life to people when things were down. It was amazing the effect he had on people on the set.

Before we left the *Gunsmoke* set Jim called me over and said, "Here, I want you to have this." And he gave me the '45 that he had been using all those years. He said, "You mean more to me than putting this into a museum somewhere." You can imagine how that made me feel, that he would want me to have that gun. It will always be in my possession and I treasure it like few other things I own.

Also, Jim later sent word by way of Bob Emme to let me know that if things got tough I was to call him because there would always be "bean money" for me.

still is. He's of the old breed, you know, they take care of their own. I'd seen him many times come on a set, things would be dragging, people would be dragging, maybe toward the end of the week or maybe just one of those days when everyone wasn't up to par. Jim would yodel a few times, maybe do a line or might even blow a line or something, then let out this yodel and laugh about it. First thing you know, everybody was "up." Everybody was up on their toes, everybody was ready and

When we started doing *The Macahans*, which later became *How the West Was Won*, I was given a pair of tennis shoes with some leather-like material over the top of them to wear instead of having boots similar to what Jim wore on the show. We were doing some scenes down an incline and I don't know if you've ever played tennis or worn tennis shoes (the old kind) very much, but you can imagine what happens to your toes when you're dig-

With Jack Elam (left) and unidentified actors on the set of *How the West Was Won***. (Arness Collection.)**

ging into rough terrain while going down a steep hill. My toes and feet became swollen and painful. Jim found out about it, but I said nothing to him, just went on. Finally, he asked me what was wrong with my feet. I told him about the modified tennis shoes and the material they had put over them to look like moccasins and the discomfort I was experiencing. Jim was upset on hearing this and the next day a Beverly Hills shoemaker was building me a set of boots like his. Jim told the people in charge that if they couldn't afford to build me a pair of shoes like his, they couldn't afford to do the show. Needless to say I was soon wearing a new pair of boots and my foot problems disappeared.

During another shoot of *The Macahans* we were on what they called the Arizona strip in Kanab, Utah, just south of Kanab near the Arizona line. We had this big Conestoga wagon and Eva Marie Saint was playing the wife of Jim's brother, played by Richard Kiley I believe. She had a whole bunch of dialogue and we were gonna wrap up the show that evening and leave the next day. It was getting a little late and it was trying to rain. The guys were all restless and got to talkin'. Well she'd get into her dialogue and somebody would say something that was not very courteous. About the second time it happened, Jim had had enough. In fact, it was the first time that I saw him really put his foot down. He told everyone to shut up. I mean you coulda heard a pin drop.

On the set of *How the West Was Won* with **Eva Marie Saint.** (**Arness Collection.**)

Later while shooting the follow-on series *How the West Was Won* in Canyon City, Colorado, we used our time off on the Fourth of July to see some rodeos. We took three days off and we visited several. At the time I was still active in the rodeo circuit, entering steer roping events. John Mantley, our executive director for *How the West Was Won*, told me that whatever I did, "Just don't get hurt!" I told him that I never get hurt but lo and behold in the next rodeo I went into, a horse reared up and jumped out over the side of the roping box and I hung my toe trying to get off him and as we hit the ground I broke my right wrist. Well I went back to work three days later with my arm in a cast. We tried to camouflage it, fix it so that I could go ahead and double for Jim. However, it got to the point where the cast had to be removed to do a scene and then put back on when we were finished. When we'd finish one of these scenes, Jim would say, "Well, we fooled them one more time." Because of the injury they were going to send me home and I told Jim, "Well, it looks like I'm going to be leaving tomorrow," and he said, "What do you mean?" I answered, "Well, they're gonna send me back to L.A." He said, "They are, are they?" I answered, "Yes sir, that's what they tell me." Well, about twenty minutes later the director walked up to me and told me, "You are now my right hand. Everywhere I go, I want you to be a shadow." I said, "O.K." I later found out that Jim had told the producer and director that if they went ahead and bought a ticket for me for L.A., they might as well buy one for him, 'cause he was leaving too. So I stayed and there was a scene where we had to stage a fight. I went to Jim and asked him if I set the scene up could he do it, 'cause I was coordinating that part of the episode. He said, "Well sure." I choreographed the fight so Jim could do it. He really did an excellent job! His punches were brisk and crisp and he just looked great on film.

Some years later I was scheduled to go to Canada to scout out locations for a follow-on series of *Gunsmoke* episodes. The first of the five shows was called *Return to Dodge*. Between 1987 and 1994 two-hour specials were aired. I was to be sent ahead to not only scout locations but recommend where it would be convenient to put Jim's mobile home once a location was determined. Also, I was to check out the horses that were going to be used, especially in a case like this where we were going to be out of the United States and didn't know what kind of horses would be made available to us. And when Jim would arrive at the location I would help him get along because of his bad leg. Before I made the trip I met with the production manager and we talked about salary, how long I was going to stay, etc. He subsequently approached me and said, "Look, we're not going to be able to take you because we're only gonna take the cast and half of our camera people. The Canadians won't let you go, won't let you in to work. They want to use their own stunt people." So I called Jim and told him that it didn't look like I was gonna be able to go to Canada with him. Right away he wanted to

know why I didn't want to go. I said, "Sure I want to go, you know that." Then I told him what was happening. He never said yea, nay, kiss my butt or anything. About 30 minutes later I got a call from the production manager wanting to know how much I wanted a week, when did I want to leave, and the whole shootin' match. Well, come to find out, I guess Jim got ahold of him and flat told him, "I've been doin' these *Gunsmokes* a lot of years and they've never done one without me, and if Ben Bates doesn't go, then I don't go!"

During a later shoot of one of the "specials," we were down in Del Rio, Texas, and I had my family with me. My son, Brandon, walked behind one of the horses and there was a burro walking along a nearby fence. Brandon's sudden appearance spooked the burro and she flopped around and knocked him down. His leg came up between the animal's hind legs and she jumped sideways and broke his leg. Brandon was in the hospital when Jim found out about it and he immediately offered to have Brandon flown out in his Learjet to any medical facility my wife and I recommended. I thanked Jim but Brandon was all right where he was, so he stayed there. Everyone on the set went to visit him while we did the show. And, as always Jim was there for all of us.

I must admit that Jim was not the only prankster on the show. We all at one time or another played tricks on each other to keep things lively. Years ago Jim, who rarely smoked, used to light up a big Macanudo cigar. Well

Ben Bates. (Arness Collection.)

to lunch I opened his book, took his Macanudo, replaced it with one of my King Edwards and lit up. Tiny returned from lunch, sat down and opened his book to find my little King Edward staring up at him. The guy went into a rage, jumping up and down (all 400 pounds of him) yelling that someone stole his cigar. I was sitting there right in front of him puffing away and he didn't catch on. Finally, when he cooled down and realized that I was the culprit he came over to me and said, "You got no class, you just got no class to take a man's cigar." Jim and the crew got a big chuckle out of the whole affair and Tiny and I eventually buried the hatchet.

I remember another time when Jim had a line that went something like, "The bridge is out, you say?" And this line struck Jim as being funny and he got to laughing about it so much that they had to go to another scene until the script could be fixed. When Jim finally did the bridge scene later he could hardly keep a straight face remembering the original line.

One occasion really sticks out in my mind. There was a pretty big scene to be played in which Milburn Stone, Kenny Curtis and Jim had to interact with a lot of dialogue. Jim looked over the script while sitting on the set and just flat rewrote the scene. He would say to the others, "Just get rid of this line, you say this, and you say this and I'll say this," and it got to the point where the frustrated director called

there was a guy that was a first assistant director, his name was Tiny Nichols. He'd been with the crew for many years and in fact during the early years of *Gunsmoke* Jim used to take him with him on personal appearances at fairs and rodeos. Tiny would take pictures of Jim and have them printed up and go through the stands selling them to Jim's fans. Tiny also smoked Macanudos and every day when he went to lunch he'd leave one in his script book. I was cutting down on my smoking at the time, using only King Edward cigars. One day when Tiny went

John Mantley down to straighten out the situation. John joined the group and the set was shut down. Together they rewrote the scene, put it together and were ready to shoot in about 45 minutes. The scene was one of the best in the episode. Jim was really sharp about such things. He knew instinctively when something just wouldn't work. I watched him time and again, shake his head over a script and call everyone together including Mantley and make suggestions about revising the script. They would all listen to what he had to say and they'd agree to change the script. The scene would be shot, printed and the end result was always better than what they had started with.

I remember one time we were down in Tucson and Jim asked, "What are you doin' this weekend?" I said, "Just laying around the motel. I don't have anything to do. I'm not working." We were both off and a lot of times they'd let Jim off and I'd do what I could for him so he could go and didn't have to be there. This weekend I didn't have anything to do for him so he asked if I'd like to join him for a run down to the Red River Cattle Company at Gila Bend. He said that John Wayne had asked him to come down and look at his operation. I jumped at the chance to go so Jim called down to "Duke" and asked if I could come along. Wayne said, "Yeah, bring your cowboy friend on. I'll show him some good horses." On the way down Jim told me, "Now whatever you do, don't talk about politics. Whatever he says about it, just agree with him." Well, evidently Wayne

was a kind of a dyed in the wool Republican and he had his own thoughts about politics and they were pretty strong. And if you didn't agree with him you'd stir up a hornet's nest. So we went down there and we had a great time. When we sat down to lunch Jim and I were treated to delicious looking T-bone steaks while Wayne was brought a tuna salad plate. Wayne was sitting between us. Jim looked over at me and asked, "How's your steak?" I said, "Oh, man it's really good, nice and tender and cooked just right." Jim then looked over at Wayne and his little old tuna salad and said something to the effect that, "it's no use asking you how your tuna is," and began to laugh. Jokingly, Wayne told us we could leave. But we just hung around for the day telling stories and having some good laughs. Before we left, Wayne showed us some really first rate horseflesh.

In the mid '70s Dinah Shore wanted Jim to appear on her show. The theme was that while Jim was on stage reading a Daniel Webster speech, Dinah would be singing "God Bless America" from a balcony. The show was to be done at the Grand Old Opry in Nashville. When they began to lay out the scene, Jim said that he would prefer to deliver the speech on screen and that to make the scene more realistic he would send his double out to appear on stage. So he called me up and wanted to know if I wanted to go to Nashville, and I said, "Yeah, when are we leaving?" He said, "*We* aren't leaving. *You* are." I said, "What's happening?" He explained everything about the show and what my role would be. He said, "Come by and pick up my tux and I'll have your plane ticket ready for you." So I flew back to Nashville and it was supposed to be that I'd fly in, work the next day and fly home. Well, I got there on a Sunday and the next day I went over to Dinah's office and in she comes with her hair in curlers and walked right by me. She quickly turned and said, "You have to be Ben Bates, James Arness' double." I said, "Yes, Ma'am." She brought me some coffee and told me that I wouldn't be working until Thursday or Friday. I answered that they told me that I was to work that day. She said that she'd take care of the miscommunication and left the office and was back in 30 minutes with a young man who was to be my driver for the week. Well, Jim sent me back there to do this thing, so I spent a week just bumming around with Jack Benny and we had a fine time. If it hadn't been for Jim I probably wouldn't have got to meet Benny, who was a great guy and a very funny person. We did the show Thursday evening and I was introduced and walked out onto the stage and stood a little to the left of a large screen which suddenly lit up and there was Jim all dressed up in his *Gunsmoke* gear starting to give the speech which he had filmed back in Hollywood. While Jim droned on, Dinah was up in the balcony singing her heart out. The audience loved it.

When we did *The Macahans* and were looking at film clips for potential cast members, Jim personally picked Bruce Boxleitner because he saw something in him that he liked and felt that

he would be comfortable working with him. When the public relations folks wanted Jim to go out and do interviews, he'd always tell them to "Send out the 'kids,' send out Boxleitner," saying that they needed the exposure and experience. He wasn't like most actors. They usually wanted to hog the spotlight. Jim felt that he didn't need the exposure. They knew who Jim Arness was and it was time that the younger members of the cast got to be known by the press and others in the business. Even when we did *McClain's Law* he did the same thing with another young actor, Marshall Colt. Colt was a tall, slim, good looking guy who turned out to be a pretty good actor. He had recently left the Navy to try his hand at acting. Unfortunately, not much happened for him after *McClain's Law* and he rejoined the Navy. It was during that time that I got my Directors Guild Card, so I could direct the second unit, which had a lot to do on the show. The first person that I had an opportunity to direct was Jim for some pick-up lines. After he did the lines, I hollered "Cut" and then turned to Jim and said, "How'd I do boss?" and he said, "That's my line, I'm supposed to be asking you how I did." We had a big laugh over that. But I thought that it was pretty fitting that when I finally got my DGA card I'd direct Jim. With that much talent how could I go wrong!

Probably one of my most vivid memories of working with Jim occurred when we were up in Canyon City, Colorado, and we were doing *The Macahans* and there was a very, very

Shot of Jim and Ricardo Montalban on the set of *How the West Was Won.* **(Taken by Janet Arness.)**

touching scene between Ricardo Montalban, who played an Indian chief, and Jim, which required a lot of dialogue. They sat there and did these lines and the scene was flawless. On the way in from the set that evening in our van, Ricardo was sitting in the front seat and I was sitting right behind him. Jim was riding in another van up ahead. Ricardo turned around to me and he said something that was probably one of the greatest tributes to Jim as an actor and the star he really was. He said, "You know, Ben, very few people in this business realize what a great talent Jim Arness is, what a great dramatic actor this man is. They take him for granted because he's done *Gunsmoke* for so many years and be-

lieve he should be doing other things besides just acting in westerns." He said, "I've worked with a lot of people in my lifetime and I've never worked with anyone with more talent than James Arness." I remembered thinking what a great compliment coming from someone like Ricardo Montalban.

I owe a great debt of gratitude and thanks to Jim for allowing me to double for him all those years. Because of the many opportunities he gave me in *Gunsmoke* and *How the West Was Won*, many doors in the picture business subsequently opened up for me. I owe it all to Jim Arness as do many others whom he helped over the years. Few people know about the many things he did for people because Jim didn't talk about such matters, he was a very private man. I think that he's one of the greatest, and I've worked with some of the finest actors in the business. The only bad thing about working for Jim Arness was that he spoiled us when we went to work for someone else.

I wish we could do it all over again. Those were unforgettable days.

Morgan Woodward

(Morgan Woodward holds the record for most appearances on *Gunsmoke*: 19. He's a superb character actor and a wonderful person. He usually played the "heavy" on our shows and I really enjoyed working with him because he was what you would call a real "pro." Morgan was born in Fort Worth, Texas, and served in the U.S. Air Force as a pilot during World War II and the Korean War. He's a collector of antique aircraft and still flies today. Morgan has appeared in over 250 television and motion picture films and in addition to *Gunsmoke* starred in 11 episodes of *Wagon Train*, *Logan's Run* (1977–1978), *Days of Our Lives* (1987–1988) and *Dallas* (1980–1988), a top rated television series in the world for several years, where he portrayed the character "Punk Anderson." He was an outstanding contender for the 1967 Motion Picture Academy Award in a supporting role for his portrayal of "the man with no eyes" in *Cool Hand Luke*, which starred Paul Newman.)

Morgan Woodward. (Morgan Woodward Collection.)

MORGAN SAYS: I think it was 1957 when I did my first *Gunsmoke*. It was a thirty minute show and I had a small part in that episode. Because of a disagreement with one of the producers on the show, I didn't return to *Gunsmoke* until 1965 when a friend of mine who I had worked with before became producer. The first show I appeared in was "Seven Hours to Dawn" in which John Drew Barrymore played a leading role. This began a long stretch of *Gunsmoke* appearances for me, 19 in all. I appeared on the show more times than any other guest performer.

Jim Arness is one of the nicest guys, if not *the* nicest guy, I worked with during my 48 year career run in Hollywood. I have never heard any bad things about him or heard him bad-mouthed by anyone who knew him or worked with him. He's a very accommodating guy. He and I got along great and I think he enjoyed working with me. I sure as hell enjoyed working with him. We were not social because he's a very private guy. He was always kind of a loner and I understand that because I've been told that I'm the same way. But when we were together we had a wonderful time. He had a great sense of humor, a dry wit, at times somewhat ribald, and loved a good story. It was a pleasure to be on the *Gunsmoke* set because Amanda Blake always liked a good joke and she had a most raucous laugh which you could hear all over the set and you could hear old Jim laughing along with her. That whole group of Milburn, Ken, and Buck Taylor and everybody on the show were all great friends. It was a very pleasant place to work and the producer, John Mantley, was a great guy to work with. It was just a wonderful show and it was the best time of my life in Hollywood in all the years I worked in show business. I was on *Dallas* for eight years and I really enjoyed that, but *Gunsmoke* was the high point of my film career, it was just sensational and Jim was a big part of that.

Jim apparently heard that I was a flier and one day we got to talking about the subject and he said he had an interest in flying. So a few days later when we both had some time off we went out to Van Nuys airport and climbed in my plane and took off. It was an absolutely perfect day and we flew up over the mountains and started out over the ocean. There was a beautiful storm coming in and I started chasing clouds. I'd dive down through the clouds and skim over the ocean and then go back up through the clouds. Old Jim was sitting in the back seat and just yelling whoa, whoa, he just had a great time. I think that ride really sold him on flying. When we got down on the ground he said, "Well, by golly, that was really great and I'm going to start flying." The next day I went to an aircraft book store and bought him his first private pilot book and I said to him jokingly, "Here's your first private flying book and that'll be five bucks." Jim, who was one of the best paid actors in Hollywood, kind of stammered and said, "Well, O.K., but I don't have any money." We both got a laugh out of that. He really did well with his flying; he went on and got his commercial license and I believe he got his instrument ticket. He eventually bought a Beechcraft "Baron" and later a de Havilland "Beaver." His buzzing of *Gunsmoke* sets almost became legendary.

I remember one time we were doing a show where I was to ride onto the set and Matt was up on a hill standing next to his horse. I was to ride up the hill and confront him about something, I don't remember exactly what it was—usually I played the heavy in the *Gunsmoke* series. They had the camera set up and I came galloping up the hill and got off to confront him and I walked up to him and as you know Jim was 6' 7" and I was no little guy myself, I was 6' 3". He was standing on the side of the hill next to his horse and it looked to me like I was speaking my lines into his belt buckle. I got tickled and ruined the shot when I turned around and said, "Excuse me but this is looking a little risque here since I'm looking right into Jim's fly, do you want to continue this scene?" Well, everyone broke up and that ended the shoot. We did it again and I rode up onto the hill to a point where we could look at each other eyeball to eyeball so I could confront him.

Another episode, "Matt Dillon Must Die," was shot up in the mountains of Utah. I played a crazy old man, Abraham Wakefield, and had a bunch of sons, one of whom had challenged Jim and drew on him. Of course, Jim shot first. My sons and I started after him to make him pay for his dastardly deed. We caught up with him and I told him that he was going to pay for what he had done and told him to start digging his grave. I was standing there watching him and my dialogue went something like, "O.K. Dillon, that's deep enough. You got any last words to say?" He was standing in this hole with a shovel in his hand and his hat on and his dialogue in the script was, "You're never going to get away with this, Wakefield, they'll catch you and your boys and you'll pay." That was rehearsed and the director said "Action" and I delivered my line. Then Jim dropped the shovel, took off his hat and looked skyward and in a very solemn voice said, "The Lord giveth and the Lord taketh away and if that ain't a square

deal I'll kiss your ass." That broke up the director and the crew and we didn't get the set back together again for another twenty minutes until people could stop laughing. But that's the kind of guy he was, blowing lines with his great sense of humor. By the way, they didn't use the retake scene in the film.

The last picture that Jim and I did together was a 1992 *Gunsmoke* TV sequel, *To the Last Man*. It was an action-packed episode. Pat Hingle was one of the other co-stars with me and he had five or six sons. Jim and I took on the whole bunch and it was one hell of a shoot out. Jim and I killed everything in sight except the cows.

I look back on those shows with affection. I just think what a remarkable achievement it was to have a show on the air and to have been that popular for 20 years. It's extraordinary ... how years after the show closed so many people come up and still talk about *Gunsmoke* saying, "God, I wish it were still on." My answer is always the same: "I wish it was on too, it was one of the best television series ever produced."

Bruce Boxleitner

(I really enjoyed working with Bruce, first in the series *How the West Was Won*, then in a *Gunsmoke* sequel and later in the made-for-television movie *Red River*. Bruce was just a young man when he was cast as my nephew in *The Macahans*, which later became the series *How the West Was*

With Gregory Harrison (left) and Bruce Boxleitner in Tucson during the filming of the 1988 TV movie *Red River*. (Arness Collection.)

Won. He was comfortable to work with, laid back like I was, and very professional for a young actor. We had many good times together and, like many of the people I worked with, he loved to laugh and thoroughly enjoyed his chosen profession. Bruce came to Los Angeles in 1972 and was given five lines on an episode of *The Mary Tyler Moore Show*. This earned him his Screen Actors Guild card and he promptly embarked on a series of screen tests and auditions which ultimately led to his joining us on *West*. Since that time he has appeared in numerous motion pictures and television productions. He starred in the adventure/espionage series *Scarecrow and Mrs. King* from 1983 to 1987 and played "Commander John Sheridan" in the syndicated series *Babylon 5*, which ran for five seasons. In 1995 he co-starred with his real life wife, Melissa Gilbert, in *Danielle Steel's Zoya*, on NBC-TV, a four hour miniseries based on the novel. In addition to his film work, Bruce is a gifted author. His most recent book is *Frontier Earth*, a science fiction novel.)

BRUCE SAYS: I was in Phoenix, Arizona, recently at an event called "Festival of the West." Buck Taylor was there and he and I competed against each other in a few events in the arena and he came in a close second to me. Well, we began to talk about Jim Arness and within two minutes we were both doubled over with laughter. We both do a mean imitation of him and whenever we get together we both talk like Jim. Buck and I worked with Jim for a long time. Buck spent a number of years with him on *Gunsmoke* and later on I worked with him on *How the West Was Won*, *Red River* and a follow-on *Gunsmoke* sequel. Both of us owe Jim a great deal of gratitude for being a strong positive influence on us early on in our careers and he was certainly an outstanding role model.

Just as an interesting sidelight there was a guy at the festival who was walking around impersonating John Wayne. Although he had all the mannerisms of Wayne and was dressed like "Duke," he bore little resemblance to the man. However, he honestly believed that he was John Wayne. Also, there was a guy there who was all over Buck and me pretending to be Festus. He had Festus' lingo down pat and evidently appears at all the western festivals and events. The *Gunsmoke* that I did was predominately with Ken Curtis and I just saw Jim fleetingly. They stuck me in the background with a mule and a plough, playing some kind of farm kid that Festus got mixed up with somehow.

I remember how generous Jim was in allowing us to take his interviews. It was kind of alarming at first 'cause I thought that he was the star of the show, and wondered why he wanted me out there. But he pushed me out there for the exposure and experience and I've been doing it ever since. It was rare that a star of his caliber would give up the spotlight to his young co-stars. I guess he did a lot of press reviews too in his early days. *Gunsmoke* had been a very popular radio show and Jim was under a lot of pressure from the fans because of William Conrad's radio voice, which conjured up an image to the listeners of an older, more rugged Matt Dillon. When it aired on television, the viewers saw a big, fresh faced guy, so he had to live up to Conrad's perceived image. When *Gunsmoke* became so popular it seemed that every stage and screen star wanted to have a guest shot on the show. So Jim found himself playing opposite some pretty talented people. The pressure on him during his early years on *Gunsmoke* must have been enormous.

When I joined *How the West Was Won* I had been bumping around Broadway, playing summer stock, and picking up parts here and there. I was very young and felt a lot of pressure doing these early performances, but I think I handled it pretty well. When I look at some of the early *West* films I looked like just a gangly kid. When I joined the cast I was in complete awe of Jim. He was a father figure for me and I think most of the young actors felt the same way. It was kind of a natural thing for me then because he was my uncle Zeb on the show. I had no trouble relating as an actor because I really loved the man. He was a strong influence because what he said was his bond and I never saw the difference between Jim Arness and Uncle Zeb. I had to be on my toes constantly when I worked with him. It was like working with Mount Rushmore and that mighty voice would come out and it all seemed like a dream come true for me. I never thought that I would be working with someone of his fame. My father was just thrilled to see me working with Jim on a show that millions of Americans watched religiously.

When Jim played Marshal Matt Dillon he was a pretty serious guy. There would be light moments when he was working with Chester or Festus, but basically they were the comedic elements and he was reacting off their antics. By the time he got to

Me and Bruce Boxleitner. (Bruce Boxleitner Collection.)

play Uncle Zeb, he let everything hang out and I sensed that he really relished not having the *Gunsmoke* restraints anymore. He really had a raucous humor. All of us younger folks on the show were kind of in awe of such a big presence. However, he instinctively became this fun loving jokester. We'd be on the set rehearsing, waiting for Jim to arrive and you could hear Jim's high cackling laugh a mile down the road. It just set everybody at ease. For me it was one of the best sets I've ever worked on because we never felt tension. Jim was a great morale booster. The guys just loved him. He was a

man's man and the women loved him. He just had this magnetic charm that drew them to him. But he treated one and all very professionally. I remember when Fionnula Flanagan joined the cast as our Irish aunt who came to look after us kids when Eva Marie Saint left the show. Fionnula was a highly trained Abbey Theater, Dublin, actress and I think Jim's charm totally disarmed her. I thought that they were wonderful together on the screen.

I think that my demeanor on the set came from Jim's example. I liked to joke around too. Some people like to work around chaos on a set. I don't respond too well to that kind of situation. Like Jim, I liked to have a light atmosphere. It's usually a long day, especially when you're doing a western and are out in the elements. It's kind of a great equalizer, even the big stars get some dirt on them.

As I mentioned Jim loved good jokes and he usually would tell one and give the punch line just as the director would yell "Action." And, of course we'd all be in tears laughing, unable to start the scene. He loved to do that. As Zeb he was just a rough mountain man who looked like he'd been shot a number of times and he used the limp caused by his game leg to good advantage on the show. To say he was a "free spirit" would be putting it mildly. I have so many publicity pictures where I'm grinning like a blithering idiot as a result of one of Jim's jokes as the pictures were taken. All he had to do was arch one eyebrow and give me a funny look and I'd be in hysterics.

One night when we were up in Utah, we were shooting a scene where we were working with the famous old Native American actor, Iron Eyes Cody. We were in this Indian encampment and my sister in the story was severely stung by an insect. Zeb took her miles and miles to this Indian medicine man to cure her. Luke, my character, insisted that we take her to a real medical doctor and it came to a point where there was a serious rift when I told Jim that I'd kill him if she died. But I go along with it and we rode way up in the middle of Kanab, Utah. It was cold and we got this camp fire going with Jim,

Will Cullen and me hunched around the fire. My sister was above us with Iron Eyes in a tent as we waited patiently below to learn of her fate. The crane went up to the tent and the director yelled "Iron Eyes, Action!" And suddenly we heard this weird chanting coming from the tent. Jim had this look on his face that had Cullen and me bent over laughing. The director yelled, "Cut, cut, cut!" Unfortunately, Iron Eyes was hard of hearing and didn't hear the order on his walkie talkie in the tent so he continued to wail away. Now all three of us were in a fit of laughter. And as was typical of Jim when he wanted to have fun he wouldn't get back to a serious demeanor until he was ready. We couldn't look at each other. We shot the master a few more times and then did some close-ups and it was even worse. I'd say, "Uncle Zeb, if Jessie dies I'm going to kill you," and he turned to me and said, "Luke, if she dies you won't have to." That was a very long night because we could hardly get through the scene.

Another scene I remember was that when Eva decided to leave the show, she was scripted as dying from a disease. I had to deliver the message to Uncle Zeb and the storyline had me making my way up into the mountains to find him and tell him that my mother was dead. I found his encampment and there he was sitting by a campfire eating some jerky or something. I rode up to where he was and he greeted me with "Luke?" as he arched his eyebrow and had this funny, perplexed look on his face. I said, "Uncle Zeb, Mother is …" and I couldn't finish the line 'cause his look or whatever it was got me laughing and he started in too, we just couldn't get serious. We finally got the line shot and it turned out to be wonderful in the final product.

When *West* went off the air I was devastated since I had hopes that it would continue on like *Gunsmoke* and I would grow up to eventually take over the show. But there came a time when Jim's leg began to bother him so much that he had to leave the show to have it taken care of. With Jim gone, *West* was finished because he *was* the show.

In 1988, I coerced him to be in the TV movie *Red River*. He had to be up on a horse again and though his leg has been somewhat repaired, Ben Bates did most of the riding in the movie. I'll always thank Jim for his participation because CBS was looking for someone else; they wanted Robert Mitchum or Kirk Douglas, or others, all of whom had just too many strings attached to them. I kept saying that James Arness was the only guy to play this part. But the production company, which obviously hadn't made any westerns, didn't want him and they didn't want me. CBS, however, forced them to put me in the movie. I insisted that Arness be hired to do the part, if he would

agree to do it since his close friend John Wayne had done the original movie, perhaps his best film. It was a tough thing for him to do but within a week's notice Jim was ready to go. I kept saying to Jim that we weren't trying to remake that movie but that a good story is a good story and it deserved to be told again. It was my favorite movie and I didn't care if the critics gave us a hard time. The crew was so happy when Jim showed up for his costume fitting. Although they had all of "Duke" Wayne's hats and western outfits, we all tried to find our own different looks; we didn't want to copy the movie. Jim jumped in there and did a wonderful job.

I owe the man a great deal as a role model and as a friend, I don't think you can get any better than that. He was a marvelous performer and much underrated as an actor. Uncle Zeb taught me a lot during our years together and his advice and example enhanced me as a man and movie professional during my career. There are only two big men in Hollywood whose presence captivated Americans of every age: John Wayne and James Arness. I doubt if we'll ever again see anyone like them.

Comments by Guest Stars[*]

Edward Asner: "It was a lovely company to be in ... an excellent show, to sit back and let the guests do the kind of situations and problems that would be found in an anthology show: Thus giving it its lasting power."

Gary Busey: "*Gunsmoke* made me feel a real part of the film community, like I had finally 'made it.' It was a classic American morality play. The first in its class."

David Carradine: "*Gunsmoke* was yet another try at the same old thing; that, because of talent, dedication and good will, managed to go right through the roof into legend status.... James Arness was a great star in an arche-typal role. The loyalty to him and the other characters was enormous."

Anne Francis: "*Gunsmoke* was a good, wholesome show with better-than-average scripts and a dedicated crew ... working with Jim was a great pleasure.... He told me that Lady Bird Johnson had Lyndon Johnson call when the network was planning to ax the show. Her favorite actors were Jim and John Wayne. This was after the show had run 13 years or so!"

Beverly Garland: "I felt it was a fine show for the kids, which made it great for the whole family. There was always a sense of family on that show. No one on it was 'the star.' They were

Permission granted by SuzAnne and Gabor Barabas to use comments from their book, Gunsmoke: A Complete History and Analysis of the Legendary Broadcast Series, McFarland & Company, Inc., Publishers, Jefferson, North Carolina, 1990.

there to make this fine show and we all worked together to find the very best in each other. Of course it was work, but it was always fun because they were the best people. I adored all of them.... I also remember I had finished my day's work, but they were still shooting and said, 'Go on, Bev. Take off your costume and then come back to the set.' When I returned, there was the most beautiful birthday cake you have ever seen ... just for me. I can't remember that ever happening on a TV show."

Darryl Hickman: "*Gunsmoke* was a beautifully devised show ... with appealing characters that the audience came to love. It had good stories, consistency of character, strong producer supervision."

Pat Hingle: "*Gunsmoke* was the best western TV series ever made, in my opinion. It gave me recognition throughout the country in a way Broadway plays, feature films and other TV never had.... I had never done a series before. *Gunsmoke* spoiled me. They were in their 17th year, I think, and by far the best organized TV production group I've been associated with in my 37 years as a professional actor."

George Kennedy: "*Gunsmoke* was the best of all TV westerns and it's still as good as it was."

Cloris Leachman: "The show ran for 20 years because of guts and thunder ... but there was always time to stop and share a kindness."

Michael Learned: "I played a Western woman named Mike, feisty, living alone, very self sufficient and quite verbose. I did all the talking and the camera was on James Arness. It was so long ago, first or second year of *The Waltons*.... I rode a horse, very badly, and felt awfully nervous about being on a show I'd watched as a young girl.... James Arness was charming and humble with a great sense of humor."

Ruta Lee: "In one episode Matt Dillon was to interrupt my seduction of him by picking me up out of the bed, slinging me over his shoulder and taking me down the hall to Miss Kitty. He did so, and in the process slammed my head against the door frame, knocking me out cold. I came to in the arms of big Jim Arness, frantic with worry—tears in his eyes, asking if I was all right. Not everyone could bring tears to Jim's eyes. I loved it!"

Guy Stockwell: "I miss doing the western.... The smell of a western set will last forever, fondly in my memory. *Gunsmoke* has images dating to my first listening to it in college—absolute fascination—it seemed so much more real! ... It never changed; like the Pacific Ocean, you could always tune in for a fix ... like visiting the family, safely, for the holidays."

Loretta Swit: "The ensemble of players were wonderful and the quality of work was always high. It was a happy company. Milburn (Millie) Stone made Jim Arness laugh and vice versa. They really enjoyed each other.... The two shows I did were such wonderful experiences. I remember so much about them so many years later."

Prominent actors and actresses who appeared on *Gunsmoke* include: Claude Akins, Jack Albertson*, Morey Amsterdam, Keith Andes, Jean Arthur**, Edward Asner, Lew Ayers**, Jim Backus, Joe Don Baker, John Drew Barrymore, Richard Basehart, Ned Beatty, Noah Beery, Jr., Ed Begley*, Ralph Bellamy**, Theodore Bikel**, Beulah Bondi**, Bruce Boxleitner, Scott Brady, Neville Brand, Beau Bridges, James Broderick, Steve Brodie, Charles Bronson, Geraldine Brooks, James Brown, Ellen Burstyn*, Gary Busey, Sebastian Cabot, Rory Calhoun, Dyan Cannon**, Harry Carey, Jr., David Carradine, John Carradine, Jack Cassidy**, Richard Chamberlain, Lee J. Cobb**, Chuck Connors, Jackie Coogan, Ellen Corby**, Robert Culp, Bette Davis*, Gloria de Haven, Bruce Dern, William Devane, Andy Devine, Angie Dickinson, Tom Drake, Richard Dreyfuss, Buddy Ebsen, Barbara Eden, Jack Elam, Sam Elliot, Nina Foch**, Harrison Ford, Steve Forrest, Jodie Foster*, Michael Fox, Anne Francis, Arthur Franz, Vincent Gardenia**, Beverly Garland, Will Geer, Melissa Gilbert, Thomas Gomez**, Alan Hale, Margaret Hamilton, Eileen Heckert*, Darryl Hickman, Pat Hingle, Earl Holliman, Dennis Hopper, Ronny Howard, Arthur Hunnicutt**, Marsha Hunt, Kim Hunter*, Betty Hutton, John Ireland**, Anne Jackson, Richard Jaeckel**, Ben Johnson*, Victor Jory, DeForest Kelley, Jack Kelly, George Kennedy*, John Kerr**, Jack Klugman, Martin Landau, Cloris Leachman*, Michael Learned, Ruta Lee, June Lockhart, Robert Loggia, Jack Lord, James MacArthur, Lee Majors, John Marley**, Marilyn Maxwell, Mercedes McCambridge*, Darren McGavin, Vera Miles, Cameron Mitchell, Ricardo Montalban, Wayne Morris, Patricia Morrow, Conrad Nagel, J. Carroll Naish**, Gene Nelson, Leslie Nielsen, Leonard Nimoy, Nick Nolte, Sheree North, France Nuyen, Warren Oates, Carroll O'Connor, Nancy Olson**, John Payne, Slim Pickens, Suzanne Pleshette, Burt Reynolds**, Wayne Rogers, Ruth Roman, Katherine Ross**, John Saxon, Evelyn Scott, William Shatner, Tom Skerritt, David Soul, Craig Stevens, Guy Stockwell, Loretta Swit, Russ Tamblyn, Forrest Tucker, Cicely Tyson**, Robert Urich, Joan Van Ark, Lee Van Cleef, Robert Vaughn, Jan-Michael Vincent, Jon Voight**, Leslie Ann Warren, Ruth Warrick, David Wayne, Adam West, Stuart Whitman, James Whitmore**, Chill Wills

Fan Letters

During our *Gunsmoke* years and up to this day I continue to receive wonderful fan letters from folks here in the States and around the world. Those from far off lands seem to be enthralled with America's western heritage. Reruns have brought new generations of *Gunsmoke* viewers and I continue to be surprised how the show captures the attention of these young people who live in a different world today.

I don't think any of us on the show realized what a lasting impact we would have on the millions of viewers who became part of our family every week. Our writers and cast members were dedicated to producing a family show which reflected the values and ethics of the times. One might say that the team was part of the "Greatest Generation" who were instilled with the high standards of Americans who went through World War II. Their sacrifices on battlefields and on the home front were accepted without fanfare. A duty was to be done and Americans met the challenge magnificently. Our cast and crew included many of these folks and they, perhaps unknowingly, set the strong standard that gave the show its staying power.

I still get letters every month though the show ended some 25 years ago. They are humbling to me in that they attribute the show's success to Marshal Dillon. However, I was just one of an ensemble of actors like Milburn Stone, Amanda Blake, Ken Curtis, Buck Taylor, Glenn Strange, James Nusser, and Burt Reynolds who were the heart of the show. For those who are no longer with us, I will be forever grateful for their professionalism, loyalty, many kindnesses and warmth they displayed to everyone on the set. How blessed I was to have such people around me.

I have selected at random a few letters I've received over the years. I hope you enjoy reading them.

From: B.K. Morrison
To: <arnessfanmail@prodigy.net>
Sent: Saturday, September 16, 2000 3:47 AM
Subject: Dear Mr. Arness—Thank you for being there.

Dear Mr. Arness,

I just wanted to take the time to write you a letter and let you know that I admire your work as an actor and as a "western" enthusiast. I too am very much interested in "the old west" in American history, in particular the period between the American Revolution and the Civil War.

I am 27 years old, am married to a wonderful woman and have 3 daughters, one of which is severely disabled. Being the last man in my family having outlived my father and grandfathers, etc., I do what I can to provide a warm and happy home for my loved ones, and let me tell you it can be a challenge sometimes, but always a pleasure and an honor.

Growing up I always looked up to certain role-models for my inspiration and my guidance in my daily life, naturally I had certain actors and such as my early heroes, but also historical figures such as Davy Crockett and Jim Bowie.

When I was 14 years old, I watched a TV movie that came out called *The Alamo—Thirteen Days to Glory* and something inside of me clicked! It helped reinforce my ideals, my morals and my values. Not only were you a big screen actor with a charismatic and larger than life presence, but you also portrayed one of my heroes, Jim Bowie.

I have read extensively all historical books I have ever come across that have to do with that early period of history, that period of adventure, opportunity and optimism. I believe that people, young people and children in particular are missing those heroes and those ideals that a great deal of us were raised upon and with. It saddens me to think that a generation and more will grow up without those essential and precious lessons and emotions bred deep within them.

… You have touched my life in a very wonderful way, and I just wanted you to know that you are appreciated and loved … not just for being an actor or a childhood hero, but as a human being. God bless you and your family sir, and know that you have made a difference in the lives of many people. Thank you for being there, Mr. Arness.

Sincerely,

Brice Kenneth Morrison

From: Margie Kron
To: <arnessfanmail@prodigy.net>
Sent: Monday, July 24, 2000 9:42 AM
Subject: Fw:To James Arness
Attach: margie.jpg

Dear James Arness,

This letter is long overdue in writing.

This is one photograph I know you do not have.

It was taken in Long Beach, Ca., in 1959.

My father was working at the Veterans Hospital in Long Beach as a medical photographer at the time. He was a Marine. He took this photograph, and recalls your comment: "This little girl should be in the movies."

My parents and I are very proud of that comment.

A friend had this photo enlarged to poster size. It is framed and hanging in my apartment.

I have kept this photograph near to my heart.

After all, I can say: "James Arness held me in his arms."

But, I always finish my comment with: "I was only 2 years old, darn it."

I hope you enjoy this photograph.

I wish you and your family, the best.

God Bless You,

Margery Kron
San Diego, Calif.

Ladies Auxiliary
Pvt Allen J. Beck, Jr. Post 5265
Veterans of Foreign Wars
Spring Grove, Pennsylvania

Dear Mr. Arness,

Congratulations on recently being presented with your Bronze Star and Purple Heart for your dedicated service during World War II. I am proud as both an American and President of my VFW Ladies Auxiliary to honor you for your contribution to preserve the freedom of our country during the war.

We are losing many of our World War II veterans every day as our population ages. It is both fitting and proper to acknowledge and thank our veterans for their service to our country while they are still here to hear it. Therefore, please allow me to offer both my personal as well as my Auxiliary's appreciation for your dedicated Army service. Our VFW Post and Ladies Auxiliary are both committed to honoring and praising our veterans for a job well done.

As a personal note, I must tell you that it is a special thrill for me to pen this letter to you, Mr. Arness. I am a lifelong *Gunsmoke* fan. In fact, my family has called me a "*Gunsmoke* Nut" on several occasions! I have collected *Gunsmoke* memorabilia for years, have videos of approximately 80% of the episodes, am an active participant on the Internet of two different *Gunsmoke* groups (TVLand and Delphi Forum), and enjoy writing original fan fiction stories based on the characters from the great western. While *Gunsmoke* premiered before I was even born, I was "raised" on it. Some of my most cherished childhood remembrances are of curling up beside my grandfather to watch "Marshal Dillon and Miss Kitty" as he would refer to the show. The series has always been my favorite and I still enjoy it immensely. I guess to say I am a huge fan would be an understatement!

Mr. Arness, thank you for your fine work in my beloved *Gunsmoke*. I appreciate your contribution to the entertainment industry. Matt Dillon has always been my fictional hero. It is a shame the young people of today do not have such a fine character of strong moral and ethical ideals to emulate. They do however, have you, Mr. Arness, and other brave men who still represent those ideals in their everyday lives. For that I am grateful. That makes you and all other veterans my real life heroes.

In closing, please accept my good wishes for your good health and happiness. If you're ever in Spring Grove, Pennsylvania, stop in at our VFW Post and say "Hello."

In Grateful Appreciation,
Sharon K. Wentz
Auxiliary President

From: Harvey Hazlewood
To: <arnessfanmail@prodigy.net>
Sent: Saturday, August 12, 2000 8:30 AM
Subject: A Fan

Hi Jim

I have enjoyed *Gunsmoke* for over 30 years. I am a busy CEO of entertainment lighting and audio companies (EFX, Broadway plays, Concerts, etc.). I relax by watching old videos of *Gunsmoke*. I am also an amateur actor and director of plays (I played the "Rainmaker" and many other roles) and my wife and I built and managed a successful theater. Unfortunately, today's TV shows do not invest time in character development, plot, or for that matter sets, lighting, and music. This was the beauty of *Gunsmoke*—the acting was superb, the sets realistic, the theme music perfect—no special effects, pyro, helicopters or other gimmicks which are prevalent today. I hope that you are enjoying your retirement and can look back with great satisfaction on the pleasure you have brought your legion of fans. No one lives forever and it is rare one can leave a legacy such as yours. You are truly blessed.

Thanks and have a great day.

Harvey Hazlewood
CEO Hubbell Entertainment Lighting/PowerFactor Audio
Sunrise, Florida 33326

From: Susan Morrill
To: <arnessfanmail@prodigy.net>
Sent: Sunday, August 13, 2000 10:32 AM
Subject: Hello Mr Arness

Dear Sir,

I cannot tell you how much you as an actor has meant to me in my life. I remember watching *Gunsmoke* with my parents. My father was in the Air Force at the time, and you reminded me so much of him. You still do. He adored you.

God bless you and thank you for all the happiness and memories you have given me and my family.

Sincerely,

Lt Col Susan Morrill, USAF

From: Cheryl Wright
To: James Arness <arnessfanmail@prodigy.net>
Sent: Friday, May 26, 2000 10:02 AM
Subject: GS: Happy Birthday Mr. Arness

Happy Birthday Mr. Jim Arness

The fans on the Delphi Gunsmoke Forum wish you a memorable birthday with family, friends, happiness and good health. And pray that you may enjoy many, many more.

Thank you for all you have given us over the last 45+ years. Your big screen movies, TV series, TV movies and special appearances over the years have entertained three generations of my home and is starting on the fourth. I personally thank you for this great entertainment, the lessons learned, the values encouraged, and the morals you have shown us through your choices of characters to portray. You are truly appreciated.

HAPPY BIRTHDAY JAMES ARNESS

"Thanks for all the wonderful years..."
(The Jailer)

Cheryl Wright

From: Cindy Costello
To: <arnessfanmail@prodigy.net>
Sent: Friday, May 26, 2000 1:18 AM
Subject: Happy Birthday!

Dear Mr. Arness:

I want to wish you the happiest of birthdays and to thank you for the countless hours of great entertainment that you have given me and millions of others.

You were my hero and champion as a child, and now as I near 40, you remain the same. My children enjoy you as well, thanks to video and TVLand.

Here's wishing the very best on your special day and every day ... once again ... thank you! I hope this message finds you and yours happy and healthy.

With respect,

Ben Costello

From: Steve Clamage
To: <arnessfanmail@prodigy.net>
Sent: Sunday, July 16, 2000 4:16 PM
Subject: To a very special person ... hello and thanks

Dear Mr. Arness,

I would just like to say hello. Congratulations on receiving the Western Heritage Award and about the Army presenting you with the medals from when you were in the service....

I am 44 years old and have only been watching *Gunsmoke* for about 18 years now. But I have grown to truly love the show. I remember when my father used to watch it during the original running of your series. He loved it too, very much.

When I found your website and email address, I just had to write you and let you know how much of an impact you have had on my life. *Gunsmoke* has become more than just a TV series to me. I know the shows were made in Hollywood, but you and the cast brought them to life.

To me, seeing you with your unbending principles, upstanding values, and your intensely fair ways, were like watching lessons of how to live a good life, full of purpose, fairness, and humanity.

I believe that the truly good actors and actresses can impart a feeling of goodness and warmth that people can walk away with. To feel good after watching a show, movie, or play is a special feeling. I hope you know how special you are to be able to leave people feeling so good after watching you.

...Watching *Gunsmoke* seemed to always instill the kind of values that my parents tried to teach me. Guess you could say you reinforced those values in a most meaningful way.

P.S. Saw some of your *Gunsmoke* movies and some of your other movies too. Always enjoyed them very much and want you to know that you will always be a special and distinguished person to all of your fans. You have left your mark and touched the world in many different, meaningful, and wonderful ways. The best to you and your family.

One of your many fans,

Most Sincerely,

Steve Clamage

Mr. Arness,

Just a short note to thank you for your wonderful work over the years, but especially for bringing Matt Dillon to the screen.

I have fond memories of watching *Gunsmoke* with my Grandpa and I suppose this is where my love of the great western series began, although the series debuted before I was even born. My love of it has never stopped, and today is stronger than ever.

The Internet has opened the whole world up and connected me to other "*Gunsmoke* Addicts" who share my interest. We are not "nut cases," just folks who have found a common interest in the old western. The Delphi Gunsmoke Board and the TVLand AOL Gunsmoke Board are interesting and a lot of fun, as they are filled with all sorts of discussions about *Gunsmoke*.

... I just think it is great that almost 50 years since its debut, *Gunsmoke* is still loved and watched faithfully by its dedicated fans. It is a fine tribute to the quality of this outstanding television show. Again, thank you Mr. Arness for being a part of that.

A Very Devoted Fan,

Sharon K. Wentz
York, PA

From:	Gloria Rigsby
To:	<arnessfanmail@prodigy.net>
Sent:	Tuesday, May 30, 2000 12:00 PM

Dear Mr. Arness,

I was so excited to find the *Gunsmoke* web page today! I will be 50 years old next month and I've watched *Gunsmoke* for 45 of them! My grandmother had a TV in the 50's so I would spend the night with her and we'd watch Marshal Dillon. Now, on Saturday nights my granddaughter spends the night with me and we watch 2 hours of Marshal Dillon/*Gunsmoke*. You have been my long time cowboy hero and I love you! ... Thank you for the best westerns ever!

Gloria Rigsby
Dallas, TX 75229

From: Ron Lipton
To: <arnessfanmail@prodigy.net>
Sent: Thursday, July 13, 2000 12:09 AM
Subject: Old friend Ron Lipton, for Jim and Janet Arness

Dear Jim and Janet:

I have gotten many pictures of Jim over the years signed by him to me. I am 54 years old now and it has been quite awhile since Jim visited me in room #610 of New York Hospital in the late 1950's.

My father had a store in the old CBS building in New York and Dennis Weaver would come in all the time. I was very sick as a child and Jim was my hero. It was arranged through the doctors and CBS people for Jim to come to see me when he made a rare trip to NY. Needless to say it was a turning point for me.

I later became a championship fighter, a lifelong police officer, and a champion shooter....

... Your body of work in bringing the integrity, honor, strength, and honesty of what Matt Dillon meant to so many of us when we were young absolutely inspired me to become an honest police officer. I will always revere you as a great American, consummate actor and a good man.... Love you Jim and God bless you always.

Ron Lipton

From: Kim Round
To: <arnessfanmail@prodigy.net>
Sent: May 11, 2000 6:08:29 PM EDT
Subject: bravo!

How wonderful it is to see you in cyberspace!

Best of luck with your web site from a life long fan, and thank you for your wonderful work!

Our youngest son's middle name is Matthew, after your character.

Kim Round
North Andover, MA (near Boston)

February 15, 2000

Mr. James Arness
PO Box 49599
Los Angeles, CA 90049

Dear Mr. Arness:

In yesterday's "Dear Abby" column one of her suggestions to celebrate Valentine's Day is to write a fan letter. I have been trying to write this letter to you for many months now since I found your address on the Internet. I just wish to express to you the profound effect you have had on my life. You are the person on this planet who most taught me my sense of right and wrong. You are truly one of the few great American heroes left on our earth.

It was during those early years of mine back in the '50s when you portrayed Matt Dillon, the legendary marshal of Dodge City, that I learned the difference between right and wrong. Matt was always on the right side of the law and he never wavered. He was always good and always against the bad. Today there are so many gray areas in people's lives that it's a wonder they find their way through life at all.

I so enjoy the re-runs of the old *Gunsmoke* episodes that are now shown on the TV Land network. I always watch when I'm home.... When I was a child, *Gunsmoke* was the only show I was permitted to stay up and watch past my bedtime. And I never missed a chance to do that.

...I just had to write and let you know that I will never, as long as I live, forget Matt Dillon or Zeb McCahan. I'm sure you have other characters to your credit but those are the two I remember most. I thank you for the 20 wonderful years of *Gunsmoke*. I thank you for instilling in a small cowgirl back in the '50s her love of horses and everything that has to do with the old west....

I just had to at least write you a letter to let you know that I always have been, and always will be, a great James Arness fan.

Sincerely,

(Mrs.) Cindy W. Walheim
Parker, PA

From: David Garcia
To: <arnessfanmail@prodigy.net>
Sent: April 27, 2000 7:51:36 PM
Subject: A special fan!

Dear Mr. Arness,

I am so glad to have found this website and an address where I can write to you to tell you how much your career has meant to me personally. I learned to love *Gunsmoke* as a child (I'm now 38) because of my grandfather, who dearly loved the show. As a result of an injury I sustained when I was 16 (during my sophomore year in high school I broke my neck in a diving accident, resulting in complete and total paralysis from the shoulders down with no feeling or movement at all since that time. I am able to type using a voice recognition program). I am confined to an electric wheelchair. However, even in the midst of a very difficult situation God has blessed me greatly. After becoming a Christian I found I was very limited in the shows on television that were not morally offensive. In a world that seems obsessed with sex and violence I found great joy in discovering the old Westerns that were so special to my father and grandfather. It is truly refreshing to have a little escape to a place where "the good guy always wins." ... I have found particular delight in *Gunsmoke* and the trustworthy Marshal, Matt Dillon. Because TV Land is now running *Gunsmoke* on a daily basis I am able enjoy the show regularly.

...Thank you so much for all that your career has meant to so many, and may God bless you richly.

In warmest regard, your friend and fan,

David Garcia
Hoover, Alabama

Mr. James Arness
PO Box 49599
Los Angeles, CA 90049

August 28, 1996

Dear Mr Arness,

I have thought about sending you fan mail for many years, but it was only recently that I was able to find where to write to you (thanks to the Internet). So, this letter may seem way overdue, nonetheless the sentiments are still just as strong.

I merely wanted to write to you to say thanks for your great work on the series *How the West Was Won*. During that show's first run, I was in high school and I would be sure to be in front of the TV each week to see the ongoing saga of the Macahan family. For several years, I have been enjoying the reruns on the TNT network.

While I know many people remember you for your role in *Gunsmoke*, I believe your portrayal of Zeb Macahan was a much more fitting and complex role for you. The dual nature of Zeb—tough as nails mountain man pioneer and yet, warm, loyal and compassionate to his friends and family. Few actors could have pulled off that duality in a convincing manner. Not only did you pull it off, but you excelled at the task. Your larger than life stature coupled with an imposing stance, grizzled look, cold stare, and gravel cold voice made Zeb a tough character. Yet, you could turn Zeb into an equally convincing warm character. After watching the shows several times, I've come to realize that your key to moving between these two sides of Zeb was through manner in which you used your eyes and voice. The warm Zeb had eyes wide open with the hint of a smile which remained as you spoke with a warm and smoother voice....

Your role in *How the West Was Won* is the reason why that series stands out in my mind as one of my favorite shows through the years. Thank you for the many years of enjoyment.

Sincerely,

Gary Haller
Park Ridge, IL

From: Jim Dunbar
To: <arnessfanmail@prodigy.net>
Sent: Friday, August 11, 2000 9:29 PM
Subject: Many Thanks

Dear Mr. Arness

I am 43 years old and an avid western movie/TV fanatic. I remember as a young boy my father faithfully watching *Gunsmoke* every week and I too continued to watch for well over 20 years.

I watch the re-runs that are available from time to time in my area (unfortunately not enough) and just yesterday I came across a new re-release of the very first *Gunsmoke* episode! I immediately purchased it and just finished watching the video.

All I can say is thank you for the many hours of enjoyment that you have been responsible for in my lifetime.

Being a fan of the western genre these days is a rarity and I was ecstatic to find this gem....

Again, many many thanks for the enjoyment you have brought myself and my family....

James Dunbar
Ontario, Canada

February 22, 2000

P.O. Box 49599
Los Angeles, CA
90049-0599

Dear Mr. Arness:

I've been a fan of yours since I could sit up, but I always felt a little intimidated, like if I would ever write a fan letter to you, either you wouldn't read it, or you'd just go "hrrmph!" and toss it with the bills and junk mail. ... But I'm 47, and I've reached a time in my life when I figure it can't hurt to tell you!

I've tried to catch as many of your performances as I could, from *The Thing* ... through *Thirteen Days to Glory*....

I was always upset about the brouhaha made about violence in *Gunsmoke*; if there was ever a program that preached that violence is a last resort, your show was it! Ten years ago, I did a caricature (I'm an artist, by profession) of how I figured the critics expected *Gunsmoke* to end. I'm sending a copy of the drawing with this letter. Please accept it, with my admiration (and appreciate that it is a joke, please!).

I hope you are in good health ... I've lifted more than a few beers toasting you (like I said, you are my favorite TV star!). Thank you for making my life richer!

Sincerely,

Ben Burgraff
North Myrtle Beach, SC

From: Mike and Cam Spear
To: <arnessfanmail@prodigy.net>
Sent: Friday, September 22, 2000 6:14 PM
Subject: Hello from a fan

Howdy Mr. Arness,

I'm pretty excited to have found your web site and to be sending this to you. My name is Mike Spear and I guess that you have had quite a bit of influence on my life. I saw you at the Houston Fat Stock Show and Rodeo, Sunday, March 8th, 1959, at the 2:00 PM matinee performance. I was 8 years old. I still have the ticket stubs (my mother saved them after all this time). We didn't save the program but I found one on ebay, believe it or not, and I was high bidder.

I'm now 49 and I would like to tell you that all of you "good guys" kept me pretty much on the right road. I think that I've done all right. I was honorably discharged after 9 years in the U.S. Army and I'm going on my 20th year with the Harris County Sheriff's Department.

I mean to tell you that there was more than one time that I used Matt/Jim as a guide!

My wife also says hello. She came from Vietnam in 1991 and you are her favorite TV lawman as well.

I sincerely hope all is well with you and your family.

Thanks,

Mike and Cam

MATT DILLON

I go to movies when I can
    But it's not quite the same
Unless Matt Dillon's on the screen,
    The action is too tame.

The Kansas Marshal and his pals
    Created characters
To satisfy the "movie mind"
    No matter his or hers.

As Chester was his deputy
    And always dragged one leg,
He clashed with Festus quite a bit
    To take him down a peg.

He only used the spoken word
    To do each playful deed.
There was no use at all to write
    'Cause Festus couldn't read.

Miss Kitty rounded out the group.
    She was Matt Dillon's girl.
They all portrayed plain country folks
    Far from the social whirl.

The writers of the "Dillon" show
    Were masters of their craft
Who always kept us entertained.
    We either groaned or laughed.

Now writers at this later time
    Can learn a thing or two
Of how to make folks love their show.
    Make it the same, but new.

You can't improve on excellence.
    Matt Dillon filled the bill.
He played the *Marshal* then so well
    That he's remembered still.

WENDELL BROWN   1999

Appendix D

Films

The Farmer's Daughter (RKO, 1947)

Man from Texas (Eagle Lions Films, Inc., 1947)

Roses Are Red (20th Century–Fox, 1947)

Battleground (MGM, 1949)

Wagonmaster (RKO, 1950)

Sierra (Universal, 1950)

Two Lost Worlds (Eagle Lions Films, Inc., 1950)

Double Crossbones (Universal, 1950)

Stars in My Crown (MGM, 1950)

Wyoming Mail (Universal, 1950)

Cavalry Scout (Monogram, 1951)

Belle Le Grand (Republic, 1951)

Iron Man (Universal, 1951)

The Thing (RKO, 1951)

The People Against O'Hara (MGM, 1951)

Carbine Williams (MGM, 1952)

Hellgate (Lippert, 1952)

The Girl in White (MGM, 1952)

Big Jim McLain (Warner, 1952)

Horizons West (Universal, 1952)

Invasion from Mars (20th Century–Fox, 1953)

Lone Hand (Universal, 1953)

Hondo (Warner, 1953)

Ride the Man Down (Republic, 1953)

Island in the Sky (Warner, 1953)

Veils of Baghdad (Universal, 1953)

Hondo (Warner, 1954)

Her Twelve Men (MGM, 1954)

Them! (Warner, 1954)

Many Rivers to Cross (MGM, 1955)

The Sea Chase (Warner, 1955)

Gun the Man Down (United Artists, 1956)

The First Traveling Saleslady (RKO, 1956)

Flame of the Islands (Republic, 1958)

Alias Jesse James (United Artists, 1959)

Appendix E

Television

The Lone Ranger (1950)
Lux Video Theater: "The Chase" (1954)
Gunsmoke (1955–75), three Emmy nominations
Front Row Center (1956)
The Red Skelton Chevy Special (1959)
The Chevrolet Golden Anniversary Show (1961)
A Salute to Television's 25th Anniversary (1972)

The Macahans (1976)
How the West Was Won (1976–79)
McClain's Law (1981)
The Alamo: 13 Days to Glory (1987)
Gunsmoke: Return to Dodge (1987)
Red River (1988)
Gunsmoke: The Last Apache (1990)
Gunsmoke: To the Last Man (1992)
Gunsmoke: The Long Ride (1993)
Gunsmoke: One Man's Justice (1994)

Honors and Awards

Plaque: "Academy of Television Arts & Sciences presents this Certificate to James Arness in recognition of Nomination for the Actor—Best Continuing Performance in a Dramatic Series: *Gunsmoke* for the year 1956," Johnny Mercer, President.

Plaque: Camp Pendleton Marine Rodeo, 1957.

Look magazine TV Award for "Best Western Series" (1958) presented to Jim Arness on behalf of *Gunsmoke* cast, producers, directors and writers.

Headliners Club Award presented by governor of Texas: "To Jim Arness, whose TV role as Marshal Matt Dillon has caught the imagination of a whole world and depicted at its very best an era of history that made our state and nation distinctly great," 1958.

Plaque (telegram), from *TV Guide*, J. T. Quick, publisher, 12/15/58: "The December 6th Issue of *TV Guide* reached a new sales high, with 6,843,585 circulation. Your personal popularity had much to do with our success. Congratulations and Best Wishes from the entire *TV Guide* staff."

Certificate: Honorary membership, Bayou Rifles Incorporated, 3/6/59.

Plaque, Reno Silver Spurs Award: "James Arness, Voted Number One Western TV Star by the TV Critics, 1959–1960."

Golden Boot Award, 1969.

Statue: "Western Heritage Wrangler Award, James Arness, Actor, *Gunsmoke*, Outstanding Fiction Television, 1971."

Honorary U.S. Marshal, 9/11/72

International Broadcasting Award, "Man of the Year," James Arness, 3/20/73.

Plaque: "*Gunsmoke* congratulates James Arness for your invaluable contribution to the 20th season of the longest running dramatic series in television history," John Mantley, John Stephens, Jack Miller, 1975.

Old West Trail Award, The Westerner, James Arness, 1977.

Western Heritage Wrangler Award from National Cowboy Hall of Fame and Western Heritage Center: "To James Arness for Outstanding Contribution to the West Through *Gunsmoke*. Elected to the Hall of Fame of Great Western Performances," 1981.

Plaque: "To James Arness, Pasadena Playhouse Alumni and Associates, Recognition Award, 1982."

Plaque: "Honorary U.S. Marshal, James Arness, 12/14/86, Los Angeles, California, Badge #2, in recognition of his unique contribution to the Image and Traditions of the U.S. Marshal's Service."

Plaque/Badge: "To James Arness in Appreciation for your help in 'Round-ing Up' the United States Marshal's Posse, Anaheim Stadium, 8/24/87."

Plaque: Honorary Citizen of Tucson, 12/10/87.

Magazine: Television's 50th Anniversary Issue, *People Weekly Extra*, Summer 1989, Top 25 Stars, James Arness (Number 6).

Badge: U.S. Marshals, "With Deep Appreciation, James Arness, 4/4/91."

Magazine: *Special Report*: Personalities, May-July 1991 Issue, The 50 Most Influential TV Characters of All Time, "Matt Dillon." Article by National Book Award recipient James Dickey, author of *Deliverance* (1970).

NAGC Gold Screen Award for Outstanding Audiovisual Production presented by the U.S. Marshal's Service. "America's Star," videotape.

Honorary Texas Ranger.

Oklahoma Hall of Fame.

Plaque, Honorary Marshal, Tucson's Marshal's Association: "Presented in grateful recognition of outstanding contributions to the City of Tucson."

Bronze Statue: Gene Autry Western Heritage Award (10/2/99).

Index

229

James Arness is recognized as one of America's most beloved actors. Generations have grown up with him as Marshal Matt Dillon on television's longest running series, *Gunsmoke*. These days Jim is busy with many projects and charity involvements, most notably United Cerebral Palsy. Jim and his wife of 23 years, Janet, live in Los Angeles and are actively involved with their family, three sons and three grandchildren. Jim loves to hear from his many fans. They can write to him through his website, *www.JamesArness.com*.

James E. Wise, Jr., became a naval aviator in 1953 following graduation from Northwestern University. He served as an intelligence officer aboard the aircraft carrier USS *America* (CVA-66) and later as commanding officer of various naval intelligence units. Since his retirement from the Navy in 1975, Wise has held senior executive posts in many private-sector companies. In addition, he has written several books and has had numerous articles published in naval and maritime journals. He lives in Alexandria, Virginia.